The Quran With Tafsir Ibn Kathir
Part 6 of 30:
An Nisaa 148 To Al Ma'idah 081

The Quran With Tafsir Ibn Kathir
Part 6 of 30:
An Nisaa 148 To Al Ma'idah 081

With
Arabic Script, Transliteration of Arabic, Meaning in English
and Ibn Kathir's Abridged Tafsir (Explanation)

Muhammad Saed Abdul-Rahman

BSc, DipHE

© Muhammad Saed Abdul-Rahman, 2012
ISBN 978-1-86179-843-5

All Rights reserved

British Library Cataloguing in Publication Data. A Catalogue record for this book is available from the British Library

Designed, Typeset and produced by:
MSA Publication Limited, 4 Bello Close, Herne Hill,
London SE24 9BW
United Kingdom

Cover design: Houriyah Abdul-Rahman

TABLE OF CONTENTS

TABLE OF CONTENTS V

PRELUDE XI

    OPENING SERMAN XI
    OUR MISSION XII
    BIOGRAPHY OF HAFIZ IBN KATHIR (701 H - 774 H) XII
        Ibn Kathir's Teachers xii
        Ibn Kathir's Students xiii
        Ibn Kathir's Books xiii
        Ibn Kathir's Death xiv

PREFACE XV

    ABOUT THIS BOOK XV
    PERFORMING PROSTRATION WHILE READING THE QUR'AN XV

PART 6 FULL ARABIC TEXT 1

INTRODUCTION TO CHAPTER (SURAH) 4: AN-NISAA (THE WOMEN) 12

    IBN KATHIR'S INTRODUCTION 12
        Virtues of Surat An-Nisa, A Madinan Surah 12

CHAPTER (SURAH) 4: AN-NISAA (THE WOMEN), VERSES 148 - 176 13

    Surah: 4 Ayah: 148 & Ayah: 149 13
        Tafsir Ibn Kathir 13
        The Permission to Utter Evil in Public, For One Who Was Wronged 13
    Surah: 4 Ayah: 150, Ayah: 151 & Ayah: 152 14
        Tafsir Ibn Kathir 15
        Believing in Some Prophets and Rejecting Others is Pure Kufr 15
    Surah: 4 Ayah: 153 & Ayah: 154 16
        Tafsir Ibn Kathir 17
        The Stubbornness of the Jews 17
    Surah: 4 Ayah: 155, Ayah: 156, Ayah: 157, Ayah: 18 & Ayah: 159 18
        Tafsir Ibn Kathir 20
        The Crimes of the Jews 20
        The Evil Accusation the Jews Uttered Against Maryam and Their Claim that They Killed `Isa 20
        All Christians Will Believe in `Isa Before He Dies 22
        The Hadiths Regarding the Descent of `Isa Just Before the Day of Judgement, and his Mission 23
        Another Hadith by Abu Hurayrah 23
        Another Hadith 24
        Another Hadith 24
        Another Hadith 25

- Another Hadith 30
- The Description of `Isa, upon him be Peace 32
- *Surah: 4 Ayah: 160, Ayah: 161 & Ayah: 162 .... 35*
  - Tafsir Ibn Kathir 36
  - Some Foods Were Made Unlawful for the Jews Because of their Injustice and Wrongdoing 36
- *Surah: 4 Ayah: 163, Ayah: 164 & Ayah: 165 .... 37*
  - Tafsir Ibn Kathir 38
  - Revelation Came to Prophet Muhammad , Just as it Came to the Prophets Before Him . 38
  - Twenty-Five Prophets Are Mentioned in the Qur'an 38
  - The Virtue of Musa 39
  - The Reason Behind Sending the Prophets is to Establish the Proof 39
- *Surah: 4 Ayah: 166, Ayah: 167, Ayah: 168, Ayah: 169 & Ayah: 170 .... 40*
  - Tafsir Ibn Kathir 41
- *Surah: 4 Ayah: 171 .... 42*
  - Tafsir Ibn Kathir 43
  - Prohibiting the People of the Book From Going to Extremes in Religion 43
  - The Meaning of "His Word and a spirit from Him 44
  - The Christian Sects 46
- *Surah: 4 Ayah: 172 & Ayah: 173 .... 47*
  - Tafsir Ibn Kathir 47
  - The Prophets and Angels Are Never too Proud to Worship Allah 47
- *Surah: 4 Ayah: 174 & Ayah: 175 .... 48*
  - Tafsir Ibn Kathir 48
  - The Description of the Revelation that Came From Allah 48
- *Surah: 4 Ayah: 176 .... 49*
  - Tafsir Ibn Kathir 49
  - This is the Last Ayah Ever Revealed, the Ruling on Al-Kalalah 49
  - The Meaning of This Ayah 50

INTRODUCTION TO CHAPTER (SURAH) 5: AL-MAIDAH (THE TABLE, THE TABLE SPREAD) 52

- IBN KATHIR'S INTRODUCTION 52
  - The Virtues of Surat Al-Ma'idah; When It was Revealed 52

CHAPTER (SURAH) 5: AL-MAIDAH (THE TABLE, THE TABLE SPREAD), VERSES 001-081 52

- *Surah: 5 Ayah: 1 & Ayah: 2 .... 53*
  - Tafsir Ibn Kathir 53
  - Explaining the Lawful and the Unlawful Beasts 54
  - The Necessity of Observing the Sanctity of the Sacred Area and the Sacred Months 55
  - Taking the Hady to the Sacred House of Allah, Al-Ka`bah 56
  - The Necessity of Preserving the Sanctity and Safety of those who Intend to Travel to the Sacred House 57
  - Hunting Game is Permissible After Ihram Ends 58
  - Justice is Always Necessary 58
- *Surah: 5 Ayah: 3 .... 59*

Table of Contents

- Tafsir Ibn Kathir 60
  - The Animals that are Unlawful to Eat 60
  - The Prohibition of Using Al-Azlam for Decision Making 63
  - Shaytan and the Disbelievers Do Not Hope that Muslims Will Ever Follow Them ... 65
  - Islam Has Been Perfected For Muslims 66
  - Permitting the Dead Animals in Conditions of Necessity 67
- *Surah: 5 Ayah: 4* 68
  - Tafsir Ibn Kathir 68
    - Clarifying the Lawful 68
    - Mention Allah's Name Upon Sending the Predators to Catch the Game 70
- *Surah: 5 Ayah: 5* 71
  - Tafsir Ibn Kathir 72
    - Permitting the Slaughtered Animals of the People of the Book 72
    - The Permission to Marry Chaste Women From the People of the Scriptures 73
- *Surah: 5 Ayah: 6* 74
  - Tafsir Ibn Kathir 75
    - The Order to Perform Wudu' 75
    - The Intention and Mentioning Allah's Name for Wudu' 76
    - Passing the Fingers through the Beard While Performing Wudu' 77
    - How to Perform Wudu' 77
    - The Necessity of Washing the Feet 79
    - The Hadiths that Indicate the Necessity of Washing the Feet 79
    - The Necessity of Washing Between the Fingers 80
    - Wiping Over the Khuffs is an Established Sunnah 80
    - Performing Tayammum with Clean earth When There is no Water and When One is Ill . 81
    - Supplicating to Allah after Wudu' 81
    - The Virtue of Wudu' 82
- *Surah: 5 Ayah: 7, Ayah: 8, Ayah: 9, Ayah: 10 & Ayah: 11* 83
  - Tafsir Ibn Kathir 84
    - Reminding the Believers of the Bounty of the Message and Islam 84
    - The Necessity of Observing Justice 85
    - Among Allah's Favors is that He Prevented the Disbelievers from Fighting the Muslims . 86
- *Surah: 5 Ayah: 12, Ayah: 13 & Ayah: 14* 87
  - Tafsir Ibn Kathir 88
    - Cursing the People of the Book for Breaking the Covenant 88
    - The Leaders of Ansar on the Night of `Aqabah 89
    - Breaking the Covenant 89
    - The Christians Also Broke their Covenant with Allah and the Repercussion of this Behavior 90
- *Surah: 5 Ayah: 15 & Ayah: 16* 91
  - Tafsir Ibn Kathir 91
    - Explaining the Truth Through the Messenger and the Qur'an 91
- *Surah: 5 Ayah: 17 & Ayah: 18* 92
  - Tafsir Ibn Kathir 93
    - The Polytheism and Disbelief of the Christians 93

- Refuting the People of the Book's Claim that they are Allah's Children 93
- *Surah: 5 Ayah: 19* *94*
  - Tafsir Ibn Kathir 94
- *Surah: 5 Ayah: 20, Ayah: 21, Ayah: 22, Ayah: 23, Ayah: 24, Ayah: 25, Ayah: 26* *97*
  - Tafsir Ibn Kathir 98
    - Musa Reminds His People of Allah's Favors on Them; The Jews Refuse to Enter the Holy Land 98
    - The Speeches of Yuwsha' (Joshua) and Kalib (Caleb) 100
    - The Righteous Response of the Companions During the Battle of Badr 101
    - Musa Supplicates to Allah Against the Jews 101
    - Forbidding the Jews from Entering the Holy Land for Forty Years 102
    - Conquering Jerusalem 102
    - Allah Comforts Musa 103
- *Surah: 5 Ayah: 27, Ayah: 28, Ayah: 29, Ayah: 30 & Ayah: 31* *103*
  - Tafsir Ibn Kathir 104
    - The Story of Habil (Abel) and Qabil (Cain) 104
    - The Swift Punishment for Transgression and Cutting the Relations of the Womb 108
- *Surah: 5 Ayah: 32, Ayah: 33 & Ayah: 34* *108*
  - Tafsir Ibn Kathir 110
    - Human Beings Should Respect the Sanctity of Other Human Beings 110
    - Warning Those who Commit Mischief 111
    - The Punishment of those Who Cause Mischief in the Land 111
    - The Punishment of those who Wage War Against Allah and His Messenger is Annulled if They Repent Before their Apprehension 114
- *Surah: 5 Ayah: 35, Ayah: 36 & Ayah: 37* *115*
  - Tafsir Ibn Kathir 116
    - Commanding Taqwa, Wasilah, and Jihad 116
    - No Amount of Ransom Shall Be Accepted from the Disbelievers on the Day of the Judgment and They Will Remain in the Fire 117
- *Surah: 5 Ayah: 38, Ayah: 39 & Ayah: 40* *118*
  - Tafsir Ibn Kathir 119
    - The Necessity of Cutting off the Hand of the Thief 119
    - When Does Cutting the Hand of the Thief Become Necessary 119
    - Repentance of the Thief is Acceptable 120
- *Surah: 5 Ayah: 41, Ayah: 42, Ayah: 43 & Ayah: 44* *122*
  - Tafsir Ibn Kathir 124
    - Do Not Feel Sad Because of the Behavior of the Jews and Hypocrites 124
    - The Jews Alter and Change the Law, Such As Stoning the Adulterer 124
    - Chastising the Jews for Their Evil Lusts and Desires, While Praising the Tawrah 127
    - Another Reason Behind Revealing these Honorable Ayat 127
- *Surah: 5 Ayah: 45* *129*
  - Tafsir Ibn Kathir 130
    - A Man is Killed for a Woman Whom He Kills 130
    - Retaliation for Wounds 131
    - An Important Ruling 131

Table of Contents

- The Pardon is Expiation for Such Offenses ... 132
- *Surah: 5 Ayah: 46 & Ayah: 47* ... *132*
  - Tafsir Ibn Kathir ... 133
  - Allah Mentions `Isa and Praises the Injil ... 133
- *Surah: 5 Ayah: 48, Ayah: 49 & Ayah: 50* ... *134*
  - Tafsir Ibn Kathir ... 135
  - Praising the Qur'an; the Command to Refer to the Qur'an for Judgment ... 135
- *Surah: 5 Ayah: 51, Ayah: 52 & Ayah: 53* ... *139*
  - Tafsir Ibn Kathir ... 140
  - The Prohibition of Taking the Jews, Christians and Enemies of Islam as Friends ... 140
- *Surah: 5 Ayah: 54, Ayah: 55 & Ayah: 56* ... *141*
  - Tafsir Ibn Kathir ... 142
  - Threatening to Replace the Believers With Another People if They Revert from Islam .. 142
- *Surah: 5 Ayah: 57 & Ayah: 58* ... *144*
  - Tafsir Ibn Kathir ... 144
  - The Prohibition of Being Loyal Friends with Disbelievers ... 144
  - The Disbelievers Mock the Prayer and the Adhan ... 145
- *Surah: 5 Ayah: 59, Ayah: 60, Ayah: 61, Ayah: 62 & Ayah: 63* ... *146*
  - Tafsir Ibn Kathir ... 147
  - The People of the Book are Enraged at the Believers Because of their Faith in Allah ... 147
  - The People of the Scriptures Deserve the Worst Torment on the Day of Resurrection .. 148
  - The Hypocrites Pretend to be Believers but Hide their Kufr ... 148
  - Criticizing Rabbis and Learned Religious Men for Giving up on Forbidding Evil ... 149
- *Surah: 5 Ayah: 64, Ayah: 65 & Ayah: 66* ... *150*
  - Tafsir Ibn Kathir ... 151
  - The Jews Say That Allah's Hand is Tied up! ... 151
  - Allah's Hands are Widely Outstretched ... 152
  - The Revelation to the Muslims only Adds to the Transgression and Disbelief of the Jews ... 153
  - Had the People of the Book Adhered to their Book, they Would Have Acquired the Good of this Life and the Hereafter ... 153
- *Surah: 5 Ayah: 67* ... *155*
  - Tafsir Ibn Kathir ... 155
  - Commanding the Prophet to Convey the Message; Promising Him Immunity and Protection ... 155
- *Surah: 5 Ayah: 68 & Ayah: 69* ... *157*
  - Tafsir Ibn Kathir ... 158
  - There is no Salvation Except through Faith in the Qur'an ... 158
- *Surah: 5 Ayah: 70 & Ayah: 71* ... *158*
  - Tafsir Ibn Kathir ... 159
- *Surah: 5 Ayah: 72, Ayah: 73, Ayah: 74 & Ayah: 75* ... *159*
  - Tafsir Ibn Kathir ... 161
  - The Disbelief of the Christians; `Isa Only called to Tawhid ... 161
  - `Isa is Allah's Servant and His Mother is a Truthful Believer ... 162
- *Surah: 5 Ayah: 76 & Ayah: 77* ... *163*

Tafsir Ibn Kathir 163
    The Prohibition of Shirk (Polytheism) and Exaggeration in the Religion 163
Surah: 5 Ayah: 78, Ayah: 79, Ayah: 80 & Ayah: 81.. 164
    Tafsir Ibn Kathir 165
        Allah Cursed the Disbelievers Among the Children of Israel 165
        Hadiths that Order Enjoining Righteousness and Forbidding Evil 165
        Censuring the Hypocrites 167

PRELUDE

Opening Serman

Indeed, all praise is due to Allah. We praise Him and seek His help and forgiveness. We seek refuge with Allah from our soul's evil and our wrong doings. He whom Allah guides, no one can misguide; and he whom He misguides, no one can guide

I bear witness that there is no (true) god except Allah – alone without a partner, and I bear witness that Muhammad (peace and blessings of Allah be upon him) is His 'abd (servant) and messenger.

يَٰٓأَيُّهَا ٱلَّذِينَ ءَامَنُوا۟ ٱتَّقُوا۟ ٱللَّهَ حَقَّ تُقَاتِهِۦ وَلَا تَمُوتُنَّ إِلَّا وَأَنتُم مُّسْلِمُونَ ۝

O you who believe! Fear Allâh (by doing all that He has ordered and by abstaining from all that He has forbidden) as He should be feared. (Obey Him, be thankful to Him, and remember Him always), and die not except in a state of Islâm (as Muslims (with complete submission to Allâh)).

يَٰٓأَيُّهَا ٱلنَّاسُ ٱتَّقُوا۟ رَبَّكُمُ ٱلَّذِى خَلَقَكُم مِّن نَّفْسٍ وَٰحِدَةٍ وَخَلَقَ مِنْهَا زَوْجَهَا وَبَثَّ مِنْهُمَا رِجَالًا كَثِيرًا وَنِسَآءً ۚ وَٱتَّقُوا۟ ٱللَّهَ ٱلَّذِى تَسَآءَلُونَ بِهِۦ وَٱلْأَرْحَامَ ۚ إِنَّ ٱللَّهَ كَانَ عَلَيْكُمْ رَقِيبًا ۝

O mankind! Be dutiful to your Lord, Who created you from a single person (Adam), and from him (Adam) He created his wife (Hawwâ (Eve)) and from them both He created many men and women; and fear Allâh through Whom you demand (your mutual rights), and (do not cut the relations of) the wombs (kinship). Surely, Allâh is Ever an All-Watcher over you.

يُصْلِحْ لَكُمْ أَعْمَٰلَكُمْ وَيَغْفِرْ لَكُمْ ذُنُوبَكُمْ ۗ وَمَن يُطِعِ ٱللَّهَ وَرَسُولَهُۥ فَقَدْ فَازَ فَوْزًا عَظِيمًا ۝

He will direct you to do righteous good deeds and will forgive you your sins. And whosoever obeys Allâh and His Messenger (peace be upon him), he has indeed achieved a great achievement (i.e. he will be saved from the Hell-fire and will be admitted to Paradise).

Indeed, the best speech is Allah's Book and the best guidance is Muhammad's () guidance. The worst affairs (of religion) are those innovated (by people), for every such innovation is an act of misguidance leading to the Fire

Our Mission

Our mission is to gather in one place, for the English-speaking public, all relevant information needed to make the Qur'an more understandable and easier to study. This book tries to do this by providing the following:

1. The Arabic Text for those who are able to read Arabic
2. Transliteration of the Arabic text for those who are unable to read the Arabic script. This will give them a sample of the sound of the Qur'an, which they could not otherwise comprehend from reading the English meaning.
3. The meaning of the qur'an (translated by Dr. Muhammad Taqi-ud-Din Al-Hilali, Ph.D. and Dr. Muhammad Muhsin Khan)
4. Explanation (abridged Tafsir) by Ibn Kathir (translated by Safi-ur-Rahman al-Mubarakpuri)

We hope that by doing this an ordinary English-speaker will be able to pick up a copy of this book and study and comprehend The Glorious Qur'an in a way that is acceptable to the understanding of the Rightly-guided Muslim Ummah (Community).

Biography of Hafiz Ibn Kathir (701 H - 774 H)

By the Honored Shaykh `Abdul-Qadir Al-Arna'ut, may Allah protect him.

He is the respected Imam, Abu Al-Fida', `Imad Ad-Din Isma il bin 'Umar bin Kathir Al-Qurashi Al-Busrawi - Busraian in origin; Dimashqi in training, learning and residence.

Ibn Kathir was born in the city of Busra in 701 H. His father was the Friday speaker of the village, but he died while Ibn Kathir was only four years old. Ibn Kathir's brother, Shaykh Abdul-Wahhab, reared him and taught him until he moved to Damascus in 706 H., when he was five years old.

Ibn Kathir's Teachers

Ibn Kathir studied Fiqh - Islamic jurisprudence - with Burhan Ad-Din, Ibrahim bin `Abdur-Rahman Al-Fizari, known as Ibn Al-Firkah (who died in 729 H). Ibn Kathir heard Hadiths from `Isa bin Al-Mutim, Ahmad bin Abi Talib, (Ibn Ash-Shahnah) (who died in 730 H), Ibn Al-Hajjar, (who died in 730 H), and the Hadith narrator of Ash-Sham (modern day Syria and surrounding areas); Baha Ad-Din Al-Qasim bin Muzaffar bin `Asakir (who died in 723 H), and Ibn Ash-Shirdzi, Ishaq bin Yahya Al-Ammuddi, also known as `Afif Ad-Din, the Zahiriyyah Shaykh who died in 725 H, and Muhammad bin Zarrad. He remained with Jamal Ad-Din, Yusuf bin Az-Zaki AlMizzi who died in 724 H, he benefited from his knowledge and also married his daughter. He also read with Shaykh Al-Islam, Taqi Ad-Din Ahmad bin `Abdul-Halim bin `Abdus-Salam bin Taymiyyah who died in 728 H. He also read with the Imam Hafiz and historian Shams Ad-Din, Muhammad bin Ahmad bin Uthman bin Qaymaz Adh-Dhahabi, who died in 748 H. Also, Abu Musa Al-Qarafai, Abu Al-Fath Ad-Dabbusi and

'Ali bin `Umar As-Suwani and others who gave him permission to transmit the knowledge he learned with them in Egypt.

In his book, Al-Mu jam Al-Mukhtas, Al-Hafiz Adh-Dhaliabi wrote that Ibn Kathir was, "The Imam, scholar of jurisprudence, skillful scholar of Hadith, renowned Faqih and scholar of Tafsir who wrote several beneficial books."

Further, in Ad-Durar Al-Kdminah, Al-Hafiz Ibn Hajar AlAsqalani said, "Ibn Kathir worked on the subject of the Hadith in the areas of texts and chains of narrators. He had a good memory, his books became popular during his lifetime, and people benefited from them after his death."

Also, the renowned historian Abu Al-Mahasin, Jamal Ad-Din Yusuf bin Sayf Ad-Din (Ibn Taghri Bardi), said in his book, AlManhal As-Safi, "He is the Shaykh, the Imam, the great scholar `Imad Ad-Din Abu Al-Fida'. He learned extensively and was very active in collecting knowledge and writing. He was excellent in the areas of Fiqh, Tafsfr and Hadith. He collected knowledge, authored (books), taught, narrated Hadith and wrote. He had immense knowledge in the fields of Hadith, Tafsir, Fiqh, the Arabic language, and so forth. He gave Fatawa (religious verdicts) and taught until he died, may Allah grant him mercy. He was known for his precision and vast knowledge, and as a scholar of history, Hadith and Tafsir."

Ibn Kathir's Students

Ibn Hajji was one of Ibn Kathir's students, and he described Ibn Kathir: "He had the best memory of the Hadith texts. He also had the most knowledge concerning the narrators and authenticity, his contemporaries and teachers admitted to these qualities. Every time I met him I gained some benefit from him."

Also, Ibn Al-`Imad Al-Hanbali said in his book, Shadhardt Adh-Dhahab, "He is the renowned Hafiz `Imad Ad-Din, whose memory was excellent, whose forgetfulness was miniscule, whose understanding was adequate, and who had good knowledge in the Arabic language." Also, Ibn Habib said about Ibn Kathir, "He heard knowledge and collected it and wrote various books. He brought comfort to the ears with his Fatwas and narrated Hadith and brought benefit to other people. The papers that contained his Fatwas were transmitted to the various (Islamic) provinces. Further, he was known for his precision and encompassing knowledge."

Ibn Kathir's Books

1 - One of the greatest books that Ibn Kathir wrote was his Tafsir of the Noble Qur'an, which is one of the best Tafsir that rely on narrations [of Ahadith, the Tafsir of the Companions, etc.]. The Tafsir by Ibn Kathir was printed many times and several scholars have summarized it.

2- The History Collection known as Al-Biddyah, which was printed in 14 volumes under the name Al-Bidayah wanNihdyah, and contained the stories of the Prophets and previous nations, the Prophet's Seerah (life story) and Islamic history until his time. He also added a book Al-Fitan, about the Signs of the Last Hour.

3- At-Takmil ft Ma`rifat Ath-Thiqat wa Ad-Du'afa wal Majdhil which Ibn Kathir collected from the books of his two Shaykhs Al-Mizzi and Adh-Dhahabi; Al-Kdmal and Mizan Al-Ftiddl. He added several benefits regarding the subject of Al-Jarh and AtT'adil.

4- Al-Hadi was-Sunan ft Ahadith Al-Masdnfd was-Sunan which is also known by, Jami` Al-Masdnfd. In this book, Ibn Kathir collected the narrations of Imams Ahmad bin Hanbal, Al-Bazzar, Abu Ya`la Al-Mawsili, Ibn Abi Shaybah and from the six collections of Hadith: the Two Sahihs [Al-Bukhari and Muslim] and the Four Sunan [Abu Dawud, At-Tirmidhi, AnNasa and Ibn Majah]. Ibn Kathir divided this book according to areas of Fiqh.

5-Tabaqat Ash-Shaf iyah which also contains the virtues of Imam Ash-Shafi.

6- Ibn Kathir wrote references for the Ahadith of Adillat AtTanbfh, from the Shafi school of Fiqh.

7- Ibn Kathir began an explanation of Sahih Al-Bukhari, but he did not finish it.

8- He started writing a large volume on the Ahkam (Laws), but finished only up to the Hajj rituals.

9- He summarized Al-Bayhaqi's 'Al-Madkhal. Many of these books were not printed.

10- He summarized `Ulum Al-Hadith, by Abu `Amr bin AsSalah and called it Mukhtasar `Ulum Al-Hadith. Shaykh Ahmad Shakir, the Egyptian Muhaddith, printed this book along with his commentary on it and called it Al-Ba'th Al-Hathfth fi Sharh Mukhtasar `Ulum Al-Hadith.

11- As-Sfrah An-Nabawiyyah, which is contained in his book Al-Biddyah, and both of these books are in print.

12- A research on Jihad called Al-Ijtihad ft Talabi Al-Jihad, which was printed several times.

Ibn Kathir's Death

Al-Hafiz Ibn Hajar Al-Asgalani said, "Ibn Kathir lost his sight just before his life ended. He died in Damascus in 774 H." May Allah grant mercy upon Ibn Kathir and make him among the residents of His Paradise.

PREFACE

In the name of Allah, Most Gracious, Most Merciful.

About this book

The previous publication of this book included some background information to the chapters of the Qur'an by an Islamic scholar known as Abul Ala Maududi. This information was used to shed more light on the chapters by giving a summery of why each chapter was given its name, It's period of revelation and the circumstances surrounding its revelatiom. However, some Muslims objected to the inclusion of the contributions of Maududi.

In this new publication of Tafsir Ibn Kathir, we have removed all traces of the contribution of Abul Ala Maududi. Personally, I do not know the reasons for the objections to Maududi, but this work concerns only the tafsir of Ibn Kathir, so we have not included anything from Maududi in it. We have also corrected all the typing and formatting errors found in the previous publication. We have not alter the structure of the book. The reader is still able to read the full Arabic Text of the thirty Parts of the Qur'an and follow its meanings in the English language. The transliteration of the Arabic text should also give the reader a taste of the sound of the original Arabic.

May Almighty Allah accept this effort from us, and make it a source of blessings for us in this world and in the next. I bear witness that there is none worthy of worship but Allah and I bear witness that Muhammad (may the peace and blessings of Allah be upon him) is the slave and messenger of Allah.

Performing Prostration While Reading the Qur'an

Question:

Could you please give a list of the Qur'anic verses when a prostration is recommended? What happens if we read these verses and not perform a prostration?

A. Jalil

Answer:

There are 15 verses in the Qur'an that mention prostration before God Almighty as a good action by God-fearing believers. Therefore, it is strongly recommended to perform such a prostration when we read or listen to any of these verses, whether during prayer or in any situation.

Some scholars are of the view that even if one has not performed ablution, one should prostrate oneself. These verses are given here, starting with the Arabic title of the surah which is followed by two numbers, the first indicating the surah, and the second indicating the verse,: Al-Araf 7: 206; Al-Raad 13: 15; Al-Nahl 16: 50; Al-Isra 17: 109; Maryam 19: 58; Al-Hajj 22: 18 & 22: 77; Al-Furqan 25: 60; Al-Naml 27: 26;

Al-Sajdah 32: 15; Saad 38: 25; Fussilat 41: 38; Al-Najm 53: 62; Al-Inshiqaq 84: 21 and Al-Alaq 96: 19.

If you do not perform a prostration when you read or listen to any of these verses, you have done badly because you miss out on the reward of performing a prostration for God. You incur no sin and violate no divine order.

Reference:
http://archive.arabnews.com/?page=5&section=0&article=97811&d=1&m=7&y=2007

The Glorious Qur'an Juz' 6 (Part 6): Chapter (Surah) 4: An-Nisaa (The Women) 148 To Chapter (Surah) 5: Al-Ma'idah (The Table, The Table Spread) 081

PART 6 FULL ARABIC TEXT

Chapter (Surah) 4: An-Nisaa 148-176

﴿ ۞ لَّا يُحِبُّ ٱللَّهُ ٱلْجَهْرَ بِٱلسُّوٓءِ مِنَ ٱلْقَوْلِ إِلَّا مَن ظُلِمَ ۚ وَكَانَ ٱللَّهُ سَمِيعًا عَلِيمًا ۝ إِن تُبْدُواْ خَيْرًا أَوْ تُخْفُوهُ أَوْ تَعْفُواْ عَن سُوٓءٍ فَإِنَّ ٱللَّهَ كَانَ عَفُوًّا قَدِيرًا ۝ إِنَّ ٱلَّذِينَ يَكْفُرُونَ بِٱللَّهِ وَرُسُلِهِ وَيُرِيدُونَ أَن يُفَرِّقُواْ بَيْنَ ٱللَّهِ وَرُسُلِهِ وَيَقُولُونَ نُؤْمِنُ بِبَعْضٍ وَنَكْفُرُ بِبَعْضٍ وَيُرِيدُونَ أَن يَتَّخِذُواْ بَيْنَ ذَٰلِكَ سَبِيلًا ۝ أُوْلَٰٓئِكَ هُمُ ٱلْكَٰفِرُونَ حَقًّا ۚ وَأَعْتَدْنَا لِلْكَٰفِرِينَ عَذَابًا مُّهِينًا ۝ وَٱلَّذِينَ ءَامَنُواْ بِٱللَّهِ وَرُسُلِهِ وَلَمْ يُفَرِّقُواْ بَيْنَ أَحَدٍ مِّنْهُمْ أُوْلَٰٓئِكَ سَوْفَ يُؤْتِيهِمْ أُجُورَهُمْ ۗ وَكَانَ ٱللَّهُ غَفُورًا رَّحِيمًا ۝ يَسْـَٔلُكَ أَهْلُ ٱلْكِتَٰبِ أَن تُنَزِّلَ عَلَيْهِمْ كِتَٰبًا مِّنَ ٱلسَّمَآءِ ۚ فَقَدْ سَأَلُواْ مُوسَىٰٓ أَكْبَرَ مِن ذَٰلِكَ فَقَالُوٓاْ أَرِنَا ٱللَّهَ جَهْرَةً فَأَخَذَتْهُمُ ٱلصَّٰعِقَةُ بِظُلْمِهِمْ ۚ ثُمَّ ٱتَّخَذُواْ ٱلْعِجْلَ مِنۢ بَعْدِ مَا جَآءَتْهُمُ ٱلْبَيِّنَٰتُ فَعَفَوْنَا عَن ذَٰلِكَ ۚ وَءَاتَيْنَا مُوسَىٰ سُلْطَٰنًا مُّبِينًا ۝ وَرَفَعْنَا فَوْقَهُمُ ٱلطُّورَ بِمِيثَٰقِهِمْ وَقُلْنَا لَهُمُ ٱدْخُلُواْ ٱلْبَابَ سُجَّدًا وَقُلْنَا لَهُمْ لَا تَعْدُواْ فِى ٱلسَّبْتِ وَأَخَذْنَا مِنْهُم مِّيثَٰقًا غَلِيظًا ۝ فَبِمَا نَقْضِهِم مِّيثَٰقَهُمْ وَكُفْرِهِم بِـَٔايَٰتِ ٱللَّهِ وَقَتْلِهِمُ ٱلْأَنۢبِيَآءَ بِغَيْرِ حَقٍّ وَقَوْلِهِمْ قُلُوبُنَا غُلْفٌۢ ۚ بَلْ طَبَعَ ٱللَّهُ عَلَيْهَا بِكُفْرِهِمْ فَلَا يُؤْمِنُونَ إِلَّا قَلِيلًا ۝ وَبِكُفْرِهِمْ وَقَوْلِهِمْ عَلَىٰ مَرْيَمَ بُهْتَٰنًا عَظِيمًا ۝ وَقَوْلِهِمْ إِنَّا قَتَلْنَا ٱلْمَسِيحَ عِيسَى ٱبْنَ مَرْيَمَ رَسُولَ ٱللَّهِ وَمَا قَتَلُوهُ

وَمَا صَلَبُوهُ وَلَـٰكِن شُبِّهَ لَهُمْ ۚ وَإِنَّ ٱلَّذِينَ ٱخْتَلَفُوا۟ فِيهِ لَفِى شَكٍّ مِّنْهُ ۚ مَا لَهُم بِهِۦ مِنْ عِلْمٍ إِلَّا ٱتِّبَاعَ ٱلظَّنِّ ۚ وَمَا قَتَلُوهُ يَقِينًۢا ۝ بَل رَّفَعَهُ ٱللَّهُ إِلَيْهِ ۚ وَكَانَ ٱللَّهُ عَزِيزًا حَكِيمًا ۝ وَإِن مِّنْ أَهْلِ ٱلْكِتَٰبِ إِلَّا لَيُؤْمِنَنَّ بِهِۦ قَبْلَ مَوْتِهِۦ ۖ وَيَوْمَ ٱلْقِيَٰمَةِ يَكُونُ عَلَيْهِمْ شَهِيدًا ۝ فَبِظُلْمٍ مِّنَ ٱلَّذِينَ هَادُوا۟ حَرَّمْنَا عَلَيْهِمْ طَيِّبَٰتٍ أُحِلَّتْ لَهُمْ وَبِصَدِّهِمْ عَن سَبِيلِ ٱللَّهِ كَثِيرًا ۝ وَأَخْذِهِمُ ٱلرِّبَوٰا۟ وَقَدْ نُهُوا۟ عَنْهُ وَأَكْلِهِمْ أَمْوَٰلَ ٱلنَّاسِ بِٱلْبَٰطِلِ ۚ وَأَعْتَدْنَا لِلْكَٰفِرِينَ مِنْهُمْ عَذَابًا أَلِيمًا ۝ لَّـٰكِنِ ٱلرَّٰسِخُونَ فِى ٱلْعِلْمِ مِنْهُمْ وَٱلْمُؤْمِنُونَ يُؤْمِنُونَ بِمَآ أُنزِلَ إِلَيْكَ وَمَآ أُنزِلَ مِن قَبْلِكَ ۚ وَٱلْمُقِيمِينَ ٱلصَّلَوٰةَ ۚ وَٱلْمُؤْتُونَ ٱلزَّكَوٰةَ وَٱلْمُؤْمِنُونَ بِٱللَّهِ وَٱلْيَوْمِ ٱلْـَٔاخِرِ أُو۟لَـٰٓئِكَ سَنُؤْتِيهِمْ أَجْرًا عَظِيمًا ۝ ۞ إِنَّآ أَوْحَيْنَآ إِلَيْكَ كَمَآ أَوْحَيْنَآ إِلَىٰ نُوحٍ وَٱلنَّبِيِّـۧنَ مِنۢ بَعْدِهِۦ ۚ وَأَوْحَيْنَآ إِلَىٰٓ إِبْرَٰهِيمَ وَإِسْمَٰعِيلَ وَإِسْحَٰقَ وَيَعْقُوبَ وَٱلْأَسْبَاطِ وَعِيسَىٰ وَأَيُّوبَ وَيُونُسَ وَهَٰرُونَ وَسُلَيْمَٰنَ ۚ وَءَاتَيْنَا دَاوُۥدَ زَبُورًا ۝ وَرُسُلًا قَدْ قَصَصْنَٰهُمْ عَلَيْكَ مِن قَبْلُ وَرُسُلًا لَّمْ نَقْصُصْهُمْ عَلَيْكَ ۚ وَكَلَّمَ ٱللَّهُ مُوسَىٰ تَكْلِيمًا ۝ رُّسُلًا مُّبَشِّرِينَ وَمُنذِرِينَ لِئَلَّا يَكُونَ لِلنَّاسِ عَلَى ٱللَّهِ حُجَّةٌۢ بَعْدَ ٱلرُّسُلِ ۚ وَكَانَ ٱللَّهُ عَزِيزًا حَكِيمًا ۝ لَّـٰكِنِ ٱللَّهُ يَشْهَدُ بِمَآ أَنزَلَ إِلَيْكَ ۖ أَنزَلَهُۥ بِعِلْمِهِۦ ۖ وَٱلْمَلَـٰٓئِكَةُ يَشْهَدُونَ ۚ وَكَفَىٰ بِٱللَّهِ شَهِيدًا ۝ إِنَّ ٱلَّذِينَ كَفَرُوا۟ وَصَدُّوا۟ عَن سَبِيلِ ٱللَّهِ قَدْ ضَلُّوا۟ ضَلَـٰلًۢا بَعِيدًا ۝ إِنَّ ٱلَّذِينَ كَفَرُوا۟ وَظَلَمُوا۟ لَمْ يَكُنِ ٱللَّهُ لِيَغْفِرَ لَهُمْ وَلَا لِيَهْدِيَهُمْ طَرِيقًا ۝ إِلَّا طَرِيقَ جَهَنَّمَ خَٰلِدِينَ فِيهَآ أَبَدًا ۚ وَكَانَ ذَٰلِكَ عَلَى ٱللَّهِ يَسِيرًا ۝ يَـٰٓأَيُّهَا ٱلنَّاسُ قَدْ جَآءَكُمُ ٱلرَّسُولُ بِٱلْحَقِّ مِن رَّبِّكُمْ فَـَٔامِنُوا۟ خَيْرًا لَّكُمْ ۚ وَإِن تَكْفُرُوا۟ فَإِنَّ لِلَّهِ مَا فِى ٱلسَّمَٰوَٰتِ وَٱلْأَرْضِ ۚ وَكَانَ ٱللَّهُ عَلِيمًا حَكِيمًا ۝ يَـٰٓأَهْلَ ٱلْكِتَٰبِ لَا تَغْلُوا۟ فِى دِينِكُمْ وَلَا تَقُولُوا۟ عَلَى ٱللَّهِ إِلَّا ٱلْحَقَّ ۚ إِنَّمَا

ٱلْمَسِيحُ عِيسَى ٱبْنُ مَرْيَمَ رَسُولُ ٱللَّهِ وَكَلِمَتُهُۥٓ أَلْقَىٰهَآ إِلَىٰ مَرْيَمَ وَرُوحٌ مِّنْهُ ۖ فَـَٔامِنُوا۟ بِٱللَّهِ وَرُسُلِهِۦ ۖ وَلَا تَقُولُوا۟ ثَلَـٰثَةٌ ۚ ٱنتَهُوا۟ خَيْرًا لَّكُمْ ۚ إِنَّمَا ٱللَّهُ إِلَـٰهٌ وَٰحِدٌ ۖ سُبْحَـٰنَهُۥٓ أَن يَكُونَ لَهُۥ وَلَدٌ ۘ لَّهُۥ مَا فِى ٱلسَّمَـٰوَٰتِ وَمَا فِى ٱلْأَرْضِ ۗ وَكَفَىٰ بِٱللَّهِ وَكِيلًا ۝١٧١ لَّن يَسْتَنكِفَ ٱلْمَسِيحُ أَن يَكُونَ عَبْدًا لِّلَّهِ وَلَا ٱلْمَلَـٰٓئِكَةُ ٱلْمُقَرَّبُونَ ۚ وَمَن يَسْتَنكِفْ عَنْ عِبَادَتِهِۦ وَيَسْتَكْبِرْ فَسَيَحْشُرُهُمْ إِلَيْهِ جَمِيعًا ۝١٧٢ فَأَمَّا ٱلَّذِينَ ءَامَنُوا۟ وَعَمِلُوا۟ ٱلصَّـٰلِحَـٰتِ فَيُوَفِّيهِمْ أُجُورَهُمْ وَيَزِيدُهُم مِّن فَضْلِهِۦ ۖ وَأَمَّا ٱلَّذِينَ ٱسْتَنكَفُوا۟ وَٱسْتَكْبَرُوا۟ فَيُعَذِّبُهُمْ عَذَابًا أَلِيمًا وَلَا يَجِدُونَ لَهُم مِّن دُونِ ٱللَّهِ وَلِيًّا وَلَا نَصِيرًا ۝١٧٣ يَـٰٓأَيُّهَا ٱلنَّاسُ قَدْ جَآءَكُم بُرْهَـٰنٌ مِّن رَّبِّكُمْ وَأَنزَلْنَآ إِلَيْكُمْ نُورًا مُّبِينًا ۝١٧٤ فَأَمَّا ٱلَّذِينَ ءَامَنُوا۟ بِٱللَّهِ وَٱعْتَصَمُوا۟ بِهِۦ فَسَيُدْخِلُهُمْ فِى رَحْمَةٍ مِّنْهُ وَفَضْلٍ وَيَهْدِيهِمْ إِلَيْهِ صِرَٰطًا مُّسْتَقِيمًا ۝١٧٥ يَسْتَفْتُونَكَ قُلِ ٱللَّهُ يُفْتِيكُمْ فِى ٱلْكَلَـٰلَةِ ۚ إِنِ ٱمْرُؤٌا۟ هَلَكَ لَيْسَ لَهُۥ وَلَدٌ وَلَهُۥٓ أُخْتٌ فَلَهَا نِصْفُ مَا تَرَكَ ۚ وَهُوَ يَرِثُهَآ إِن لَّمْ يَكُن لَّهَا وَلَدٌ ۚ فَإِن كَانَتَا ٱثْنَتَيْنِ فَلَهُمَا ٱلثُّلُثَانِ مِمَّا تَرَكَ ۚ وَإِن كَانُوٓا۟ إِخْوَةً رِّجَالًا وَنِسَآءً فَلِلذَّكَرِ مِثْلُ حَظِّ ٱلْأُنثَيَيْنِ ۗ يُبَيِّنُ ٱللَّهُ لَكُمْ أَن تَضِلُّوا۟ ۗ وَٱللَّهُ بِكُلِّ شَىْءٍ عَلِيمٌۢ ۝١٧٦

(An-Nisaa 148-176)

Chapter (Surah) 5: Al-Maidah 001-081

﴿يَـٰٓأَيُّهَا ٱلَّذِينَ ءَامَنُوٓاْ أَوْفُواْ بِٱلْعُقُودِ ۚ أُحِلَّتْ لَكُم بَهِيمَةُ ٱلْأَنْعَـٰمِ إِلَّا مَا يُتْلَىٰ عَلَيْكُمْ غَيْرَ مُحِلِّى ٱلصَّيْدِ وَأَنتُمْ حُرُمٌ ۗ إِنَّ ٱللَّهَ يَحْكُمُ مَا يُرِيدُ ۝ يَـٰٓأَيُّهَا ٱلَّذِينَ ءَامَنُواْ لَا تُحِلُّواْ شَعَـٰٓئِرَ ٱللَّهِ وَلَا ٱلشَّهْرَ ٱلْحَرَامَ وَلَا ٱلْهَدْىَ وَلَا ٱلْقَلَـٰٓئِدَ وَلَآ ءَآمِّينَ ٱلْبَيْتَ ٱلْحَرَامَ يَبْتَغُونَ فَضْلًا مِّن رَّبِّهِمْ وَرِضْوَٰنًا ۚ وَإِذَا حَلَلْتُمْ فَٱصْطَادُواْ ۚ وَلَا يَجْرِمَنَّكُمْ شَنَـَٔانُ قَوْمٍ أَن صَدُّوكُمْ عَنِ ٱلْمَسْجِدِ ٱلْحَرَامِ أَن تَعْتَدُواْ ۘ وَتَعَاوَنُواْ عَلَى ٱلْبِرِّ وَٱلتَّقْوَىٰ ۖ وَلَا تَعَاوَنُواْ عَلَى ٱلْإِثْمِ وَٱلْعُدْوَٰنِ ۚ وَٱتَّقُواْ ٱللَّهَ ۖ إِنَّ ٱللَّهَ شَدِيدُ ٱلْعِقَابِ ۝ حُرِّمَتْ عَلَيْكُمُ ٱلْمَيْتَةُ وَٱلدَّمُ وَلَحْمُ ٱلْخِنزِيرِ وَمَآ أُهِلَّ لِغَيْرِ ٱللَّهِ بِهِۦ وَٱلْمُنْخَنِقَةُ وَٱلْمَوْقُوذَةُ وَٱلْمُتَرَدِّيَةُ وَٱلنَّطِيحَةُ وَمَآ أَكَلَ ٱلسَّبُعُ إِلَّا مَا ذَكَّيْتُمْ وَمَا ذُبِحَ عَلَى ٱلنُّصُبِ وَأَن تَسْتَقْسِمُواْ بِٱلْأَزْلَـٰمِ ۚ ذَٰلِكُمْ فِسْقٌ ۗ ٱلْيَوْمَ يَئِسَ ٱلَّذِينَ كَفَرُواْ مِن دِينِكُمْ فَلَا تَخْشَوْهُمْ وَٱخْشَوْنِ ۚ ٱلْيَوْمَ أَكْمَلْتُ لَكُمْ دِينَكُمْ وَأَتْمَمْتُ عَلَيْكُمْ نِعْمَتِى وَرَضِيتُ لَكُمُ ٱلْإِسْلَـٰمَ دِينًا ۚ فَمَنِ ٱضْطُرَّ فِى مَخْمَصَةٍ غَيْرَ مُتَجَانِفٍ لِّإِثْمٍ ۙ فَإِنَّ ٱللَّهَ غَفُورٌ رَّحِيمٌ ۝ يَسْـَٔلُونَكَ مَاذَآ أُحِلَّ لَهُمْ ۖ قُلْ أُحِلَّ لَكُمُ ٱلطَّيِّبَـٰتُ ۙ وَمَا عَلَّمْتُم مِّنَ ٱلْجَوَارِحِ مُكَلِّبِينَ تُعَلِّمُونَهُنَّ مِمَّا عَلَّمَكُمُ ٱللَّهُ ۖ فَكُلُواْ مِمَّآ أَمْسَكْنَ عَلَيْكُمْ وَٱذْكُرُواْ ٱسْمَ ٱللَّهِ عَلَيْهِ ۖ وَٱتَّقُواْ ٱللَّهَ ۚ إِنَّ ٱللَّهَ سَرِيعُ ٱلْحِسَابِ ۝ ٱلْيَوْمَ أُحِلَّ لَكُمُ ٱلطَّيِّبَـٰتُ ۖ وَطَعَامُ ٱلَّذِينَ أُوتُواْ ٱلْكِتَـٰبَ حِلٌّ لَّكُمْ وَطَعَامُكُمْ حِلٌّ لَّهُمْ ۖ وَٱلْمُحْصَنَـٰتُ مِنَ ٱلْمُؤْمِنَـٰتِ وَٱلْمُحْصَنَـٰتُ مِنَ ٱلَّذِينَ أُوتُواْ ٱلْكِتَـٰبَ مِن قَبْلِكُمْ إِذَآ ءَاتَيْتُمُوهُنَّ أُجُورَهُنَّ مُحْصِنِينَ غَيْرَ مُسَـٰفِحِينَ وَلَا مُتَّخِذِىٓ أَخْدَانٍ ۗ وَمَن يَكْفُرْ بِٱلْإِيمَـٰنِ فَقَدْ حَبِطَ عَمَلُهُۥ وَهُوَ فِى ٱلْأَخِرَةِ مِنَ ٱلْخَـٰسِرِينَ ۝ يَـٰٓأَيُّهَا ٱلَّذِينَ ءَامَنُوٓاْ إِذَا قُمْتُمْ إِلَى ٱلصَّلَوٰةِ فَٱغْسِلُواْ وُجُوهَكُمْ

وَأَيْدِيَكُمْ إِلَى ٱلْمَرَافِقِ وَٱمْسَحُوا۟ بِرُءُوسِكُمْ وَأَرْجُلَكُمْ إِلَى ٱلْكَعْبَيْنِ ۚ وَإِن كُنتُمْ جُنُبًا فَٱطَّهَّرُوا۟ ۚ وَإِن كُنتُم مَّرْضَىٰٓ أَوْ عَلَىٰ سَفَرٍ أَوْ جَآءَ أَحَدٌ مِّنكُم مِّنَ ٱلْغَآئِطِ أَوْ لَـٰمَسْتُمُ ٱلنِّسَآءَ فَلَمْ تَجِدُوا۟ مَآءً فَتَيَمَّمُوا۟ صَعِيدًا طَيِّبًا فَٱمْسَحُوا۟ بِوُجُوهِكُمْ وَأَيْدِيكُم مِّنْهُ ۚ مَا يُرِيدُ ٱللَّهُ لِيَجْعَلَ عَلَيْكُم مِّنْ حَرَجٍ وَلَـٰكِن يُرِيدُ لِيُطَهِّرَكُمْ وَلِيُتِمَّ نِعْمَتَهُۥ عَلَيْكُمْ لَعَلَّكُمْ تَشْكُرُونَ ۝٦ وَٱذْكُرُوا۟ نِعْمَةَ ٱللَّهِ عَلَيْكُمْ وَمِيثَـٰقَهُ ٱلَّذِى وَاثَقَكُم بِهِۦٓ إِذْ قُلْتُمْ سَمِعْنَا وَأَطَعْنَا ۖ وَٱتَّقُوا۟ ٱللَّهَ ۚ إِنَّ ٱللَّهَ عَلِيمٌۢ بِذَاتِ ٱلصُّدُورِ ۝٧ يَـٰٓأَيُّهَا ٱلَّذِينَ ءَامَنُوا۟ كُونُوا۟ قَوَّٰمِينَ لِلَّهِ شُهَدَآءَ بِٱلْقِسْطِ ۖ وَلَا يَجْرِمَنَّكُمْ شَنَـَٔانُ قَوْمٍ عَلَىٰٓ أَلَّا تَعْدِلُوا۟ ۚ ٱعْدِلُوا۟ هُوَ أَقْرَبُ لِلتَّقْوَىٰ ۖ وَٱتَّقُوا۟ ٱللَّهَ ۚ إِنَّ ٱللَّهَ خَبِيرٌۢ بِمَا تَعْمَلُونَ ۝٨ وَعَدَ ٱللَّهُ ٱلَّذِينَ ءَامَنُوا۟ وَعَمِلُوا۟ ٱلصَّـٰلِحَـٰتِ ۙ لَهُم مَّغْفِرَةٌ وَأَجْرٌ عَظِيمٌ ۝٩ وَٱلَّذِينَ كَفَرُوا۟ وَكَذَّبُوا۟ بِـَٔايَـٰتِنَآ أُو۟لَـٰٓئِكَ أَصْحَـٰبُ ٱلْجَحِيمِ ۝١٠ يَـٰٓأَيُّهَا ٱلَّذِينَ ءَامَنُوا۟ ٱذْكُرُوا۟ نِعْمَتَ ٱللَّهِ عَلَيْكُمْ إِذْ هَمَّ قَوْمٌ أَن يَبْسُطُوٓا۟ إِلَيْكُمْ أَيْدِيَهُمْ فَكَفَّ أَيْدِيَهُمْ عَنكُمْ ۖ وَٱتَّقُوا۟ ٱللَّهَ ۚ وَعَلَى ٱللَّهِ فَلْيَتَوَكَّلِ ٱلْمُؤْمِنُونَ ۝١١ ۞ وَلَقَدْ أَخَذَ ٱللَّهُ مِيثَـٰقَ بَنِىٓ إِسْرَٰٓءِيلَ وَبَعَثْنَا مِنْهُمُ ٱثْنَىْ عَشَرَ نَقِيبًا ۖ وَقَالَ ٱللَّهُ إِنِّى مَعَكُمْ ۖ لَئِنْ أَقَمْتُمُ ٱلصَّلَوٰةَ وَءَاتَيْتُمُ ٱلزَّكَوٰةَ وَءَامَنتُم بِرُسُلِى وَعَزَّرْتُمُوهُمْ وَأَقْرَضْتُمُ ٱللَّهَ قَرْضًا حَسَنًا لَّأُكَفِّرَنَّ عَنكُمْ سَيِّـَٔاتِكُمْ وَلَأُدْخِلَنَّكُمْ جَنَّـٰتٍ تَجْرِى مِن تَحْتِهَا ٱلْأَنْهَـٰرُ ۚ فَمَن كَفَرَ بَعْدَ ذَٰلِكَ مِنكُمْ فَقَدْ ضَلَّ سَوَآءَ ٱلسَّبِيلِ ۝١٢ فَبِمَا نَقْضِهِم مِّيثَـٰقَهُمْ لَعَنَّـٰهُمْ وَجَعَلْنَا قُلُوبَهُمْ قَـٰسِيَةً ۖ يُحَرِّفُونَ ٱلْكَلِمَ عَن مَّوَاضِعِهِۦ ۙ وَنَسُوا۟ حَظًّا مِّمَّا ذُكِّرُوا۟ بِهِۦ ۚ وَلَا تَزَالُ تَطَّلِعُ عَلَىٰ خَآئِنَةٍ مِّنْهُمْ إِلَّا قَلِيلًا مِّنْهُمْ ۖ فَٱعْفُ عَنْهُمْ وَٱصْفَحْ ۚ إِنَّ ٱللَّهَ يُحِبُّ ٱلْمُحْسِنِينَ ۝١٣ وَمِنَ ٱلَّذِينَ قَالُوٓا۟ إِنَّا نَصَـٰرَىٰٓ أَخَذْنَا مِيثَـٰقَهُمْ فَنَسُوا۟ حَظًّا مِّمَّا ذُكِّرُوا۟ بِهِۦ

فَأَغْرَيْنَا بَيْنَهُمُ ٱلْعَدَاوَةَ وَٱلْبَغْضَآءَ إِلَىٰ يَوْمِ ٱلْقِيَٰمَةِ ۚ وَسَوْفَ يُنَبِّئُهُمُ ٱللَّهُ بِمَا كَانُوا۟ يَصْنَعُونَ ۝ يَٰٓأَهْلَ ٱلْكِتَٰبِ قَدْ جَآءَكُمْ رَسُولُنَا يُبَيِّنُ لَكُمْ كَثِيرًا مِّمَّا كُنتُمْ تُخْفُونَ مِنَ ٱلْكِتَٰبِ وَيَعْفُوا۟ عَن كَثِيرٍ ۚ قَدْ جَآءَكُم مِّنَ ٱللَّهِ نُورٌ وَكِتَٰبٌ مُّبِينٌ ۝ يَهْدِى بِهِ ٱللَّهُ مَنِ ٱتَّبَعَ رِضْوَٰنَهُۥ سُبُلَ ٱلسَّلَٰمِ وَيُخْرِجُهُم مِّنَ ٱلظُّلُمَٰتِ إِلَى ٱلنُّورِ بِإِذْنِهِۦ وَيَهْدِيهِمْ إِلَىٰ صِرَٰطٍ مُّسْتَقِيمٍ ۝ لَّقَدْ كَفَرَ ٱلَّذِينَ قَالُوٓا۟ إِنَّ ٱللَّهَ هُوَ ٱلْمَسِيحُ ٱبْنُ مَرْيَمَ ۚ قُلْ فَمَن يَمْلِكُ مِنَ ٱللَّهِ شَيْـًٔا إِنْ أَرَادَ أَن يُهْلِكَ ٱلْمَسِيحَ ٱبْنَ مَرْيَمَ وَأُمَّهُۥ وَمَن فِى ٱلْأَرْضِ جَمِيعًا ۗ وَلِلَّهِ مُلْكُ ٱلسَّمَٰوَٰتِ وَٱلْأَرْضِ وَمَا بَيْنَهُمَا ۚ يَخْلُقُ مَا يَشَآءُ ۚ وَٱللَّهُ عَلَىٰ كُلِّ شَىْءٍ قَدِيرٌ ۝ وَقَالَتِ ٱلْيَهُودُ وَٱلنَّصَٰرَىٰ نَحْنُ أَبْنَٰٓؤُا۟ ٱللَّهِ وَأَحِبَّٰٓؤُهُۥ ۚ قُلْ فَلِمَ يُعَذِّبُكُم بِذُنُوبِكُم ۖ بَلْ أَنتُم بَشَرٌ مِّمَّنْ خَلَقَ ۚ يَغْفِرُ لِمَن يَشَآءُ وَيُعَذِّبُ مَن يَشَآءُ ۚ وَلِلَّهِ مُلْكُ ٱلسَّمَٰوَٰتِ وَٱلْأَرْضِ وَمَا بَيْنَهُمَا ۖ وَإِلَيْهِ ٱلْمَصِيرُ ۝ يَٰٓأَهْلَ ٱلْكِتَٰبِ قَدْ جَآءَكُمْ رَسُولُنَا يُبَيِّنُ لَكُمْ عَلَىٰ فَتْرَةٍ مِّنَ ٱلرُّسُلِ أَن تَقُولُوا۟ مَا جَآءَنَا مِنۢ بَشِيرٍ وَلَا نَذِيرٍ ۖ فَقَدْ جَآءَكُم بَشِيرٌ وَنَذِيرٌ ۗ وَٱللَّهُ عَلَىٰ كُلِّ شَىْءٍ قَدِيرٌ ۝ وَإِذْ قَالَ مُوسَىٰ لِقَوْمِهِۦ يَٰقَوْمِ ٱذْكُرُوا۟ نِعْمَةَ ٱللَّهِ عَلَيْكُمْ إِذْ جَعَلَ فِيكُمْ أَنۢبِيَآءَ وَجَعَلَكُم مُّلُوكًا وَءَاتَىٰكُم مَّا لَمْ يُؤْتِ أَحَدًا مِّنَ ٱلْعَٰلَمِينَ ۝ يَٰقَوْمِ ٱدْخُلُوا۟ ٱلْأَرْضَ ٱلْمُقَدَّسَةَ ٱلَّتِى كَتَبَ ٱللَّهُ لَكُمْ وَلَا تَرْتَدُّوا۟ عَلَىٰٓ أَدْبَارِكُمْ فَتَنقَلِبُوا۟ خَٰسِرِينَ ۝ قَالُوا۟ يَٰمُوسَىٰٓ إِنَّ فِيهَا قَوْمًا جَبَّارِينَ وَإِنَّا لَن نَّدْخُلَهَا حَتَّىٰ يَخْرُجُوا۟ مِنْهَا فَإِن يَخْرُجُوا۟ مِنْهَا فَإِنَّا دَٰخِلُونَ ۝ قَالَ رَجُلَانِ مِنَ ٱلَّذِينَ يَخَافُونَ أَنْعَمَ ٱللَّهُ عَلَيْهِمَا ٱدْخُلُوا۟ عَلَيْهِمُ ٱلْبَابَ فَإِذَا دَخَلْتُمُوهُ فَإِنَّكُمْ غَٰلِبُونَ ۚ وَعَلَى ٱللَّهِ فَتَوَكَّلُوٓا۟ إِن كُنتُم مُّؤْمِنِينَ ۝ قَالُوا۟ يَٰمُوسَىٰٓ إِنَّا لَن نَّدْخُلَهَآ أَبَدًا مَّا دَامُوا۟ فِيهَا ۖ فَٱذْهَبْ أَنتَ وَرَبُّكَ فَقَٰتِلَآ إِنَّا

هَـٰهُنَا قَـٰعِدُونَ ۝ قَالَ رَبِّ إِنِّى لَآ أَمْلِكُ إِلَّا نَفْسِى وَأَخِى ۖ فَٱفْرُقْ بَيْنَنَا وَبَيْنَ ٱلْقَوْمِ ٱلْفَـٰسِقِينَ ۝ قَالَ فَإِنَّهَا مُحَرَّمَةٌ عَلَيْهِمْ ۛ أَرْبَعِينَ سَنَةً ۛ يَتِيهُونَ فِى ٱلْأَرْضِ ۚ فَلَا تَأْسَ عَلَى ٱلْقَوْمِ ٱلْفَـٰسِقِينَ ۝ ۞ وَٱتْلُ عَلَيْهِمْ نَبَأَ ٱبْنَىْ ءَادَمَ بِٱلْحَقِّ إِذْ قَرَّبَا قُرْبَانًا فَتُقُبِّلَ مِنْ أَحَدِهِمَا وَلَمْ يُتَقَبَّلْ مِنَ ٱلْءَاخَرِ قَالَ لَأَقْتُلَنَّكَ ۖ قَالَ إِنَّمَا يَتَقَبَّلُ ٱللَّهُ مِنَ ٱلْمُتَّقِينَ ۝ لَئِنۢ بَسَطتَ إِلَىَّ يَدَكَ لِتَقْتُلَنِى مَآ أَنَا۠ بِبَاسِطٍ يَدِىَ إِلَيْكَ لِأَقْتُلَكَ ۖ إِنِّىٓ أَخَافُ ٱللَّهَ رَبَّ ٱلْعَـٰلَمِينَ ۝ إِنِّىٓ أُرِيدُ أَن تَبُوٓأَ بِإِثْمِى وَإِثْمِكَ فَتَكُونَ مِنْ أَصْحَـٰبِ ٱلنَّارِ ۚ وَذَٰلِكَ جَزَٰٓؤُا۟ ٱلظَّـٰلِمِينَ ۝ فَطَوَّعَتْ لَهُۥ نَفْسُهُۥ قَتْلَ أَخِيهِ فَقَتَلَهُۥ فَأَصْبَحَ مِنَ ٱلْخَـٰسِرِينَ ۝ فَبَعَثَ ٱللَّهُ غُرَابًا يَبْحَثُ فِى ٱلْأَرْضِ لِيُرِيَهُۥ كَيْفَ يُوَٰرِى سَوْءَةَ أَخِيهِ ۚ قَالَ يَـٰوَيْلَتَىٰٓ أَعَجَزْتُ أَنْ أَكُونَ مِثْلَ هَـٰذَا ٱلْغُرَابِ فَأُوَٰرِىَ سَوْءَةَ أَخِى ۖ فَأَصْبَحَ مِنَ ٱلنَّـٰدِمِينَ ۝ مِنْ أَجْلِ ذَٰلِكَ كَتَبْنَا عَلَىٰ بَنِىٓ إِسْرَٰٓءِيلَ أَنَّهُۥ مَن قَتَلَ نَفْسًۢا بِغَيْرِ نَفْسٍ أَوْ فَسَادٍ فِى ٱلْأَرْضِ فَكَأَنَّمَا قَتَلَ ٱلنَّاسَ جَمِيعًا وَمَنْ أَحْيَاهَا فَكَأَنَّمَآ أَحْيَا ٱلنَّاسَ جَمِيعًا ۚ وَلَقَدْ جَآءَتْهُمْ رُسُلُنَا بِٱلْبَيِّنَـٰتِ ثُمَّ إِنَّ كَثِيرًا مِّنْهُم بَعْدَ ذَٰلِكَ فِى ٱلْأَرْضِ لَمُسْرِفُونَ ۝ إِنَّمَا جَزَٰٓؤُا۟ ٱلَّذِينَ يُحَارِبُونَ ٱللَّهَ وَرَسُولَهُۥ وَيَسْعَوْنَ فِى ٱلْأَرْضِ فَسَادًا أَن يُقَتَّلُوٓا۟ أَوْ يُصَلَّبُوٓا۟ أَوْ تُقَطَّعَ أَيْدِيهِمْ وَأَرْجُلُهُم مِّنْ خِلَـٰفٍ أَوْ يُنفَوْا۟ مِنَ ٱلْأَرْضِ ۚ ذَٰلِكَ لَهُمْ خِزْىٌ فِى ٱلدُّنْيَا ۖ وَلَهُمْ فِى ٱلْءَاخِرَةِ عَذَابٌ عَظِيمٌ ۝ إِلَّا ٱلَّذِينَ تَابُوا۟ مِن قَبْلِ أَن تَقْدِرُوا۟ عَلَيْهِمْ ۖ فَٱعْلَمُوٓا۟ أَنَّ ٱللَّهَ غَفُورٌ رَّحِيمٌ ۝ يَـٰٓأَيُّهَا ٱلَّذِينَ ءَامَنُوا۟ ٱتَّقُوا۟ ٱللَّهَ وَٱبْتَغُوٓا۟ إِلَيْهِ ٱلْوَسِيلَةَ وَجَـٰهِدُوا۟ فِى سَبِيلِهِۦ لَعَلَّكُمْ تُفْلِحُونَ ۝ إِنَّ ٱلَّذِينَ كَفَرُوا۟ لَوْ أَنَّ لَهُم مَّا فِى ٱلْأَرْضِ جَمِيعًا وَمِثْلَهُۥ مَعَهُۥ لِيَفْتَدُوا۟ بِهِۦ مِنْ عَذَابِ يَوْمِ ٱلْقِيَـٰمَةِ مَا تُقُبِّلَ مِنْهُمْ ۖ وَلَهُمْ عَذَابٌ أَلِيمٌ ۝ يُرِيدُونَ أَن

تَخْرُجُوا۟ مِنَ ٱلنَّارِ وَمَا هُم بِخَـٰرِجِينَ مِنْهَا ۖ وَلَهُمْ عَذَابٌ مُّقِيمٌ ۝ وَٱلسَّارِقُ وَٱلسَّارِقَةُ فَٱقْطَعُوٓا۟ أَيْدِيَهُمَا جَزَآءًۢ بِمَا كَسَبَا نَكَـٰلًا مِّنَ ٱللَّهِ ۗ وَٱللَّهُ عَزِيزٌ حَكِيمٌ ۝ فَمَن تَابَ مِنۢ بَعْدِ ظُلْمِهِۦ وَأَصْلَحَ فَإِنَّ ٱللَّهَ يَتُوبُ عَلَيْهِ ۗ إِنَّ ٱللَّهَ غَفُورٌ رَّحِيمٌ ۝ أَلَمْ تَعْلَمْ أَنَّ ٱللَّهَ لَهُۥ مُلْكُ ٱلسَّمَـٰوَٰتِ وَٱلْأَرْضِ يُعَذِّبُ مَن يَشَآءُ وَيَغْفِرُ لِمَن يَشَآءُ ۗ وَٱللَّهُ عَلَىٰ كُلِّ شَىْءٍ قَدِيرٌ ۝ ۞ يَـٰٓأَيُّهَا ٱلرَّسُولُ لَا يَحْزُنكَ ٱلَّذِينَ يُسَـٰرِعُونَ فِى ٱلْكُفْرِ مِنَ ٱلَّذِينَ قَالُوٓا۟ ءَامَنَّا بِأَفْوَٰهِهِمْ وَلَمْ تُؤْمِن قُلُوبُهُمْ ۛ وَمِنَ ٱلَّذِينَ هَادُوا۟ ۛ سَمَّـٰعُونَ لِلْكَذِبِ سَمَّـٰعُونَ لِقَوْمٍ ءَاخَرِينَ لَمْ يَأْتُوكَ ۖ يُحَرِّفُونَ ٱلْكَلِمَ مِنۢ بَعْدِ مَوَاضِعِهِۦ ۖ يَقُولُونَ إِنْ أُوتِيتُمْ هَـٰذَا فَخُذُوهُ وَإِن لَّمْ تُؤْتَوْهُ فَٱحْذَرُوا۟ ۚ وَمَن يُرِدِ ٱللَّهُ فِتْنَتَهُۥ فَلَن تَمْلِكَ لَهُۥ مِنَ ٱللَّهِ شَيْـًٔا ۚ أُو۟لَـٰٓئِكَ ٱلَّذِينَ لَمْ يُرِدِ ٱللَّهُ أَن يُطَهِّرَ قُلُوبَهُمْ ۚ لَهُمْ فِى ٱلدُّنْيَا خِزْىٌ ۖ وَلَهُمْ فِى ٱلْـَٔاخِرَةِ عَذَابٌ عَظِيمٌ ۝ سَمَّـٰعُونَ لِلْكَذِبِ أَكَّـٰلُونَ لِلسُّحْتِ ۚ فَإِن جَآءُوكَ فَٱحْكُم بَيْنَهُمْ أَوْ أَعْرِضْ عَنْهُمْ ۖ وَإِن تُعْرِضْ عَنْهُمْ فَلَن يَضُرُّوكَ شَيْـًٔا ۖ وَإِنْ حَكَمْتَ فَٱحْكُم بَيْنَهُم بِٱلْقِسْطِ ۚ إِنَّ ٱللَّهَ يُحِبُّ ٱلْمُقْسِطِينَ ۝ وَكَيْفَ يُحَكِّمُونَكَ وَعِندَهُمُ ٱلتَّوْرَىٰةُ فِيهَا حُكْمُ ٱللَّهِ ثُمَّ يَتَوَلَّوْنَ مِنۢ بَعْدِ ذَٰلِكَ ۚ وَمَآ أُو۟لَـٰٓئِكَ بِٱلْمُؤْمِنِينَ ۝ إِنَّآ أَنزَلْنَا ٱلتَّوْرَىٰةَ فِيهَا هُدًى وَنُورٌ ۚ يَحْكُمُ بِهَا ٱلنَّبِيُّونَ ٱلَّذِينَ أَسْلَمُوا۟ لِلَّذِينَ هَادُوا۟ وَٱلرَّبَّـٰنِيُّونَ وَٱلْأَحْبَارُ بِمَا ٱسْتُحْفِظُوا۟ مِن كِتَـٰبِ ٱللَّهِ وَكَانُوا۟ عَلَيْهِ شُهَدَآءَ ۚ فَلَا تَخْشَوُا۟ ٱلنَّاسَ وَٱخْشَوْنِ وَلَا تَشْتَرُوا۟ بِـَٔايَـٰتِى ثَمَنًا قَلِيلًا ۚ وَمَن لَّمْ يَحْكُم بِمَآ أَنزَلَ ٱللَّهُ فَأُو۟لَـٰٓئِكَ هُمُ ٱلْكَـٰفِرُونَ ۝ وَكَتَبْنَا عَلَيْهِمْ فِيهَآ أَنَّ ٱلنَّفْسَ بِٱلنَّفْسِ وَٱلْعَيْنَ بِٱلْعَيْنِ وَٱلْأَنفَ بِٱلْأَنفِ وَٱلْأُذُنَ بِٱلْأُذُنِ وَٱلسِّنَّ بِٱلسِّنِّ وَٱلْجُرُوحَ قِصَاصٌ ۚ فَمَن تَصَدَّقَ بِهِۦ فَهُوَ كَفَّارَةٌ لَّهُۥ ۚ وَمَن لَّمْ يَحْكُم بِمَآ أَنزَلَ ٱللَّهُ فَأُو۟لَـٰٓئِكَ هُمُ ٱلظَّـٰلِمُونَ

۞ وَقَفَّيْنَا عَلَىٰ ءَاثَٰرِهِم بِعِيسَى ٱبْنِ مَرْيَمَ مُصَدِّقًا لِّمَا بَيْنَ يَدَيْهِ مِنَ ٱلتَّوْرَىٰةِ ۖ وَءَاتَيْنَٰهُ ٱلْإِنجِيلَ فِيهِ هُدًى وَنُورٌ وَمُصَدِّقًا لِّمَا بَيْنَ يَدَيْهِ مِنَ ٱلتَّوْرَىٰةِ وَهُدًى وَمَوْعِظَةً لِّلْمُتَّقِينَ ۝ وَلْيَحْكُمْ أَهْلُ ٱلْإِنجِيلِ بِمَآ أَنزَلَ ٱللَّهُ فِيهِ ۚ وَمَن لَّمْ يَحْكُم بِمَآ أَنزَلَ ٱللَّهُ فَأُوْلَٰٓئِكَ هُمُ ٱلْفَٰسِقُونَ ۝ وَأَنزَلْنَآ إِلَيْكَ ٱلْكِتَٰبَ بِٱلْحَقِّ مُصَدِّقًا لِّمَا بَيْنَ يَدَيْهِ مِنَ ٱلْكِتَٰبِ وَمُهَيْمِنًا عَلَيْهِ ۖ فَٱحْكُم بَيْنَهُم بِمَآ أَنزَلَ ٱللَّهُ ۖ وَلَا تَتَّبِعْ أَهْوَآءَهُمْ عَمَّا جَآءَكَ مِنَ ٱلْحَقِّ ۚ لِكُلٍّ جَعَلْنَا مِنكُمْ شِرْعَةً وَمِنْهَاجًا ۚ وَلَوْ شَآءَ ٱللَّهُ لَجَعَلَكُمْ أُمَّةً وَٰحِدَةً وَلَٰكِن لِّيَبْلُوَكُمْ فِى مَآ ءَاتَىٰكُمْ ۖ فَٱسْتَبِقُواْ ٱلْخَيْرَٰتِ ۚ إِلَى ٱللَّهِ مَرْجِعُكُمْ جَمِيعًا فَيُنَبِّئُكُم بِمَا كُنتُمْ فِيهِ تَخْتَلِفُونَ ۝ وَأَنِ ٱحْكُم بَيْنَهُم بِمَآ أَنزَلَ ٱللَّهُ وَلَا تَتَّبِعْ أَهْوَآءَهُمْ وَٱحْذَرْهُمْ أَن يَفْتِنُوكَ عَنۢ بَعْضِ مَآ أَنزَلَ ٱللَّهُ إِلَيْكَ ۖ فَإِن تَوَلَّوْاْ فَٱعْلَمْ أَنَّمَا يُرِيدُ ٱللَّهُ أَن يُصِيبَهُم بِبَعْضِ ذُنُوبِهِمْ ۗ وَإِنَّ كَثِيرًا مِّنَ ٱلنَّاسِ لَفَٰسِقُونَ ۝ أَفَحُكْمَ ٱلْجَٰهِلِيَّةِ يَبْغُونَ ۚ وَمَنْ أَحْسَنُ مِنَ ٱللَّهِ حُكْمًا لِّقَوْمٍ يُوقِنُونَ ۝ ۞ يَٰٓأَيُّهَا ٱلَّذِينَ ءَامَنُواْ لَا تَتَّخِذُواْ ٱلْيَهُودَ وَٱلنَّصَٰرَىٰٓ أَوْلِيَآءَ ۘ بَعْضُهُمْ أَوْلِيَآءُ بَعْضٍ ۚ وَمَن يَتَوَلَّهُم مِّنكُمْ فَإِنَّهُۥ مِنْهُمْ ۗ إِنَّ ٱللَّهَ لَا يَهْدِى ٱلْقَوْمَ ٱلظَّٰلِمِينَ ۝ فَتَرَى ٱلَّذِينَ فِى قُلُوبِهِم مَّرَضٌ يُسَٰرِعُونَ فِيهِمْ يَقُولُونَ نَخْشَىٰٓ أَن تُصِيبَنَا دَآئِرَةٌ ۚ فَعَسَى ٱللَّهُ أَن يَأْتِىَ بِٱلْفَتْحِ أَوْ أَمْرٍ مِّنْ عِندِهِۦ فَيُصْبِحُواْ عَلَىٰ مَآ أَسَرُّواْ فِىٓ أَنفُسِهِمْ نَٰدِمِينَ ۝ وَيَقُولُ ٱلَّذِينَ ءَامَنُوٓاْ أَهَٰٓؤُلَآءِ ٱلَّذِينَ أَقْسَمُواْ بِٱللَّهِ جَهْدَ أَيْمَٰنِهِمْ ۙ إِنَّهُمْ لَمَعَكُمْ ۚ حَبِطَتْ أَعْمَٰلُهُمْ فَأَصْبَحُواْ خَٰسِرِينَ ۝ يَٰٓأَيُّهَا ٱلَّذِينَ ءَامَنُواْ مَن يَرْتَدَّ مِنكُمْ عَن دِينِهِۦ فَسَوْفَ يَأْتِى ٱللَّهُ بِقَوْمٍ يُحِبُّهُمْ وَيُحِبُّونَهُۥٓ أَذِلَّةٍ عَلَى ٱلْمُؤْمِنِينَ أَعِزَّةٍ عَلَى ٱلْكَٰفِرِينَ يُجَٰهِدُونَ فِى سَبِيلِ ٱللَّهِ وَلَا يَخَافُونَ لَوْمَةَ لَآئِمٍ ۚ ذَٰلِكَ فَضْلُ ٱللَّهِ يُؤْتِيهِ مَن يَشَآءُ ۚ وَٱللَّهُ وَٰسِعٌ عَلِيمٌ ۝ إِنَّمَا وَلِيُّكُمُ

ٱللَّهُ وَرَسُولُهُ وَٱلَّذِينَ ءَامَنُوا۟ ٱلَّذِينَ يُقِيمُونَ ٱلصَّلَوٰةَ وَيُؤْتُونَ ٱلزَّكَوٰةَ وَهُمْ رَٰكِعُونَ ۝ وَمَن يَتَوَلَّ ٱللَّهَ وَرَسُولَهُۥ وَٱلَّذِينَ ءَامَنُوا۟ فَإِنَّ حِزْبَ ٱللَّهِ هُمُ ٱلْغَٰلِبُونَ ۝ يَٰٓأَيُّهَا ٱلَّذِينَ ءَامَنُوا۟ لَا تَتَّخِذُوا۟ ٱلَّذِينَ ٱتَّخَذُوا۟ دِينَكُمْ هُزُوًا وَلَعِبًا مِّنَ ٱلَّذِينَ أُوتُوا۟ ٱلْكِتَٰبَ مِن قَبْلِكُمْ وَٱلْكُفَّارَ أَوْلِيَآءَ ۚ وَٱتَّقُوا۟ ٱللَّهَ إِن كُنتُم مُّؤْمِنِينَ ۝ وَإِذَا نَادَيْتُمْ إِلَى ٱلصَّلَوٰةِ ٱتَّخَذُوهَا هُزُوًا وَلَعِبًا ۚ ذَٰلِكَ بِأَنَّهُمْ قَوْمٌ لَّا يَعْقِلُونَ ۝ قُلْ يَٰٓأَهْلَ ٱلْكِتَٰبِ هَلْ تَنقِمُونَ مِنَّآ إِلَّآ أَنْ ءَامَنَّا بِٱللَّهِ وَمَآ أُنزِلَ إِلَيْنَا وَمَآ أُنزِلَ مِن قَبْلُ وَأَنَّ أَكْثَرَكُمْ فَٰسِقُونَ ۝ قُلْ هَلْ أُنَبِّئُكُم بِشَرٍّ مِّن ذَٰلِكَ مَثُوبَةً عِندَ ٱللَّهِ ۚ مَن لَّعَنَهُ ٱللَّهُ وَغَضِبَ عَلَيْهِ وَجَعَلَ مِنْهُمُ ٱلْقِرَدَةَ وَٱلْخَنَازِيرَ وَعَبَدَ ٱلطَّٰغُوتَ ۚ أُو۟لَٰٓئِكَ شَرٌّ مَّكَانًا وَأَضَلُّ عَن سَوَآءِ ٱلسَّبِيلِ ۝ وَإِذَا جَآءُوكُمْ قَالُوٓا۟ ءَامَنَّا وَقَد دَّخَلُوا۟ بِٱلْكُفْرِ وَهُمْ قَدْ خَرَجُوا۟ بِهِۦ ۚ وَٱللَّهُ أَعْلَمُ بِمَا كَانُوا۟ يَكْتُمُونَ ۝ وَتَرَىٰ كَثِيرًا مِّنْهُمْ يُسَٰرِعُونَ فِى ٱلْإِثْمِ وَٱلْعُدْوَٰنِ وَأَكْلِهِمُ ٱلسُّحْتَ ۚ لَبِئْسَ مَا كَانُوا۟ يَعْمَلُونَ ۝ لَوْلَا يَنْهَىٰهُمُ ٱلرَّبَّٰنِيُّونَ وَٱلْأَحْبَارُ عَن قَوْلِهِمُ ٱلْإِثْمَ وَأَكْلِهِمُ ٱلسُّحْتَ ۚ لَبِئْسَ مَا كَانُوا۟ يَصْنَعُونَ ۝ وَقَالَتِ ٱلْيَهُودُ يَدُ ٱللَّهِ مَغْلُولَةٌ ۚ غُلَّتْ أَيْدِيهِمْ وَلُعِنُوا۟ بِمَا قَالُوا۟ ۘ بَلْ يَدَاهُ مَبْسُوطَتَانِ يُنفِقُ كَيْفَ يَشَآءُ ۚ وَلَيَزِيدَنَّ كَثِيرًا مِّنْهُم مَّآ أُنزِلَ إِلَيْكَ مِن رَّبِّكَ طُغْيَٰنًا وَكُفْرًا ۚ وَأَلْقَيْنَا بَيْنَهُمُ ٱلْعَدَٰوَةَ وَٱلْبَغْضَآءَ إِلَىٰ يَوْمِ ٱلْقِيَٰمَةِ ۚ كُلَّمَآ أَوْقَدُوا۟ نَارًا لِّلْحَرْبِ أَطْفَأَهَا ٱللَّهُ ۚ وَيَسْعَوْنَ فِى ٱلْأَرْضِ فَسَادًا ۚ وَٱللَّهُ لَا يُحِبُّ ٱلْمُفْسِدِينَ ۝ وَلَوْ أَنَّ أَهْلَ ٱلْكِتَٰبِ ءَامَنُوا۟ وَٱتَّقَوْا۟ لَكَفَّرْنَا عَنْهُمْ سَيِّـَٔاتِهِمْ وَلَأَدْخَلْنَٰهُمْ جَنَّٰتِ ٱلنَّعِيمِ ۝ وَلَوْ أَنَّهُمْ أَقَامُوا۟ ٱلتَّوْرَىٰةَ وَٱلْإِنجِيلَ وَمَآ أُنزِلَ إِلَيْهِم مِّن رَّبِّهِمْ لَأَكَلُوا۟ مِن فَوْقِهِمْ وَمِن تَحْتِ أَرْجُلِهِم ۚ مِّنْهُمْ أُمَّةٌ مُّقْتَصِدَةٌ ۖ وَكَثِيرٌ مِّنْهُمْ سَآءَ مَا يَعْمَلُونَ ۝ يَٰٓأَيُّهَا ٱلرَّسُولُ بَلِّغْ مَآ أُنزِلَ إِلَيْكَ مِن رَّبِّكَ ۖ وَإِن لَّمْ تَفْعَلْ فَمَا بَلَّغْتَ رِسَالَتَهُۥ ۚ وَٱللَّهُ

يَعْصِمُكَ مِنَ ٱلنَّاسِ ۗ إِنَّ ٱللَّهَ لَا يَهْدِى ٱلْقَوْمَ ٱلْكَٰفِرِينَ ۝ قُلْ يَٰٓأَهْلَ ٱلْكِتَٰبِ لَسْتُمْ عَلَىٰ شَىْءٍ حَتَّىٰ تُقِيمُوا۟ ٱلتَّوْرَىٰةَ وَٱلْإِنجِيلَ وَمَآ أُنزِلَ إِلَيْكُم مِّن رَّبِّكُمْ ۗ وَلَيَزِيدَنَّ كَثِيرًا مِّنْهُم مَّآ أُنزِلَ إِلَيْكَ مِن رَّبِّكَ طُغْيَٰنًا وَكُفْرًا ۖ فَلَا تَأْسَ عَلَى ٱلْقَوْمِ ٱلْكَٰفِرِينَ ۝ إِنَّ ٱلَّذِينَ ءَامَنُوا۟ وَٱلَّذِينَ هَادُوا۟ وَٱلصَّٰبِـُٔونَ وَٱلنَّصَٰرَىٰ مَنْ ءَامَنَ بِٱللَّهِ وَٱلْيَوْمِ ٱلْءَاخِرِ وَعَمِلَ صَٰلِحًا فَلَا خَوْفٌ عَلَيْهِمْ وَلَا هُمْ يَحْزَنُونَ ۝ لَقَدْ أَخَذْنَا مِيثَٰقَ بَنِىٓ إِسْرَٰٓءِيلَ وَأَرْسَلْنَآ إِلَيْهِمْ رُسُلًا ۖ كُلَّمَا جَآءَهُمْ رَسُولٌۢ بِمَا لَا تَهْوَىٰٓ أَنفُسُهُمْ فَرِيقًا كَذَّبُوا۟ وَفَرِيقًا يَقْتُلُونَ ۝ وَحَسِبُوٓا۟ أَلَّا تَكُونَ فِتْنَةٌ فَعَمُوا۟ وَصَمُّوا۟ ثُمَّ تَابَ ٱللَّهُ عَلَيْهِمْ ثُمَّ عَمُوا۟ وَصَمُّوا۟ كَثِيرٌ مِّنْهُمْ ۚ وَٱللَّهُ بَصِيرٌۢ بِمَا يَعْمَلُونَ ۝ لَقَدْ كَفَرَ ٱلَّذِينَ قَالُوٓا۟ إِنَّ ٱللَّهَ هُوَ ٱلْمَسِيحُ ٱبْنُ مَرْيَمَ ۖ وَقَالَ ٱلْمَسِيحُ يَٰبَنِىٓ إِسْرَٰٓءِيلَ ٱعْبُدُوا۟ ٱللَّهَ رَبِّى وَرَبَّكُمْ ۖ إِنَّهُۥ مَن يُشْرِكْ بِٱللَّهِ فَقَدْ حَرَّمَ ٱللَّهُ عَلَيْهِ ٱلْجَنَّةَ وَمَأْوَىٰهُ ٱلنَّارُ ۖ وَمَا لِلظَّٰلِمِينَ مِنْ أَنصَارٍ ۝ لَّقَدْ كَفَرَ ٱلَّذِينَ قَالُوٓا۟ إِنَّ ٱللَّهَ ثَالِثُ ثَلَٰثَةٍ ۘ وَمَا مِنْ إِلَٰهٍ إِلَّآ إِلَٰهٌ وَٰحِدٌ ۚ وَإِن لَّمْ يَنتَهُوا۟ عَمَّا يَقُولُونَ لَيَمَسَّنَّ ٱلَّذِينَ كَفَرُوا۟ مِنْهُمْ عَذَابٌ أَلِيمٌ ۝ أَفَلَا يَتُوبُونَ إِلَى ٱللَّهِ وَيَسْتَغْفِرُونَهُۥ ۚ وَٱللَّهُ غَفُورٌ رَّحِيمٌ ۝ مَّا ٱلْمَسِيحُ ٱبْنُ مَرْيَمَ إِلَّا رَسُولٌ قَدْ خَلَتْ مِن قَبْلِهِ ٱلرُّسُلُ وَأُمُّهُۥ صِدِّيقَةٌ ۖ كَانَا يَأْكُلَانِ ٱلطَّعَامَ ۗ ٱنظُرْ كَيْفَ نُبَيِّنُ لَهُمُ ٱلْءَايَٰتِ ثُمَّ ٱنظُرْ أَنَّىٰ يُؤْفَكُونَ ۝ قُلْ أَتَعْبُدُونَ مِن دُونِ ٱللَّهِ مَا لَا يَمْلِكُ لَكُمْ ضَرًّا وَلَا نَفْعًا ۚ وَٱللَّهُ هُوَ ٱلسَّمِيعُ ٱلْعَلِيمُ ۝ قُلْ يَٰٓأَهْلَ ٱلْكِتَٰبِ لَا تَغْلُوا۟ فِى دِينِكُمْ غَيْرَ ٱلْحَقِّ وَلَا تَتَّبِعُوٓا۟ أَهْوَآءَ قَوْمٍ قَدْ ضَلُّوا۟ مِن قَبْلُ وَأَضَلُّوا۟ كَثِيرًا وَضَلُّوا۟ عَن سَوَآءِ ٱلسَّبِيلِ ۝ لُعِنَ ٱلَّذِينَ كَفَرُوا۟ مِنۢ بَنِىٓ إِسْرَٰٓءِيلَ عَلَىٰ لِسَانِ دَاوُۥدَ وَعِيسَى ٱبْنِ مَرْيَمَ ۚ ذَٰلِكَ بِمَا عَصَوا۟

وَّكَانُوا۟ يَعْتَدُونَ ۝ كَانُوا۟ لَا يَتَنَاهَوْنَ عَن مُّنكَرٍ فَعَلُوهُ ۚ لَبِئْسَ مَا كَانُوا۟ يَفْعَلُونَ ۝ تَرَىٰ كَثِيرًا مِّنْهُمْ يَتَوَلَّوْنَ ٱلَّذِينَ كَفَرُوا۟ ۚ لَبِئْسَ مَا قَدَّمَتْ لَهُمْ أَنفُسُهُمْ أَن سَخِطَ ٱللَّهُ عَلَيْهِمْ وَفِى ٱلْعَذَابِ هُمْ خَٰلِدُونَ ۝ وَلَوْ كَانُوا۟ يُؤْمِنُونَ بِٱللَّهِ وَٱلنَّبِىِّ وَمَآ أُنزِلَ إِلَيْهِ مَا ٱتَّخَذُوهُمْ أَوْلِيَآءَ وَلَٰكِنَّ كَثِيرًا مِّنْهُمْ فَٰسِقُونَ ۝

(Al-Maidah 001-081)

INTRODUCTION TO CHAPTER (SURAH) 4: AN-NISAA (THE WOMEN)

Ibn Kathir's Introduction

Virtues of Surat An-Nisa, A Madinan Surah

Al-`Awfi reported that Ibn `Abbas said that Surat An-Nisa' was revealed in Al-Madinah. Ibn Marduwyah recorded similar statements from `Abdullah bin Az-Zubayr and Zayd bin Thabit. In his Mustadrak, Al-Hakim recorded that `Abdullah bin Mas`ud said, "There are five Ayat in Surat An-Nisa' that I would prefer to the life of this world and all that is in it,

(Surely, Allah wrongs not even the weight of an atom,) (4:40),

(If you avoid the great sins which you are forbidden to do) (4:31),

(Verily, Allah forgives not that partners should be set up with Him (in worship), but He forgives except that (anything else) to whom He wills) (4:48),

(If they (hypocrites), when they had been unjust to themselves, had come to you) (4:64), and,

(And whoever does evil or wrongs himself, but afterwards seeks Allah's forgiveness, he will find Allah Oft-Forgiving, Most Merciful) (4:110)." Al-Hakim recorded that Ibn `Abbas said, "Ask me about Surat An-Nisa', for I learned the Qur'an when I was still young." Al-Hakim said, "This Hadith is Sahih according to the criteria of the Two Sahihs, and they did not collect it."

CHAPTER (SURAH) 4: AN-NISAA (THE WOMEN), VERSES 148 - 176

Surah: 4 Ayah: 148 & Ayah: 149

﴿ ۞ لَّا يُحِبُّ ٱللَّهُ ٱلْجَهْرَ بِٱلسُّوٓءِ مِنَ ٱلْقَوْلِ إِلَّا مَن ظُلِمَ ۚ وَكَانَ ٱللَّهُ سَمِيعًا عَلِيمًا ۱٤۸ ﴾

148. Allâh does not like that the evil should be uttered in public except by him who has been wronged. And Allâh is Ever All-Hearer, All-Knower.

﴿ إِن تُبْدُوا۟ خَيْرًا أَوْ تُخْفُوهُ أَوْ تَعْفُوا۟ عَن سُوٓءٍ فَإِنَّ ٱللَّهَ كَانَ عَفُوًّا قَدِيرًا ۱٤۹ ﴾

149. Whether you (mankind) disclose (by good words of thanks) a good deed (done to you in the form of a favor by someone), or conceal it, or pardon an evil, ... verily, Allâh is Ever Oft-Pardoning, All-Powerful.

Transliteration

148. La yuhibbu Allahu aljahra bialssoo-i mina alqawli illa man thulima wakana Allahu sameeAAan AAaleeman 149. In tubdoo khayran aw tukhfoohu aw taAAfoo AAan soo-in fa-inna Allaha kana AAafuwwan qadeeran

Tafsir Ibn Kathir

The Permission to Utter Evil in Public, For One Who Was Wronged

`Ali bin Abi Talhah said that Ibn `Abbas commented on the Ayah,

(Allah does not like that the evil should be uttered in public) "Allah does not like that any one should invoke Him against anyone else, unless one was wronged. In this case, Allah allows one to invoke Him against whoever wronged him. Hence Allah's statement,

(except by him who has been wronged.) Yet, it is better for one if he observes patience." Al-Hasan Al-Basri commented, "One should not invoke Allah (for curses) against whoever wronged him. Rather, he should supplicate, `O Allah! Help me against him and take my right from him.'" In another narration, Al-Hasan said, "Allah has allowed one to invoke Him against whoever wronged him without transgressing the limits." `Abdul-Karim bin Malik Al-Jazari said about this Ayah; "When a man curses you, you could curse him in retaliation. But if he lies about you, you may not lie about him.

(And indeed whosoever takes revenge after he has suffered wrong, for such there is no way (of blame) against them.)" Abu Dawud recorded that Abu Hurayrah said that the Messenger of Allah said,

«الْمُسْتَبَّانِ مَا قَالَا، فَعَلَى الْبَادِئِ مِنْهُمَا مَا لَمْ يَعْتَدِ الْمَظْلُومُ»

(Whatever words are uttered by those who curse each other, then he who started it will carry the burden thereof, unless the one who was wronged transgresses the limit.) Allah said,

(Whether you disclose a good deed, or conceal it, or pardon an evil; verily, Allah is Ever Pardoning, All-Powerful.) Meaning when you, mankind, admit to a good favor done to you, or conceal it, and forgive those who wrong you, then this will bring you closer to Allah and increase your reward with Him. Among Allah's attributes is that He forgives and pardons His servants, although He is able to punish them. Hence Allah's statement,

(Verily, Allah is Ever Pardoning, All-Powerful.) It was reported that some of the angels who carry Allah's Throne praise Him saying, "All praise is due to You for Your forbearing even though You have perfect knowledge (in all evil committed)." Some of them supplicate, "All praise is due to You for Your forgiving even though You have perfect ability (to punish)." An authentic Hadith states,

«مَا نَقَصَ مَالٌ مِنْ صَدَقَةٍ، وَلَا زَادَ اللهُ عَبْدًا بِعَفْوٍ إِلَّا عِزًّا، وَمَنْ تَوَاضَعَ لِلَّهِ رَفَعَهُ اللهُ»

(No charity shall ever decrease wealth, and Allah will only increase the honor of a servant who pardons, and he who is humble for Allah's sake, then Allah will elevate his grade.)

Surah: 4 Ayah: 150, Ayah: 151 & Ayah: 152

﴿ إِنَّ ٱلَّذِينَ يَكْفُرُونَ بِٱللَّهِ وَرُسُلِهِ وَيُرِيدُونَ أَن يُفَرِّقُوا۟ بَيْنَ ٱللَّهِ وَرُسُلِهِ وَيَقُولُونَ نُؤْمِنُ بِبَعْضٍ وَنَكْفُرُ بِبَعْضٍ وَيُرِيدُونَ أَن يَتَّخِذُوا۟ بَيْنَ ذَٰلِكَ سَبِيلًا ﴿١٥٠﴾

150. Verily, those who disbelieve in Allâh and His Messengers and wish to make distinction between Allâh and His Messengers (by believing in Allâh and disbelieving in His Messengers) saying, "We believe in some but reject others," and wish to adopt a way in between.

﴿ أُو۟لَٰٓئِكَ هُمُ ٱلْكَٰفِرُونَ حَقًّا ۚ وَأَعْتَدْنَا لِلْكَٰفِرِينَ عَذَابًا مُّهِينًا ﴿١٥١﴾

151. They are in truth disbelievers. And We have prepared for the disbelievers a humiliating torment.

﴿ وَٱلَّذِينَ ءَامَنُواْ بِٱللَّهِ وَرُسُلِهِۦ وَلَمْ يُفَرِّقُواْ بَيْنَ أَحَدٍ مِّنْهُمْ أُوْلَـٰٓئِكَ سَوْفَ يُؤْتِيهِمْ أُجُورَهُمْ ۗ وَكَانَ ٱللَّهُ غَفُورًا رَّحِيمًا ﴿١٥٢﴾ ﴾

152. And those who believe in Allâh and His Messengers and make no distinction between any of them (Messengers), We shall give them their rewards; and Allâh is Ever Oft-Forgiving, Most Merciful.

Transliteration

150. Inna allatheena yakfuroona biAllahi warusulihi wayureedoona an yufarriqoo bayna Allahi warusulihi wayaqooloona nu/minu bibaAAdin wanakfuru bibaAAdin wayureedoona an yattakhithoo bayna thalika sabeelan 151. Ola-ika humu alkafiroona haqqan waaAAtadna lilkafireena AAathaban muheenan 152. Waallatheena amanoo biAllahi warusulihi walam yufarriqoo bayna ahadin minhum ola-ika sawfa yu/teehim ojoorahum wakana Allahu ghafooran raheeman

Tafsir Ibn Kathir

Believing in Some Prophets and Rejecting Others is Pure Kufr

Allah threatens those who disbelieve in Him and in His Messengers, such as the Jews and Christians, who differentiate between Allah and His Messengers regarding faith. They believe in some Prophets and reject others, following their desires, lusts and the practices of their forefathers. They do not follow any proof for such distinction, because there is no such proof. Rather, they follow their lusts and prejudices. The Jews, may Allah curse them, believe in the Prophets, except `Isa and Muhammad, peace be upon them. The Christians believe in the Prophets but reject their Final and Seal, and the most honored among the prophets, Muhammad, peace be upon him. In addition, the Samirah (Samaritans) do not believe in any Prophet after Yuwsha` (Joshua), the successor of Musa bin `Imran. The Majus (Zoroastrians) are said to believe only in a Prophet called Zoroaster, although they do not believe in the law he brought them casting it behind them, and Allah knows best. Therefore, whoever rejects only one of Allah's Prophets, he will have disbelieved in all of them, because it is required from mankind to believe in every prophet whom Allah sent to the people of the earth. And whoever rejects one Prophet, out of envy, bias and personal whim, he only demonstrates that his faith in other Prophets is not valid, but an act of following desire and whim. This is why Allah said,

(Verily, those who disbelieve in Allah and His Messengers...) Thus, Allah describes these people as disbelievers in Allah and His Messengers;

(and wish to make distinction between Allah and His Messengers) in faith,

(saying, "We believe in some but reject others," and wish to adopt a way in between.) Allah then describes them;

(They are in truth disbelievers.) meaning, their disbelief in the Prophet they claim to believe in is clear. This is because their claimed faith in a certain Messenger is not true, for had they truly believed in him, they would have believed in other

Messengers, especially if the other Messenger has a stronger proof for his truthfulness. Or at least, they would have strived hard to acquire knowledge of the truth of the other Messenger. Allah said,

(And We have prepared for the disbelievers a humiliating torment.) This is just punishment for belittling the Prophets whom they disbelieved in, by ignoring what the Prophet brought to them from Allah, and because they are interested in the insignificant possessions of this world. Or, their behavior could be the result of their disbelief in the Prophet after they were aware of his truth, just as the Jewish rabbis did during the time of Muhammad, the Messenger of Allah . The Jews envied the Messenger because of the great prophethood that Allah gave him, and as a consequence, they denied the Messenger, defied him, became his enemies and fought against him. Allah sent humiliation upon them in this life, that shall be followed by disgrace in the Hereafter,

(And they were covered with humiliation and misery, and they drew on themselves the wrath of Allah.) in this life and the Hereafter. Allah's statement,

(And those who believe in Allah and His Messengers and make no distinction between any of them,) This refers to the Ummah of Muhammad who believe in every Book that Allah has revealed and in every Prophet whom Allah has sent. Allah said,

(The Messenger believes in what has been revealed to him from his Lord, and (so do) the believers. All of them believe in Allah.) (2:285). Allah then states that He has prepared great rewards for them, tremendous favor and a handsome bounty,

(We shall give them their rewards;) because of their faith in Allah and His Messengers,

(and Allah is Ever Forgiving, Most Merciful.) for their sin, if they have any.

Surah: 4 Ayah: 153 & Ayah: 154

﴿يَسْـَٔلُكَ أَهْلُ ٱلْكِتَٰبِ أَن تُنَزِّلَ عَلَيْهِمْ كِتَٰبًا مِّنَ ٱلسَّمَآءِ فَقَدْ سَأَلُواْ مُوسَىٰٓ أَكْبَرَ مِن ذَٰلِكَ فَقَالُوٓاْ أَرِنَا ٱللَّهَ جَهْرَةً فَأَخَذَتْهُمُ ٱلصَّٰعِقَةُ بِظُلْمِهِمْ ثُمَّ ٱتَّخَذُواْ ٱلْعِجْلَ مِنۢ بَعْدِ مَا جَآءَتْهُمُ ٱلْبَيِّنَٰتُ فَعَفَوْنَا عَن ذَٰلِكَ وَءَاتَيْنَا مُوسَىٰ سُلْطَٰنًا مُّبِينًا ۝﴾

153. The people of the Scripture (Jews) ask you to cause a book to descend upon them from heaven. Indeed they asked Mûsâ (Moses) for even greater than that, when they said: "Show us Allâh in public," but they were struck with thunderclap and lightning for their wickedness. Then they worshipped the calf even after clear proofs, evidences, and signs had come to them. (Even) so We forgave them. And We gave Mûsâ (Moses) a clear proof of authority.

Chapter 4: An-Nisaa (The Women), Verses 148-176

﴿ وَرَفَعْنَا فَوْقَهُمُ ٱلطُّورَ بِمِيثَٰقِهِمْ وَقُلْنَا لَهُمُ ٱدْخُلُوا۟ ٱلْبَابَ سُجَّدًا وَقُلْنَا لَهُمْ لَا تَعْدُوا۟ فِى ٱلسَّبْتِ وَأَخَذْنَا مِنْهُم مِّيثَٰقًا غَلِيظًا ۞ ﴾

154. And for their covenant, We raised over them the Mount and (on the other occasion) We said: "Enter the gate prostrating (or bowing) with humility;" and We commanded them: "Transgress not (by doing worldly works) on the Sabbath (Saturday)." And We took from them a firm covenant.

Transliteration

153. Yas-aluka ahlu alkitabi an tunazzila AAalayhim kitaban mina alssama-i faqad saaloo moosa akbara min thalika faqaloo arina Allaha jahratan faakhathat-humu alssaAAiqatu bithulmihim thumma ittakhathoo alAAijla min baAAdi ma jaat-humu albayyinatu faAAafawna AAan thalika waatayna moosa sultanan mubeenan 154. WarafaAAna fawqahumu alttoora bimeethaqihim waqulna lahumu odkhuloo albaba sujjadan waqulna lahum la taAAdoo fee alssabti waakhathna minhum meethaqan ghaleethan

Tafsir Ibn Kathir

The Stubbornness of the Jews

Muhammad bin Ka`b Al-Qurazi, As-Suddi and Qatadah said that the Jews asked the Messenger of Allah to cause a book to come down to them from heaven, just as the Tawrah was sent down to Musa. Ibn Jurayj said that the Jews asked the Messenger to cause books to come down to them addressed to so-and-so among them, testifying to the truth of what he was sent with. The Jews only asked for this because of their stubbornness, defiance, rejection and disbelief. The disbelievers of Quraysh also asked for similar things from the Prophet, as is mentioned in Surat Al-Isra',

(And they say: "We shall not believe in you, until you cause a spring to gush forth from the earth for us;) (17:90) Allah said,

(Indeed, they asked Musa for even greater than that, when they said, "Show us Allah in public," but they were struck with a bolt of lightning for their wickedness.) injustice, transgression, defiance and rebellion. This part was explained in Surat Al-Baqarah,

(And (remember) when you said: "O Musa! We shall never believe in you until we see Allah plainly." But you were struck by a bolt of lightning while you were looking. Then We raised you up after your death, so that you might be grateful.) (2:55,56) Allah's statement,

(Then they worshipped the calf even after Al-Bayyinat had come to them.) meaning, after they witnessed the tremendous miracles and unequivocal proofs at the hand of Musa in Egypt. They also witnessed the demise of their enemy, Fir`awn and his soldiers, when they all drowned in the sea. Yet soon after, when they passed by a people who were worshipping idols, they said to Musa,

(Make for us a god as they have gods.) Allah explains the story of the Jews worshipping the calf in Surat Al-A`raf (7) and Surah Ta Ha (20) after Musa went to meet with his Lord. When Musa returned, Allah decreed that in order for the Jews to earn accepted repentance, then those who did not worship the calf would have to kill those who worshipped it. They complied with this command, and Allah resurrected them afterwards. Allah said here,

((Even) so We forgave them. And We gave Musa a clear proof of authority.) Allah then said,

(And for their covenant, We raised over them the mount,) This was when they refrained from implementing the rulings of the Tawrah and refused what Musa brought them from Allah. So Allah raised the mountain above their heads and they were ordered to prostrate, which they did. Even so, they were looking above when they were prostrating for fear that the mountain might fall on them,

(And (remember) when We raised the mountain over them as if it had been a canopy, and they thought that it was going to fall on them. (We said): "Hold firmly to what We have given you.") Allah then said,

(and We said, "Enter the gate prostrating (or bowing) with humility;") meaning that they also defied this command in word and action. They were commanded to enter Bayt Al-Quds (in Jerusalem) while bowing and saying "Hittah", meaning: `O Allah! take from us our sin of abandoning Jihad.' This was the cause of their wandering in the desert of Tih for forty years. Yet, they entered the House while crawling on their rear ends and saying `Hintah (a wheat grain) in Sha`rah (the hair)'.

(and We commanded them, "Transgress not the Sabbath (Saturday).") meaning, We commanded them to honor the Sabbath and honor what Allah prohibited them on that day.

t(And We took from them a firm covenant.) meaning, strong covenant. They rebelled, transgressed and committed what Allah prohibited by using deceit and trickery, as is mentioned in Surat Al-A`raf (7), (And ask them about the town that was by the sea.)

Surah: 4 Ayah: 155, Ayah: 156, Ayah: 157, Ayah: 18 & Ayah: 159

﴿ فَبِمَا نَقْضِهِم مِّيثَـٰقَهُمْ وَكُفْرِهِم بِـَٔايَـٰتِ ٱللَّهِ وَقَتْلِهِمُ ٱلْأَنۢبِيَآءَ بِغَيْرِ حَقٍّ وَقَوْلِهِمْ قُلُوبُنَا غُلْفٌۢ بَلْ طَبَعَ ٱللَّهُ عَلَيْهَا بِكُفْرِهِمْ فَلَا يُؤْمِنُونَ إِلَّا قَلِيلًا ﴾

155. Because of their breaking the covenant, and of their rejecting the Ayât (proofs, evidences, verses, lessons, signs, revelations, etc.) of Allâh, and of their killing the Prophets unjustly, and of their saying: "Our hearts are wrapped (with coverings, i.e. we do not understand what the Messengers say)" - nay, Allâh has set a seal upon their hearts because of their disbelief, so they believe not but a little.

Chapter 4: An-Nisaa (The Women), Verses 148-176

﴿ وَبِكُفْرِهِمْ وَقَوْلِهِمْ عَلَىٰ مَرْيَمَ بُهْتَٰنًا عَظِيمًا ۝ ﴾

156. And because of their (Jews) disbelief and uttering against Maryam (Mary (peace be upon her)) a grave false charge (that she has committed illegal sexual intercourse);

﴿ وَقَوْلِهِمْ إِنَّا قَتَلْنَا ٱلْمَسِيحَ عِيسَى ٱبْنَ مَرْيَمَ رَسُولَ ٱللَّهِ وَمَا قَتَلُوهُ وَمَا صَلَبُوهُ وَلَٰكِن شُبِّهَ لَهُمْ ۚ وَإِنَّ ٱلَّذِينَ ٱخْتَلَفُوا۟ فِيهِ لَفِى شَكٍّ مِّنْهُ ۚ مَا لَهُم بِهِۦ مِنْ عِلْمٍ إِلَّا ٱتِّبَاعَ ٱلظَّنِّ ۚ وَمَا قَتَلُوهُ يَقِينًۢا ۝ ﴾

157. And because of their saying (in boast), "We killed Messiah 'Isâ (Jesus), son of Maryam (Mary), the Messenger of Allâh," - but they killed him not, nor crucified him, but the resemblance of 'Isâ (Jesus) was put over another man (and they killed that man), and those who differ therein are full of doubts. They have no (certain) knowledge, they follow nothing but conjecture. For surely; they killed him not (i.e. 'Isâ (Jesus), son of Maryam (Mary) (peace be upon them))

﴿ بَل رَّفَعَهُ ٱللَّهُ إِلَيْهِ ۚ وَكَانَ ٱللَّهُ عَزِيزًا حَكِيمًا ۝ ﴾

158. But Allâh raised him ('Isâ (Jesus)) up (with his body and soul) unto Himself (and he (peace be upon him) is in the heavens). And Allâh is Ever All-Powerful, All-Wise.

﴿ وَإِن مِّنْ أَهْلِ ٱلْكِتَٰبِ إِلَّا لَيُؤْمِنَنَّ بِهِۦ قَبْلَ مَوْتِهِۦ ۖ وَيَوْمَ ٱلْقِيَٰمَةِ يَكُونُ عَلَيْهِمْ شَهِيدًا ۝ ﴾

159. And there is none of the people of the Scripture (Jews and Christians), but must believe in him ('Isâ (Jesus), son of Maryam (Mary), as only a Messenger of Allâh and a human being), before his ('Isâ (Jesus) (peace be upon him)or a Jew's or a Christian's) death (at the time of the appearance of the angel of death). And on the Day of Resurrection, he ('Isâ (Jesus)) will be a witness against them.

Transliteration

155. Fabima naqdihim meethaqahum wakufrihim bi-ayati Allahi waqatlihimu al-anbiyaa bighayri haqqin waqawlihim quloobuna ghulfun bal tabaAAa Allahu AAalayha bikufrihim fala yu/minoona illa qaleelan   156. Wabikufrihim waqawlihim AAala maryama buhtanan AAatheeman   157. Waqawlihim inna qatalna almaseeha AAeesa ibna maryama rasoola Allahi wama qataloohu wama salaboohu walakin shubbiha lahum wa-inna allatheena ikhtalafoo feehi lafee shakkin minhu ma lahum bihi min AAilmin illa ittibaAAa alththanni wama qataloohu yaqeenan   158. Bal rafaAAahu Allahu ilayhi wakana Allahu AAazeezan hakeeman   159. Wa-in min ahli alkitabi illa layu/minanna bihi qabla mawtihi wayawma alqiyamati yakoonu AAalayhim shaheedan

Tafsir Ibn Kathir

The Crimes of the Jews

The sins mentioned here are among the many sins that the Jews committed, which caused them to be cursed and removed far away from right guidance. The Jews broke the promises and vows that Allah took from them, and also rejected Allah's Ayat, meaning His signs and proofs, and the miracles that they witnessed at the hands of their Prophets. Allah said,

(and their killing the Prophets unjustly,) because their many crimes and offenses against the Prophets of Allah, for they killed many Prophets, may Allah's peace be upon them Their saying:

("Our hearts are Ghulf,") meaning, wrapped with covering, according to Ibn `Abbas, Mujahid, Sa`id bin Jubayr, `Ikrimah, As-Suddi and Qatadah. This is similar to the what the idolators said,

(And they say: "Our hearts are under coverings (screened) from that to which you invite us.") Allah said,

(nay, Allah has set a seal upon their hearts because of their disbelief,) It is as if they had given an excuse that their hearts do not understand what the Prophet says since their hearts are wrapped with coverings, so they claim. Allah said that their hearts are sealed because of their disbelief, as we mentioned before in the explanation of Surat Al-Baqarah. Allah then said,

(so they believe not but a little.) for their hearts became accustomed to Kufr, transgression and weak faith.

The Evil Accusation the Jews Uttered Against Maryam and Their Claim that They Killed `Isa

Allah said,

(And because of their (Jews) disbelief and uttering against Maryam a grave false charge.) `Ali bin Abi Talhah said that Ibn `Abbas stated that the Jews accused Maryam of fornication.This is also the saying of As-Suddi, Juwaybir, Muhammad bin Ishaq and several others. This meaning is also apparent in the Ayah, as the Jews accused Maryam and her son of grave accusations: They accused her of fornication and claimed that `Isa was an illegitimate son. Some of them even claimed that she was menstruating while fornicating. May Allah's continued curse be upon them until the Day of Resurrection. The Jews also said,

("We killed Al-Masih, `Isa, son of Maryam, the Messenger of Allah,") meaning, we killed the person who claimed to be the Messenger of Allah. The Jews only uttered these words in jest and mockery, just as the polytheists said,

(O you to whom the Dhikr (the Qur'an) has been sent down! Verily, you are a mad man!) When Allah sent `Isa with proofs and guidance, the Jews, may Allah's curses, anger, torment and punishment be upon them, envied him because of his

Chapter 4: An-Nisaa (The Women), Verses 148-176   21

prophethood and obvious miracles; curing the blind and leprous and bringing the dead back to life, by Allah's leave. He also used to make the shape of a bird from clay and blow in it, and it became a bird by Allah's leave and flew. `Isa performed other miracles that Allah honored him with, yet the Jews defied and bellied him and tried their best to harm him. Allah's Prophet `Isa could not live in any one city for long and he had to travel often with his mother, peace be upon them. Even so, the Jews were not satisfied, and they went to the king of Damascus at that time, a Greek polytheist who worshipped the stars. They told him that there was a man in Bayt Al-Maqdis misguiding and dividing the people in Jerusalem and stirring unrest among the king's subjects. The king became angry and wrote to his deputy in Jerusalem to arrest the rebel leader, stop him from causing unrest, crucify him and make him wear a crown of thorns. When the king's deputy in Jerusalem received these orders, he went with some Jews to the house that `Isa was residing in, and he was then with twelve, thirteen or seventeen of his companions. That day was a Friday, in the evening. They surrounded `Isa in the house, and when he felt that they would soon enter the house or that he would sooner or later have to leave it, he said to his companions, "Who volunteers to be made to look like me, for which he will be my companion in Paradise" A young man volunteered, but `Isa thought that he was too young. He asked the question a second and third time, each time the young man volunteering, prompting `Isa to say, "Well then, you will be that man." Allah made the young man look exactly like `Isa, while a hole opened in the roof of the house, and `Isa was made to sleep and ascended to heaven while asleep. Allah said,

(And (remember) when Allah said: "O `Isa! I will take you and raise you to Myself.") When `Isa ascended, those who were in the house came out. When those surrounding the house saw the man who looked like `Isa, they thought that he was `Isa. So they took him at night, crucified him and placed a crown of thorns on his head. The Jews then boasted that they killed `Isa and some Christians accepted their false claim, due to their ignorance and lack of reason. As for those who were in the house with `Isa, they witnessed his ascension to heaven, while the rest thought that the Jews killed `Isa by crucifixion. They even said that Maryam sat under the corpse of the crucified man and cried, and they say that the dead man spoke to her. All this was a test from Allah for His servants out of His wisdom. Allah explained this matter in the Glorious Qur'an which He sent to His honorable Messenger, whom He supported with miracles and clear, unequivocal evidence. Allah is the Most Truthful, and He is the Lord of the worlds Who knows the secrets, what the hearts conceal, the hidden matters in heaven and earth, what has occurred, what will occur, and what would occur if it was decreed. He said,

(but they killed him not, nor crucified him, but it appeared as that to them,) referring to the person whom the Jews thought was `Isa. This is why Allah said afterwards,

(and those who differ therein are full of doubts. They have no (certain) knowledge, they follow nothing but conjecture.) referring to the Jews who claimed to kill `Isa and the ignorant Christians who believed them. Indeed they are all in confusion, misguidance and bewilderment. This is why Allah said,

(For surely; they killed him not.) meaning they are not sure that `Isa was the one whom they killed. Rather, they are in doubt and confusion over this matter.

(But Allah raised him up unto Himself. And Allah is Ever All-Powerful,) meaning, He is the Almighty, and He is never weak, nor will those who seek refuge in Him ever be subjected to disgrace,

(All-Wise.) in all that He decides and ordains for His creatures. Indeed, Allah's is the clearest wisdom, unequivocal proof and the most glorious authority. Ibn Abi Hatim recorded that Ibn `Abbas said, "Just before Allah raised `Isa to the heavens, `Isa went to his companions, who were twelve inside the house. When he arrived, his hair was dripping water and he said, `There are those among you who will disbelieve in me twelve times after he had believed in me.' He then asked, `Who volunteers that his image appear as mine, and be killed in my place. He will be with me (in Paradise)' One of the youngest ones among them volunteered and `Isa asked him to sit down. `Isa again asked for a volunteer, and the young man kept volunteering and `Isa asking him to sit down. Then the young man volunteered again and `Isa said, `You will be that man,' and the resemblance of `Isa was cast over that man while `Isa ascended to heaven from a hole in the house. When the Jews came looking for `Isa, they found that young man and crucified him. Some of `Isa's followers disbelieved in him twelve times after they had believed in him. They then divided into three groups. One group, Al-Ya`qubiyyah (Jacobites), said, `Allah remained with us as long as He willed and then ascended to heaven.' Another group, An-Nasturiyyah (Nestorians), said, `The son of Allah was with us as long as he willed and Allah took him to heaven.' Another group, Muslims, said, `The servant and Messenger of Allah remained with us as long as Allah willed, and Allah then took him to Him.' The two disbelieving groups cooperated against the Muslim group and they killed them. Ever since that happened, Islam was then veiled until Allah sent Muhammad ." This statement has an authentic chain of narration leading to Ibn `Abbas, and An-Nasa'i narrated it through Abu Kurayb who reported it from Abu Mu`awiyah. Many among the Salaf stated that `Isa asked if someone would volunteer for his appearance to be cast over him, and that he will be killed instead of `Isa, for which he would be his companion in Paradise.

All Christians Will Believe in `Isa Before He Dies

Allah said,

(And there is none of the People of the Scripture, but must believe in him, before his death. And on the Day of Resurrection, he will be a witness against them.) Ibn Jarir recorded that Ibn `Abbas commented,

(And there is none of the People of the Scripture, but must believe in him, before his death.) before the death of `Isa, son of Maryam, peace be upon him. Al-`Awfi reported similar from Ibn `Abbas. Abu Malik commented;

(but must believe in him, before his death.) "This occurs after `Isa returns and before he dies, as then, all of the People of the Scriptures will believe in him."

Chapter 4: An-Nisaa (The Women), Verses 148-176

The Hadiths Regarding the Descent of `Isa Just Before the Day of Judgement, and his Mission

In the chapter about the Prophets in his Sahih, under, "The Descent of `Isa, Son of Maryam," Al-Bukhari recorded that Abu Hurayrah said that the Messenger of Allah said,

«وَالَّذِي نَفْسِي بِيَدِهِ، لَيُوشِكَنَّ أَنْ يَنْزِلَ فِيكُمُ ابْنُ مَرْيَمَ حَكَمًا عَدْلًا، فَيَكْسِرَ الصَّلِيبَ، وَيَقْتُلَ الْخِنْزِيرَ، وَيَضَعَ الْجِزْيَةَ، وَيَفِيضَ الْمَالُ حَتَّى لَا يَقْبَلَهُ أَحَدٌ، حَتَّى تَكُونَ السَّجْدَةُ خَيْرًا لَهُمْ مِنَ الدُّنْيَا وَمَا فِيهَا»

(By Him in Whose Hands my soul is, the son of Maryam (`Isa) will shortly descend among you as a just ruler, and will break the cross, kill the pig and abolish the Jizyah. Then there will be an abundance of wealth and nobody will accept charitable gifts any more. At that time, one prostration will be better for them than this life and all that is in it.) Abu Hurayrah then said, "Read if you will,

(And there is none of the People of the Scripture, but must believe in him, before his death. And on the Day of Resurrection, he will be a witness against them.)" Muslim recorded this Hadith. So, Allah's statement,

(before his death) refers to the death of `Isa, son of Maryam.

Another Hadith by Abu Hurayrah

Imam Ahmad recorded that Abu Hurayrah said that the Messenger of Allah said,

«لَيُهِلَّنَّ عِيسَى بِفَجِّ الرَّوْحَاءِ بِالْحَجِّ أَوِ الْعُمْرَةِ، أَوْ لَيُثْنِيَنَّهُمَا جَمِيعًا»

(`Isa will say Ihlal from the mountain highway of Ar-Rawha' for Hajj, `Umrah or both.) Muslim also recorded it. Ahmad recorded that Abu Hurayrah said that the Prophet said,

«يَنْزِلُ عِيسَى ابْنُ مَرْيَمَ فَيَقْتُلُ الْخِنْزِيرَ، وَيَمْحُو الصَّلِيبَ، وَتُجْمَعُ لَهُ الصَّلَاةُ، وَيُعْطَى الْمَالُ حَتَّى لَا يُقْبَلَ، وَيَضَعُ الْخَرَاجَ، وَيَنْزِلُ الرَّوْحَاءَ فَيَحُجُّ مِنْهَا أَوْ يَعْتَمِرُ أَوْ يَجْمَعُهُمَا»

(`Isa, son of Maryam, will descend and will kill the pig, break the cross, lead the prayer in congregation and give away wealth until it is no longer accepted by anyone.

He will also abolish the Jizyah and go to Ar-Rawha' from where he will go to perform Hajj, `Umrah or both.) Abu Hurayrah then recited,

(And there is none of the People of the Scripture, but must believe in him, before his death.) Hanzalah said, "Abu Hurayrah added, `Will believe in `Isa before `Isa dies,' but I do not know if this was a part of the Prophet's Hadith or if it was something that Abu Hurayrah said on his own." Ibn Abi Hatim also recorded this Hadith.

Another Hadith

Al-Bukhari recorded that Abu Hurayrah said that the Messenger of Allah said,

«كَيْفَ بِكُمْ إِذَا نَزَلَ فِيكُمُ الْمَسِيحُ ابْنُ مَرْيَمَ وَإِمَامُكُمْ مِنْكُم»

(How will you be when Al-Masih, son of Maryam (`Isa) descends among you while your Imam is from among yourselves) Imam Ahmad and Muslim also recorded this Hadith.

Another Hadith

Imam Ahmad recorded that Abu Hurayrah said that the Prophet said,

«الْأَنْبِيَاءُ إِخْوَةٌ لِعَلَّاتٍ، أُمَّهَاتُهُمْ شَتَّى، وَدِينُهُمْ وَاحِدٌ، وَإِنِّي أَوْلَى النَّاسِ بِعِيسَى ابْنِ مَرْيَمَ، لِأَنَّهُ لَمْ يَكُنْ نَبِيٌّ بَيْنِي وَبَيْنَهُ، وَإِنَّهُ نَازِلٌ فَإِذَا رَأَيْتُمُوهُ فَاعْرِفُوهُ: رَجُلٌ مَرْبُوعٌ إِلَى الْحُمْرَةِ وَالْبَيَاضِ، عَلَيْهِ ثَوْبَانِ مُمَصَّرَانِ، كَأَنَّ رَأْسَهُ يَقْطُرُ، وَإِنْ لَمْ يُصِبْهُ بَلَلٌ، فَيَدُقُّ الصَّلِيبَ، وَيَقْتُلُ الْخِنْزِيرَ، وَيَضَعُ الْجِزْيَةَ، وَيَدْعُو النَّاسَ إِلَى الْإِسْلَامِ، وَيُهْلِكُ اللهُ فِي زَمَانِهِ الْمِلَلَ كُلَّهَا إِلَّا الْإِسْلَامَ، وَيُهْلِكُ اللهُ فِي زَمَانِهِ الْمَسِيحَ الدَّجَّالَ، ثُمَّ تَقَعُ الْأَمَنَةُ عَلَى الْأَرْضِ حَتَّى تَرْتَعَ الْأُسُودُ مَعَ الْإِبِلِ، وَالنِّمَارُ مَعَ الْبَقَرِ، وَالذِّئَابُ مَعَ الْغَنَمِ، وَيَلْعَبُ الصِّبْيَانُ بِالْحَيَّاتِ لَا تَضُرُّهُمْ، فَيَمْكُثُ أَرْبَعِينَ سَنَةً ثُمَّ يُتَوَفَّى، وَيُصَلِّي عَلَيْهِ الْمُسْلِمُون»

(The Prophets are paternal brothers; their mothers are different, but their religion is one. I, more than any of mankind, have more right to `Isa, son of Maryam, for there was no Prophet between him and I. He will descend, and if you see him, know him. He is a well-built man, (the color of his skin) between red and white. He will descend while wearing two long, light yellow garments. His head appears to be dripping water, even though no moisture touched it. He will break the cross, kill the pig, and banish the Jizyah and will call the people to Islam. During his time, Allah will destroy all religions except Islam and Allah will destroy Al-Masih Ad-Dajjal (the False Messiah). Safety will then fill the earth, so much so that the lions will mingle with camels, tigers with cattle and wolves with sheep. Children will play with snakes, and they will not harm them. `Isa will remain for forty years and then will die, and Muslims will offer the funeral prayer for him.) Abu Dawud also recorded it.

Another Hadith

In his Sahih, Muslim recorded that Abu Hurayrah related to the Messenger of Allah that he said,

«لَا تَقُومُ السَّاعَةُ حَتَّى يَنْزِلَ الرُّومُ بِالْأَعْمَاقِ أَوْ بِدَابِقَ، فَيَخْرُجُ إِلَيْهِمْ جَيْشٌ مِنَ الْمَدِينَةِ مِنْ خِيَارِ أَهْلِ الْأَرْضِ يَوْمَئِذٍ، فَإِذَا تَصَافُّوا، قَالَتِ الرُّومُ: خَلُّوا بَيْنَنَا وَبَيْنَ الَّذِينَ سَبَوْا مِنَّا نُقَاتِلْهُمْ، فَيَقُولُ الْمُسْلِمُونَ: لَا وَاللهِ، لَا نُخَلِّي بَيْنَكُمْ وَبَيْنَ إِخْوَانِنَا، فَيُقَاتِلُونَهُمْ، (فَيَنْهَزِمُ) ثُلُثٌ لَا يَتُوبُ اللهُ عَلَيْهِمْ أَبَدًا، وَيُقْتَلُ ثُلُثُهُ أَفْضَلُ الشُّهَدَاءِ عِنْدَ اللهِ، وَيَفْتَتِحُ الثُّلُثُ لَا يُفْتَنُونَ أَبَدًا، فَيَفْتَتِحُونَ قُسْطَنْطِينِيَّةَ، فَبَيْنَمَا هُمْ يَقْسِمُونَ الْغَنَائِمَ قَدْ عَلَّقُوا سُيُوفَهُمْ بِالزَّيْتُونِ، إِذْ صَاحَ فِيهِمُ الشَّيْطَانُ: إِنَّ الْمَسِيحَ قَدْ خَلَفَكُمْ فِي أَهْلِيكُمْ، فَيَخْرُجُونَ، وَذَلِكَ بَاطِلٌ، فَإِذَا جَاءُوا الشَّامَ خَرَجَ، فَبَيْنَمَا هُمْ يُعِدُّونَ لِلْقِتَالِ يُسَوُّونَ الصُّفُوفَ، إِذْ أُقِيمَتِ الصَّلَاةُ فَيَنْزِلُ عِيسَى ابْنُ مَرْيَمَ، فَأَمَّهُمْ، فَإِذَا رَآهُ عَدُوُّ اللهِ، ذَابَ كَمَا يَذُوبُ الْمِلْحُ فِي الْمَاءِ، فَلَوْ تَرَكَهُ لَانْذَابَ حَتَّى يَهْلِكَ، وَلَكِنْ يَقْتُلُهُ اللهُ بِيَدِهِ، فَيُرِيهِمْ دَمَهُ فِي حَرْبَتِهِ»

(The (Last) Hour will not start until the Romans occupy Al-A`maq or Dabiq. An army, comprised of the best of the people of the earth then, will come from Al-Madinah and challenge them. When they camp face to face, the Romans will say, `Let us fight those who captured some of us.' The Muslims will say, `Nay! By Allah, we will never let you get to our brothers.' They will fight them. A third of the (Muslim) army will flee in defeat, and those are the ones whom Allah will never forgive. Another third will be killed, and those are the best martyrs before Allah. The last third will be victorious, and this third will never be stricken with Fitnah, and they will capture Constantinople (Istanbul). While they are dividing war booty, after hanging their swords on olive trees, Shaytan will shout among them, saying, `Al-Masih (Ad-Dajjal) has cornered your people'. They will leave to meet Ad-Dajjal in Ash-Sham. This will be a false warning, and when they reach Ash-Sham, Ad-Dajjal will then appear. When the Muslims are arranging their lines for battle and the prayer is called for, `Isa, son of Maryam, will descend and lead them in prayer. When the enemy of Allah (the False Messiah) sees him, he will dissolve just as salt dissolves in water, and if any of him were left, he would continue dissolving until he died. Allah will kill him with the hand of `Isa and will show the Muslims his blood on his spear.) Muslim recorded that `Abdullah bin `Amr said that the Messenger of Allah said,

«لَتُقَاتِلُنَّ الْيَهُودَ فَلَتَقْتُلُنَّهُمْ، حَتَّى يَقُولَ الْحَجَرُ: يَامُسْلِمُ هَذَا يَهُودِيٌّ فَتَعَالَ فَاقْتُلْه»

(You will fight the Jews and will kill them, until the stone will say, `O Muslim! There is a Jew here, so come and kill him.') Muslim recorded that Abu Hurayrah said that the Messenger of Allah said,

«لَا تَقُومُ السَّاعَةُ حَتَّى يُقَاتِلَ الْمُسْلِمُونَ الْيَهُودَ، فَيَقْتُلُهُمُ الْمُسْلِمُونَ حَتَّى يَخْتَبِىءَ الْيَهُودِيُّ مِنْ وَرَاءِ الْحَجَرِ وَالشَّجَرِ، فَيَقُولُ الْحَجَرُ وَالشَّجَرُ: يَامُسْلِمُ يَاعَبْدَاللهِ هَذَا يَهُودِيٌّ خَلْفِي فَتَعَالَ فَاقْتُلْهُ إِلَّا الْغَرْقَدَ فَإِنَّهُ مِنْ شَجَرِ الْيَهُودِ»

(The Hour will not start, until after the Muslims fight the Jews and the Muslims kill them. The Jew will hide behind a stone or tree, and the tree will say, `O Muslim! O servant of Allah! This is a Jew behind me, come and kill him.' Except Al-Gharqad, for it is a tree of the Jews.) Muslim bin Al-Hajjaj recorded in his Sahih that An-Nawwas bin Sam`an said, "The Messenger of Allah , mentioned Ad-Dajjal one day and kept belittling him (because being blind, yet claiming to be Allah) and speaking in grave terms about him until we thought that he was hiding in gardens of date-trees (in Al-Madinah). When we went by the Messenger, he sensed this anxiety in us and said,

«مَا شَأْنُكُمْ؟»

(What is the matter with you) We said, `O Messenger of Allah! Earlier, you mentioned Ad-Dajjal and while belittling him you spoke gravely about him until we thought that he was hiding in gardens of date-trees (of Al-Madinah).' He said,

«غَيْرُ الدَّجَّالِ أَخْوَفُنِي عَلَيْكُمْ، إِنْ يَخْرُجْ وَأَنَا فِيكُمْ فَأَنَا حَجِيجُهُ دُونَكُمْ، وَإِنْ يَخْرُجْ وَلَسْتُ فِيكُمْ فَامْرُؤٌ حَجِيجُ نَفْسِهِ، واللهُ خَلِيفَتِي عَلَى كُلِّ مُسْلِمٍ. إِنَّهُ شَابٌ قَطَطٌ، عَيْنُهُ طَافِيَةٌ كَأَنِّي أُشَبِّهُهُ بِعَبْدِالْعُزَّى بْنِ قَطَنٍ، مَنْ أَدْرَكَهُ مِنْكُمْ فَلْيَقْرَأْ عَلَيْهِ فَوَاتِحَ سُورَةِ الْكَهْفِ، إِنَّهُ خَارِجٌ مِنْ خَلَّةٍ بَيْنَ الشَّامِ وَالْعِرَاقِ، فَعَاثَ يَمِينًا وَعَاثَ شِمَالًا، يَاعِبَادَ اللهِ فَاثْبُتُوا»

(I fear other than Ad-Dajjal for you! If he appears while I am still among you, I will be his adversary on your behalf. If he appears while I am not among you, each one will depend on himself and Allah will be the Helper of every Muslim after me. He is young, with very curly hair and his eye is smashed. I thought that he looked like `Abdul-`Uzza bin Qatan. Whoever lives long and meets Ad-Dajjal, then let him recite the beginnings of Surat Al-Kahf. He will appear on a pass between Ash-Sham (Syria) and Al-`Iraq. He will wreak havoc to the right and left. O Servants of Allah! Hold fast.) We said, `O Messenger of Allah! How long will he stay on earth' He said,

«أَرْبَعُونَ يَوْمًا، يَوْمٌ كَسَنَةٍ، وَيَوْمٌ كَشَهْرٍ، وَيَوْمٌ كَجُمْعَةٍ، وَسَائِرُ أَيَّامِهِ كَأَيَّامِكُمْ»

(Forty days: One day as long as a year, one day as long as a month and one day as long as a week. The rest of his days will be as long as one of your ordinary days.) We said, `O Messenger of Allah! As for the day that is like a year, will the prayers of one day suffice for it' He said,

«لَا، اقْدُرُوا لَهُ قَدْرَهُ»

(No. Count for its due measure.) We said, `O Messenger of Allah, how will his speed be on earth' He said,

«كَالْغَيْثِ اسْتَدْبَرَتْهُ الرِّيحُ فَيَأْتِي عَلَى قَوْمٍ فَيَدْعُوهُمْ فَيُؤْمِنُونَ بِهِ، وَيَسْتَجِيبُونَ لَهُ، فَيَأْمُرُ السَّمَاءَ فَتُمْطِرُ، وَالْأَرْضَ فَتُنْبِتُ، فَتَرُوحُ عَلَيْهِمْ سَارِحَتُهُمْ أَطْوَلَ مَا كَانَتْ ذُرًى، وَأَسْبَغَهُ ضُرُوعًا، وَأَمَدَّهُ خَوَاصِرَ، ثُمَّ يَأْتِي الْقَوْمَ فَيَدْعُوهُمْ فَيَرُدُّونَ

عَلَيْهِ قَوْلَهُ، فَيَنْصَرِفُ عَنْهُمْ فَيُصْبِحُونَ مُمْحِلِينَ لَيْسَ بِأَيْدِيهِمْ شَيْءٌ مِنْ أَمْوَالِهِمْ وَيَمُرُّ بِالْخَرِبَةِ فَيَقُولُ لَهَا: أَخْرِجِي كُنُوزَكِ، فَتَتْبَعُهُ كُنُوزُهَا كَيَعَاسِيبِ النَّحْلِ، ثُمَّ يَدْعُو رَجُلًا مُمْتَلِئًا شَبَابًا فَيَضْرِبُهُ بِالسَّيْفِ، فَيَقْطَعُهُ جِزْلَتَيْنِ رَمْيَةَ الْغَرَضِ، ثُمَّ يَدْعُوهُ، فَيُقْبِلُ وَيَتَهَلَّلُ وَجْهُهُ وَيَضْحَكُ، فَبَيْنَمَا هُوَ كَذَلِكَ إِذْ بَعَثَ اللهُ الْمَسِيحَ ابْنَ مَرْيَمَ عَلَيْهِ السَّلَامُ، فَيَنْزِلُ عِنْدَ الْمَنَارَةِ الْبَيْضَاءِ شَرْقِيَّ دِمَشْقَ بَيْنَ مَهْرُودَتَيْنِ، وَاضِعًا كَفَّيْهِ عَلَى أَجْنِحَةِ مَلَكَيْنِ، إِذَا طَأْطَأَ رَأْسَهُ قَطَرَ، وَإِذَا رَفَعَهُ تَحَدَّرَ مِنْهُ جُمَانٌ كَاللُّؤْلُؤِ، وَلَا يَحِلُّ لِكَافِرٍ يَجِدُ رِيحَ نَفْسِهِ إِلَّا مَاتَ، وَنَفَسُهُ يَنْتَهِي حَيْثُ يَنْتَهِي طَرْفُهُ، فَيَطْلُبُهُ حَتَّى يُدْرِكَهُ بِبَابِ لُدٍّ، فَيَقْتُلُهُ، ثُمَّ يَأْتِي عِيسَى عَلَيْهِ السَّلَامُ قَوْمًا قَدْ عَصَمَهُمُ اللهُ مِنْهُ، فَيَمْسَحُ عَنْ وُجُوهِهِمْ، وَيُحَدِّثُهُمْ بِدَرَجَاتِهِمْ فِي الْجَنَّةِ، فَبَيْنَمَا هُوَ كَذَلِكَ إِذْ أَوْحَى اللهُ عَزَّ وَجَلَّ إِلَى عِيسَى: إِنِّي قَدْ أَخْرَجْتُ عِبَادًا لِي لَا يَدَانِ لِأَحَدٍ بِقِتَالِهِمْ، فَحَرِّزْ عِبَادِي إِلَى الطُّورِ، وَيَبْعَثُ اللهُ يَأْجُوجَ وَمَأْجُوجَ وَهُمْ مِنْ كُلِّ حَدَبٍ يَنْسِلُونَ، فَيَمُرُّ أَوَّلُهُمْ عَلَى بُحَيْرَةِ طَبَرِيَّةَ فَيَشْرَبُونَ مَا فِيهَا، وَيَمُرُّ آخِرُهُمْ فَيَقُولُونَ: لَقَدْ كَانَ بِهَذِهِ مَرَّةً مَاءٌ، وَيُحْصَرُ نَبِيُّ اللهِ عِيسَى وَأَصْحَابُهُ، حَتَّى يَكُونَ رَأْسُ الثَّوْرِ لِأَحَدِهِمْ خَيْرًا مِنْ مِائَةِ دِينَارٍ لِأَحَدِكُمُ الْيَوْمَ، فَيَرْغَبُ نَبِيُّ اللهِ عِيسَى وَأَصْحَابُهُ، فَيُرْسِلُ اللهُ عَلَيْهِمُ النَّغَفَ فِي رِقَابِهِمْ، فَيُصْبِحُونَ فَرْسَى كَمَوْتِ نَفْسٍ وَاحِدَةٍ، ثُمَّ يَهْبِطُ نَبِيُّ اللهِ عِيسَى وَأَصْحَابُهُ إِلَى الْأَرْضِ، فَلَا يَجِدُونَ فِي الْأَرْضِ مَوْضِعَ شِبْرٍ إِلَّا مَلَأَهُ زَهَمُهُمْ وَنَتْنُهُمْ، فَيَرْغَبُ نَبِيُّ اللهِ عِيسَى وَأَصْحَابُهُ إِلَى اللهِ، فَيُرْسِلُ اللهُ طَيْرًا كَأَعْنَاقِ الْبُخْتِ، فَتَحْمِلُهُمْ فَتَطْرَحُهُمْ حَيْثُ شَاءَ اللهُ، ثُمَّ يُرْسِلُ اللهُ مَطَرًا

لَا يَكُنْ مِنْهُ بَيْتُ مَدَرٍ، وَلَا وَبَرٍ، فَيَغْسِلُ الْأَرْضَ حَتَّى يَتْرُكَهَا كَالزَّلَفَةِ، ثُمَّ يُقَالُ لِلْأَرْضِ: أَخْرِجِي ثَمَرَكِ وَرُدِّي بَرَكَتَكِ، فَيَوْمَئِذٍ تَأْكُلُ الْعِصَابَةُ مِنَ الرُّمَّانَةِ، وَيَسْتَظِلُّونَ بِقِحْفِهَا، وَيُبَارِكُ اللهُ فِي الرِّسْلِ حَتَّى إِنَّ اللِّقْحَةَ مِنَ الْإِبِلِ لَتَكْفِي الْفِئَامَ، (مِنَ النَّاسِ وَاللِّقْحَةَ مِنَ الْبَقَرِ لَتَكْفِي الْقَبِيلَةَ مِنَ النَّاسِ، وَاللِّقْحَةَ مِنَ الْغَنَمِ لَتَكْفِي الْفَخِذَ مِنَ النَّاسِ)، فَبَيْنَمَا هُمْ كَذَلِكَ إِذْ بَعَثَ اللهُ رِيحًا طَيِّبَةً، فَتَأْخُذُهُمْ تَحْتَ آبَاطِهِمْ، فَتَقْبِضُ رُوحَ كُلِّ مُؤْمِنٍ وَكُلِّ مُسْلِمٍ، وَيَبْقَى شِرَارُ النَّاسِ يَتَهَارَجُونَ فِيهَا تَهَارُجَ الْحُمُرِ، فَعَلَيْهِمْ تَقُومُ السَّاعَةُ»

(Like the storm when driven by the wind. He will come to a people and will call them (to his worship), and they will believe in him and accept his call. He will order the sky and it will rain, the land and it will grow (vegetation). Their cattle will return to them with their hair the longest, their udders the fullest (with milk) and their stomachs the fattest. He will come to a different people and will call them (to his worship), and they will reject his call. He will then leave them. They will wake up in the morning destitute, missing all of their possessions. He will pass by a deserted land and will say to it, `Bring out your treasures', and its treasures will follow him just like swarms of bees. He will summon a man full of youth and will strike him with the sword once and will cut him into two pieces (and will separate between them like) the distance (between the hunter and) the game. He will call the dead man and he will come, and his face will radiant with pleasure and laughter. Afterwards (while all this is happening with Ad-Dajjal), Allah will send Al-Masih (`Isa), son of Maryam down. He will descend close to the white minaret to the east of Damascus. He will be wearing garments lightly colored with saffron and his hands will be placed on the wings of two angels. Whenever he lowers his head droplets fall. Whenever he raises his head, precious stones that look like pearls fall. No disbeliever can survive `Isa's breath, which reaches the distance of his sight. He will pursue Ad-Dajjal and will follow him to the doors of (the Palestinian city of) Ludd where he will kill him. A group of people who, by Allah's help, resisted and survived Ad-Dajjal, will pass by `Isa and he will anoint their faces and inform them about their grades in Paradise. Shortly afterwards, while this is happening with `Isa, Allah will reveal to him, `I raised a people of My creation that no one can fight. Therefore, gather My servants to At-Tur (the mountain of Musa in Sinai).' Then, Allah will raise Gog and Magog and they will swiftly swarm from every mound. Their front forces will reach Lake Tabariah (Sea of Galilee) and will drink all its water. The last of their forces will say as they pass by the lake, `This lake once had water!'

Meanwhile, `Isa, Allah's Prophet, will be cornered along with his companions until the head of a bull will be more precious to them than a hundred Dinars to you today.

`Isa, Allah's Prophet, and his companions will invoke Allah for help and Allah will send An-Naghaf (a worm) into the necks of Gog and Magog! The morning will come, and they will all be dead as if it was the death of one soul. Afterwards, `Isa, the Prophet of Allah, will come down with his companions to the low grounds (from Mount At-Tur). They will find that no space of a hand-span on the earth was free of their fat and rot (rotten corpses). `Isa, the Prophet of Allah, and his companions will seek Allah in supplication. Allah will send birds as large as the necks of camels. They will carry them (the corpses of Gog and Magog) and will throw them wherever Allah wills. Afterwards, Allah will send rain that no house made of mud or animal hair will be saved from, and it will cleanse the earth until it is as clean as a mirror. The earth will be commanded (by Allah), `Produce your fruits and regain your blessing.' Then, the group will eat from a pomegranate and will take shelter under the shade of its skin. Milk will be blessed, so much so that the milk-producing camel will yield large amounts that suffice for a large group of people. Meanwhile, Allah will send a pure wind that will overcome Muslims from under their arms and will take the soul of every believer and Muslim. Only the evildoers among people will remain. They will indulge in shameless public sex like that of donkeys. On them, the Hour will begin.)

Imam Ahmad and the collectors of the Sunan also recorded this Hadith. We will mention this Hadith again using the chain of narration collected by Ahmad explaining Allah's statement in Surat Al-Anbiya' (chapter 21),

(Until, when Ya`juj and Ma`juj (Gog and Magog people) are let loose (from their barrier).) In our time, in the year seven hundred and forty-one, a white minaret was built in the Umayyad Masjid (in Damascus) made of stone, in place of the minaret that was destroyed by a fire which the Christians were suspected to have started. May Allah's continued curses descend on the Christians until the Day of Resurrection. There is a strong feeling that this minaret is the one that `Isa will descend on, according to this Hadith.

Another Hadith

Muslim recorded in his Sahih that Ya`qub bin `Asim bin `Urwah bin Mas`ud Ath-Thaqafi said, "I heard `Abdullah bin `Amr saying to a man who asked him, `What is this Hadith that you are narrating You claim that the Hour will start on such and such date.' He said, `Subhan Allah (glory be to Allah),' or he said, `There is no deity worthy of worship except Allah.' I almost decided to never narrate anything to anyone. I only said, "Soon, you will witness tremendous incidents, the House (the Ka`bah) will be destroyed by fire, and such and such things will occur." He then said, `The Messenger of Allah said,

»يَخْرُجُ الدَّجَّالُ فِي أُمَّتِي فَيَمْكُثُ أَرْبَعِينَ، لَا أَدْرِي أَرْبَعِينَ يَوْمًا أَوْ أَرْبَعِينَ شَهْرًا أَوْ أَرْبَعِينَ عَامًا، فَيَبْعَثُ اللهُ تَعَالَى عِيسَى ابْنَ مَرْيَمَ كَأَنَّهُ عُرْوَةُ بْنُ مَسْعُودٍ، فَيَطْلُبُهُ فَيُهْلِكُهُ، ثُمَّ يَمْكُثُ النَّاسُ سَبْعَ سِنِينَ لَيْسَ بَيْنَ اثْنَيْنِ عَدَاوَةٌ، ثُمَّ يُرْسِلُ

Chapter 4: An-Nisaa (The Women), Verses 148-176

اللهُ رِيحًا بَارِدَةً مِنْ قِبَلِ الشَّامِ، فَلَا يَبْقَى عَلَى وَجْهِ الْأَرْضِ أَحَدٌ فِي قَلْبِهِ مِثْقَالُ ذَرَّةٍ مِنْ خَيْرٍ أَوْ إِيمَانٍ إِلَّا قَبَضَتْهُ، حَتَّى لَوْ أَنَّ أَحَدَكُمْ دَخَلَ فِي كَبِدِ جَبَلٍ لَدَخَلَتْهُ عَلَيْهِ حَتَّى تَقْبِضَهُ»

(Ad-Dajjal will appear in my nation and will remain for forty. (The narrator doubts whether it is forty days, months, or years).Then, Allah will send down `Isa, son of Maryam, looking just like `Urwah bin Mas`ud and he will seek Ad-Dajjal and will kill him. People will remain for seven years with no enmity between any two. Allah will send a cool wind from As-Sham that will leave no man on the face of the earth who has even the weight of an atom of good or faith, but will capture (his soul). Even if one of you takes refuge in the middle of a mountain, it will find him and capture (his soul).

«فَيَبْقَى شِرَارُ النَّاسِ فِي خِفَّةِ الطَّيْرِ وَأَحْلَامِ السِّبَاعِ، وَلَا يَعْرِفُونَ مَعْرُوفًا، وَلَا يُنْكِرُونَ مُنْكَرًا، فَيَتَمَثَّلُ لَهُمُ الشَّيْطَانُ فَيَقُولُ: أَلَا تَسْتَجِيبُونَ؟ فَيَقُولُونَ: فَمَا تَأْمُرُنَا؟ فَيَأْمُرُهُمْ بِعِبَادَةِ الْأَوْثَانِ، وَهُمْ فِي ذَلِكَ دَارٌّ رِزْقُهُمْ، حَسَنٌ عَيْشُهُمْ، ثُمَّ يُنْفَخُ فِي الصُّورِ فَلَا يَسْمَعُهُ أَحَدٌ إِلَّا أَصْغَى لِيتًا وَرَفَعَ لِيتًا،قَالَ: وَأَوَّلُ مَنْ يَسْمَعُهُ رَجُلٌ يَلُوطُ حَوْضَ إِبِلِهِ، قَالَ: فَيَصْعَقُ وَيَصْعَقُ النَّاسُ، ثُمَّ يُرْسِلُ اللهُ أَوْ قَالَ: يُنْزِلُ اللهُ مَطَرًا كَأَنَّهُ الطَّلُّ أَوْ قَالَ الظِّلُّ نُعْمَانُ الشَّاكُّ فَتَنْبُتُ مِنْهُ أَجْسَادُ النَّاسِ، ثُمَّ يُنْفَخُ فِيهِ أُخْرَى فَإِذَا هُمْ قِيَامٌ يَنْظُرُونَ. ثُمَّ يُقَالُ: أَيُّهَا النَّاسُ: هَلُمُّوا إِلَى رَبِّكُمْ»

Afterwards, only the most evil people will remain. They will be as light as birds, with the comprehension of beasts. They will not know or enjoin righteousness or forbid or know evil. Shaytan will appear to them and will say to them, `Would you follow me.' They will say, `What do you command us' He will command them to worship the idols. Meanwhile, their provision will come to them in abundance and their life will be good. Then the Trumpet will be blown and every person who hears it, will lower one side of his head and raise the other side (trying to hear that distant sound). The first man who will hear the Trumpet is someone who is preparing the water pool for his camels, and he and the people will swoon away. Allah will send down heavy rain and the bodies of people will grow with it. The Trumpet will be blown in again and the people will be resurrected and looking all about, staring. It will be said to them, `O people! Come to your Lord,'

(But stop them, verily, they are to be questioned.)

«ثم يقال: أخرجوا بعث النار، فيقال: من كم؟ فيقال: من كل ألف تسعمائة وتسعة وتسعين، قال: فذلك يوم»

(It will then be said, `Bring forth the share of the Fire.' It will be asked, `How many' It will be said, `From every one thousand, nine hundred and ninety-nine.' That Day is when,)

(the children will turn grey-headed,) and,

(The Day when the Shin shall be laid bare).)"

The Description of `Isa, upon him be Peace

As mentioned earlier, `Abdur-Rahman bin Adam narrated that Abu Hurayrah said that the Prophet said,

«فَإِذَا رَأَيْتُمُوهُ فَاعْرِفُوهُ: رَجُلٌ مَرْبُوعٌ إِلَى الْحُمْرَةِ وَالْبَيَاضِ، عَلَيْهِ ثَوْبَانِ مُمَصَّرَانِ، كَأَنَّ رَأْسَهُ يَقْطُرُ وَإِنْ لَمْ يُصِبْهُ بَلَلٌ»

(If you see `Isa, know him. He is a well-built man, (the color of his skin) between red and white. He will descend while wearing light yellow garments. His head looks like it is dripping water, even though no moisture touched it.) In the Hadith that An-Nawwas bin Sam`an narrated,

«فَيَنْزِلُ عِنْدَ الْمَنَارَةِ الْبَيْضَاءِ شَرْقِيَّ دِمَشْقَ بَيْنَ مَهْرُودَتَيْنِ وَاضِعًا كَفَّيْهِ عَلَى أَجْنِحَةِ مَلَكَيْنِ، إِذَا طَأْطَأَ رَأْسَهُ قَطَرَ، وَإِذَا رَفَعَهُ تَحَدَّرَ مِنْهُ مِثْلُ جُمَانِ اللُّؤْلُؤِ، لَا يَحِلُّ لِكَافِرٍ يَجِدُ رِيحَ نَفْسِهِ إِلَّا مَاتَ، وَنَفَسُهُ يَنْتَهِي حَيْثُ يَنْتَهِي طَرْفُهُ»

(He will descend close to the white minaret to the east of Damascus. He will be wearing two garments lightly colored with saffron, having his hands on the wings of two angels. Whenever he lowers his head, drops will fall off of it. Whenever he raises his head, precious jewels like pearls will fall off of it. No disbeliever can survive `Isa's breath, and his breath reaches the distance of his sight.) Al-Bukhari and Muslim recorded that Abu Hurayrah said that the Messenger of Allah said,

Chapter 4: An-Nisaa (The Women), Verses 148-176

«لَيْلَةَ أُسْرِيَ بِي لَقِيتُ مُوسَى»

(I met Musa on the night of my Ascension to heaven.) The Prophet then described him saying, as I think,

«مُضْطَرِبٌ، رَجِلُ الرَّأْسِ كَأَنَّهُ مِنْ رِجَالِ شَنُوءَةٍ»

(He was a tall person with hair as if he was one of the men from the tribe of Shanu'ah.) The Prophet further said,

«وَلَقِيتُ عِيسَى»

(`I met `Isa.' The Prophet described him saying,

«رَبْعَةٌ أَحْمَرُ كَأَنَّهُ خَرَجَ مِنْ دِيمَاسٍ»

`He was of moderate height and was red-faced as if he had just come out of a bathroom.

«وَرَأَيْتُ إِبْرَاهِيمَ وَأَنَا أَشْبَهُ وَلَدِهِ بِهِ»

I saw Ibrahim whom I resembled more than any of his children did.') Al-Bukhari recorded that Mujahid said that Ibn `Umar said that the Messenger of Allah said,

«رَأَيْتُ مُوسَى وَعِيسَى وَإِبْرَاهِيمَ، فَأَمَّا عِيسَى فَأَحْمَرُ جَعْدٌ عَرِيضُ الصَّدْرِ، وَأَمَّا مُوسَى فَآدَمُ جَسِيمٌ سَبْطٌ، كَأَنَّهُ مِنْ رِجَالِ الزُّطِّ»

(I saw Musa, `Isa and Ibrahim. `Isa was of red complexion and had curly hair and a broad chest. Musa was of brown complexion and had straight hair and a tall stature, as if he was from the people of Az-Zutt.) Al-Bukhari and Muslim recorded that Ibrahim said that `Abdullah bin `Umar said, "The Prophet once mentioned the False Messiah (Al-Masih Ad-Dajjal) to people, saying,

«إِنَّ اللهَ لَيْسَ بِأَعْوَرَ، أَلَا إِنَّ الْمَسِيحَ الدَّجَّالَ أَعْوَرُ الْعَيْنِ الْيُمْنَى، كَأَنَّ عَيْنَهُ عِنَبَةٌ طَافِيَةٌ»

(Allah is not blind in His Eye. Al-Masih Ad-Dajjal is blind in his right eye. His eye is like a protruding grape.)" Muslim recorded that the Messenger of Allah said,

«وَأَرَانِي اللهُ عِنْدَ الْكَعْبَةِ فِي الْمَنَامِ، فَإِذَا رَجُلٌ آدَمُ كَأَحْسَنِ مَا تَرَى مِنْ أُدْمِ الرِّجَالِ، تَضْرِبُ لِمَّتُهُ بَيْنَ مَنْكِبَيْهِ، رَجِلُ الشَّعْرِ، يَقْطُرُ رَأْسُهُ مَاءً، وَاضِعًا يَدَيْهِ عَلَى مَنْكِبَيْ رَجُلَيْنِ، وَهُوَ يَطُوفُ بِالْبَيْتِ، فَقُلْتُ: مَنْ هَذَا؟ فَقَالُوا: هُوَ الْمَسِيحُ ابْنُ مَرْيَمَ، ثُمَّ رَأَيْتُ وَرَاءَهُ رَجُلًا جَعْدًا قَطِطًا، أَعْوَرَ الْعَيْنِ الْيُمْنَى، كَأَشْبَهِ مَنْ رَأَيْتُ بِابْنِ قَطَنٍ، وَاضِعًا يَدَيْهِ عَلَى مَنْكِبَيْ رَجُلٍ، يَطُوفُ بِالْبَيْتِ، فَقُلْتُ: مَنْ هَذَا؟ قَالُوا: الْمَسِيحُ الدَّجَّالُ»

(In a dream, I was at the Ka`bah and Allah made me see a light - colored man, a color that is as beautiful as a light - colored man could be, with combed hair that reached his shoulders. His hair was dripping water, and he was leaning on the shoulders of two men while circling the Ka`bah. I asked, `Who is this man' I was told, `This is the Al-Masih, son of Maryam.' Behind him, I saw a man with very curly hair who was blind in his right eye. He looked exactly as Ibn Qatan, and he was leaning on the shoulder of a man while circling the House. I asked, `Who is this man' I was told, `He is Al-Masih Ad-Dajjal.') Al-Bukhari recorded that Salim said that his father said, "No, By Allah! The Prophet did not say that `Isa was of red complexion but said,

«بَيْنَمَا أَنَا نَائِمٌ أَطُوفُ بِالْكَعْبَةِ، فَإِذَا رَجُلٌ آدَمُ سَبْطُ الشَّعْرِ، يَتَهَادَى بَيْنَ رَجُلَيْنِ، يَنْطُفُ رَأْسُهُ مَاءً أَوْ يُهَرَاقُ رَأْسُهُ مَاءً فَقُلْتُ: مَنْ هَذَا؟ فَقَالُوا: ابْنُ مَرْيَمَ، فَذَهَبْتُ أَلْتَفِتُ، فَإِذَا رَجُلٌ أَحْمَرُ جَسِيمٌ، جَعْدُ الرَّأْسِ، أَعْوَرُ عَيْنِهِ الْيُمْنَى، كَأَنَّ عَيْنَهُ عِنَبَةٌ طَافِيَةٌ، قُلْتُ: مَنْ هَذَا؟ قَالُو: الدَّجَّالُ، وَأَقْرَبُ النَّاسِ بِهِ شَبَهًا ابْنُ قَطَنٍ»

(While I was asleep circumambulating the Ka`bah (in my dream), I suddenly saw a man of brown complexion and ample hair walking between two men with water dripping from his head. I asked, `Who is this' The people said, `He is the son of Maryam.' Then I looked behind and I saw a red-complexioned, fat, curly-haired man, blind in the right eye, which looked like a bulging out grape. I asked, `Who is this' They replied, `He is Ad-Dajjal.' The person he most resembled is Ibn Qatan.)" Az-

Zuhri commented that Ibn Qatan was a man from the tribe of Khuza`ah who died during the time of Jahiliyyah. This is the wording of Al-Bukhari. Allah's statement,

(And on the Day of Resurrection, he (`Isa) will be a witness against them) Qatadah said, "He will bear witness before them that he has delivered the Message from Allah and that he is but a servant of His." In a similar statement in the end of Surat Al-Ma'idah,

And (remember) when Allâh will say (on the Day of Resurrection): "O 'Iesa (Jesus), son of Maryam (Mary)! Did you say unto men: 'Worship me and my mother as two gods besides Allâh?'" He will say: "Glory be to You! It was not for me to say what I had no right (to say). Had I said such a thing, You would surely have known it. You know what is in my innerself though I do not know what is in Yours, truly, You, only You, are the AllKnower of all that is hidden and unseen

Surah: 4 Ayah: 160, Ayah: 161 & Ayah: 162

﴿ فَبِظُلْمٍ مِّنَ ٱلَّذِينَ هَادُوا۟ حَرَّمْنَا عَلَيْهِمْ طَيِّبَٰتٍ أُحِلَّتْ لَهُمْ وَبِصَدِّهِمْ عَن سَبِيلِ ٱللَّهِ كَثِيرًا ﴾

160. For the wrong-doing of the Jews, We made unlawful to them certain good foods which had been lawful to them, and for their hindering many from Allâh's Way;

﴿ وَأَخْذِهِمُ ٱلرِّبَوٰا۟ وَقَدْ نُهُوا۟ عَنْهُ وَأَكْلِهِمْ أَمْوَٰلَ ٱلنَّاسِ بِٱلْبَٰطِلِ وَأَعْتَدْنَا لِلْكَٰفِرِينَ مِنْهُمْ عَذَابًا أَلِيمًا ﴾

161. And their taking of Ribâ (usury) though they were forbidden from taking it and their devouring of men's substance wrongfully (bribery). And We have prepared for the disbelievers among them a painful torment.

﴿ لَّٰكِنِ ٱلرَّٰسِخُونَ فِى ٱلْعِلْمِ مِنْهُمْ وَٱلْمُؤْمِنُونَ يُؤْمِنُونَ بِمَآ أُنزِلَ إِلَيْكَ وَمَآ أُنزِلَ مِن قَبْلِكَ وَٱلْمُقِيمِينَ ٱلصَّلَوٰةَ وَٱلْمُؤْتُونَ ٱلزَّكَوٰةَ وَٱلْمُؤْمِنُونَ بِٱللَّهِ وَٱلْيَوْمِ ٱلْءَاخِرِ أُو۟لَٰٓئِكَ سَنُؤْتِيهِمْ أَجْرًا عَظِيمًا ﴾

162. But those among them who are well-grounded in knowledge, and the believers, believe in what has been sent down to you (Muhammad (peace be upon him)) and what was sent down before you; and those who perform As-Salât (Iqâmat-as-Salât), and give Zakât and believe in Allâh and in the Last Day, it is they to whom We shall give a great reward.

Transliteration

160. Fabithulmin mina allatheena hadoo harramna AAalayhim tayyibatin ohillat lahum wabisaddihim AAan sabeeli Allahi katheeran 161. Waakhthihimu alrriba waqad nuhoo

AAanhu waaklihim amwala alnnasi bialbatili waaAAtadna lilkafireena minhum AAathaban aleeman 162. Lakini alrrasikhoona fee alAAilmi minhum waalmu/minoona yu/minoona bima onzila ilayka wama onzila min qablika waalmuqeemeena alssalata waalmu/toona alzzakata waalmu/minoona biAllahi waalyawmi al-akhiri ola-ika sanu/teehim ajran AAatheeman

Tafsir Ibn Kathir

Some Foods Were Made Unlawful for the Jews Because of their Injustice and Wrongdoing

Allah states that because of the injustice and transgression of the Jews, demonstrated by committing major sins, He prohibited some of the lawful, pure things which were previously allowed for them. This prohibition could be only that of decree, meaning that Allah allowed the Jews to falsely interpret their Book and change and alter the information about what was allowed for them. They thus, out of exaggeration and extremism in the religion, prohibited some things for themselves. It could also mean that in the Tawrah, Allah prohibited things that were allowed for them before. Allah said,

(All food was lawful to the Children of Israel, except what Isra'il made unlawful for himself before the Tawrah was revealed.) We mentioned this Ayah before, which means that all types of food were allowed for the Children of Israel before the Tawrah was revealed, except the camel's meat and milk that Isra'il prohibited for himself. Later, Allah prohibited many things in the Tawrah. Allah said in Surat Al-An`am (chapter 6),

(And unto those who are Jews, We forbade every (animal) with undivided hoof, and We forbade them the fat of the ox and the sheep except what adheres to their backs or their entrails, or is mixed up with a bone. Thus We recompensed them for their rebellion. And verily, We are Truthful.) This means, We prohibited these things for them because they deserved it due to their transgression, injustice, defying their Messenger and disputing with him. So Allah said;

(For the wrongdoing of the Jews, We made unlawful to them certain good foods which had been lawful to them, and for their hindering many from Allah's way.) This Ayah states that they hindered themselves and others from following the truth, and this is the behavior that they brought from the past to the present. This is why they were and still are the enemies of the Messengers, killing many of the Prophets. They also denied Muhammad and `Isa, peace be upon them. mAllah said,

(And their taking of Riba' though they were forbidden from taking it,) Allah prohibited them from taking Riba', yet they did so using various kinds of tricks, ploys and cons, thus devouring people's property unjustly. Allah said,

(And We have prepared for the disbelievers among them a painful torment.) Allah then said,

(But those among them who are well-grounded in knowledge...) firm in the religion and full of beneficial knowledge. We mentioned this subject when we explained Surah Al `Imran (3). The Ayah;

(and the believers...) refers to the well-grounded in knowledge;

(believe in what has been sent down to you and what was sent down before you;) Ibn `Abbas said, "This Ayah was revealed concerning `Abdullah bin Salam, Tha`labah bin Sa`yah, Zayd bin Sa`yah and Asad bin `Ubayd who embraced Islam and believed what Allah sent Muhammad with. Allah said,

(and give Zakah,) This could be referring to the obligatory charity due on one's wealth and property, or those who purify themselves, or both. Allah knows best.

(and believe in Allah and in the Last Day,) They believe that there is no deity worthy of worship except Allah, believe in Resurrection after death and the reward or punishment for the good or evil deeds. Allah's statement,

(It is they,) those whom the Ayah described above,

(To whom We shall give a great reward.) means Paradise.

Surah: 4 Ayah: 163, Ayah: 164 & Ayah: 165

﴿ ۞ إِنَّآ أَوْحَيْنَآ إِلَيْكَ كَمَآ أَوْحَيْنَآ إِلَىٰ نُوحٍ وَالنَّبِيِّـۧنَ مِنۢ بَعْدِهِۦ ۚ وَأَوْحَيْنَآ إِلَىٰٓ إِبْرَٰهِيمَ وَإِسْمَٰعِيلَ وَإِسْحَٰقَ وَيَعْقُوبَ وَالْأَسْبَاطِ وَعِيسَىٰ وَأَيُّوبَ وَيُونُسَ وَهَٰرُونَ وَسُلَيْمَٰنَ ۚ وَءَاتَيْنَا دَاوُۥدَ زَبُورًا ﴿١٦٣﴾ ﴾

163. Verily, We have sent the revelation to you (O Muhammad (peace be upon him)) as We sent the revelation to Nûh (Noah) and the Prophets after him; We (also) sent the revelation to Ibrâhîm (Abraham), Ismâ'îl (Ishmael), Ishâque (Isaac), Ya'qûb (Jacob), and Al-Asbât (the twelve sons of Ya'qûb (Jacob)) 'Isâ (Jesus), Ayyûb (Job), Yûnus (Jonah), Hârûn (Aaron), and Sulaimân (Solomon), and to Dawûd (David) We gave the Zabûr (Psalms).

﴿ وَرُسُلًا قَدْ قَصَصْنَٰهُمْ عَلَيْكَ مِن قَبْلُ وَرُسُلًا لَّمْ نَقْصُصْهُمْ عَلَيْكَ ۚ وَكَلَّمَ ٱللَّهُ مُوسَىٰ تَكْلِيمًا ﴿١٦٤﴾ ﴾

164. And Messengers We have mentioned to you before, and Messengers We have not mentioned to you, - and to Mûsâ (Moses) Allâh spoke directly.

﴿ رُّسُلًا مُّبَشِّرِينَ وَمُنذِرِينَ لِئَلَّا يَكُونَ لِلنَّاسِ عَلَى ٱللَّهِ حُجَّةٌۢ بَعْدَ ٱلرُّسُلِ ۚ وَكَانَ ٱللَّهُ عَزِيزًا حَكِيمًا ﴿١٦٥﴾ ﴾

165. Messengers as bearers of good news as well as of warning in order that mankind should have no plea against Allâh after the (coming of) Messengers. And Allâh is Ever All-Powerful, All-Wise.

Transliteration

163. Inna awhayna ilayka kama awhayna ila noohin waalnnabiyyeena min baAAdihi waawhayna ila ibraheema wa-ismaAAeela wa-ishaqa wayaAAqooba waal-asbati waAAeesa waayyooba wayoonusa waharoona wasulaymana waatayna dawooda zabooran 164. Warusulan qad qasasnahum AAalayka min qablu warusulan lam naqsushum AAalayka wakallama Allahu moosa takleeman 165. Rusulan mubashshireena wamunthireena li-alla yakoona lilnnasi AAala Allahi hujjatun baAAda alrrusuli wakana Allahu AAazeezan hakeeman

Tafsir Ibn Kathir

Revelation Came to Prophet Muhammad , Just as it Came to the Prophets Before Him

Muhammad bin Ishaq narrated that Muhammad bin Abi Muhammad said that `Ikrimah, or Sa`id bin Jubayr, related to Ibn `Abbas that he said, "Sukayn and `Adi bin Zayd said, `O Muhammad! We do not know that Allah sent down anything to any human after Musa.' Allah sent down a rebuttal of their statement,

(Verily, We have inspired you (O Muhammad) as We inspired Nuh and the Prophets after him.)" Allah states that He sent down revelation to His servant and Messenger Muhammad just as He sent down revelation to previous Prophets. Allah said,

(Verily, We have inspired you (O Muhammad) as We inspired Nuh and the Prophets after him,) until,

(...and to Dawud We gave the Zabur.) The `Zabur' (Psalms) is the name of the Book revealed to Prophet Dawud, peace be upon him.

Twenty-Five Prophets Are Mentioned in the Qur'an

Allah said,

(And Messengers We have mentioned to you before, and Messengers We have not mentioned to you) Before the revelation of this Ayah. The following are the names of the Prophets whom Allah named in the Qur'an. They are: Adam, Idris, Nuh (Noah), Hud, Salih, Ibrahim (Abraham), Lut, Isma`il (Ishmael), Ishaq (Isaac), Ya`qub (Jacob), Yusuf (Joesph), Ayyub (Job), Shu`ayb, Musa (Moses), Harun (Aaron), Yunus (Jonah), Dawud (David), Sulayman (Solomon), Ilyas (Elias), Al-Yasa` (Elisha), Zakariya (Zachariya), Yahya (John) and `Isa (Jesus), and their leader, Muhammad . Several scholars of Tafsir also listed Dhul-Kifl among the Prophets. Allah's statement,

(and Messengers We have not mentioned to you,) means, `there are other Prophets whom We did not mention to you in the Qur'an.'

The Virtue of Musa

Allah said,

(and to Musa Allah spoke directly.) This is an honor to Musa, and this is why he is called the Kalim, he whom Allah spoke to directly. Al-Hafiz Abu Bakr bin Marduwyah recorded that `Abdul-Jabbar bin `Abdullah said, "A man came to Abu Bakr bin `Ayyash and said, `I heard a man recite (this Ayah this way): "and to Allah, Musa spoke directly." Abu Bakr said, `Only a disbeliever would recite it like this.' Al-A`mash recited it with Yahya bin Withab, who recited it with Abu `Abdur-Rahman As-Sulami who recited it with `Ali bin Abi Talib who recited with the Messenger of Allah ,

(and to Musa Allah spoke directly.)'" Abu Bakr bin Abi Ayyash was so angry with the man who recited the Ayah differently, because he altered its words and meanings. That person was from the group of Mu`tazilah who denied that Allah spoke to Musa or that He speaks to any of His creation. We were told that some of the Mu`tazilah once recited the Ayah that way, so one teacher present said to him, "O son of a stinking woman! What would you do concerning Allah's statement,

(And when Musa came at the time and place appointed by Us, and his Lord spoke to him,) (7:143)" The Shaykh meant that the later Ayah cannot be altered or changed.

The Reason Behind Sending the Prophets is to Establish the Proof

Allah said,

(Messengers as bearers of good news as well as of warning,) meaning, the Prophets bring good news to those who obey Allah and practice the good things that please Him. They also warn against His punishment and torment for those who defy His commandments. Allah said next,

(in order that mankind should have no plea against Allah after the Messengers. And Allah is Ever All-Powerful, All-Wise.) Allah sent down His Books and sent His Messengers with good news and warnings. He explained what He likes and is pleased with and what He dislikes and is displeased with. This way, no one will have an excuse with Allah. Allah said in other Ayat,

(And if We had destroyed them with a torment before this, they would surely have said: "Our Lord! If only You had sent us a Messenger, we should certainly have followed Your Ayat, before we were humiliated and disgraced.") and,

(And if (We had) not (sent you to the people of Makkah) in case a calamity should seize them for (the deeds) that their hands have sent forth.) It is recorded in the Two Sahihs that Ibn Mas`ud said that the Messenger of Allah said,

«لَا أَحَدَ أَغْيَرُ مِنَ اللهِ، مِنْ أَجْلِ ذلِكَ حَرَّمَ الْفَوَاحِشَ مَا ظَهَرَ مِنْهَا وَمَا بَطَنَ، وَلَا أَحَدَ أَحَبُّ إِلَيْهِ الْمَدْحُ مِنَ اللهِ عَزَّ وَجَلَّ، مِنْ أَجْلِ ذلِكَ مَدَحَ

نَفْسُهُ، وَلَا أَحَدَ أَحَبُّ إِلَيْهِ الْعُذْرُ مِنَ اللهِ، مِنْ أَجْلِ ذَلِكَ بَعَثَ النَّبِيِّينَ مُبَشِّرِينَ وَمُنْذِرِينَ

(No one is more jealous than Allah. This is why He prohibited all types of sin committed in public or secret. No one likes praise more than Allah, and this is why He has praised Himself. No one likes to give excuse more than Allah, and this is why He sent the Prophets as bearers of good news and as warners.) In another narration, the Prophet said,

مِنْ أَجْلِ ذَلِكَ أَرْسَلَ رُسُلَهُ وَأَنْزَلَ كُتُبَهُ

(And this is why He sent His Messengers and revealed His Books.)

Surah: 4 Ayah: 166, Ayah: 167, Ayah: 168, Ayah: 169 & Ayah: 170

﴿لَّكِنِ ٱللَّهُ يَشْهَدُ بِمَآ أَنزَلَ إِلَيْكَ أَنزَلَهُۥ بِعِلْمِهِۦ وَٱلْمَلَٰٓئِكَةُ يَشْهَدُونَ وَكَفَىٰ بِٱللَّهِ شَهِيدًا﴾

166. But Allâh bears witness to that which He has sent down (the Qur'ân) unto you (O Muhammad (peace be upon him)) He has sent it down with His Knowledge, and the angels bear witness. And Allâh is All-Sufficient as a Witness.

﴿إِنَّ ٱلَّذِينَ كَفَرُوا۟ وَصَدُّوا۟ عَن سَبِيلِ ٱللَّهِ قَدْ ضَلُّوا۟ ضَلَٰلًۢا بَعِيدًا﴾

167. Verily, those who disbelieve (by concealing the truth about Prophet Muhammad (peace be upon him) and his message of true Islâmic Monotheism written in the Taurât (Torah) and the Injeel (Gospel) with them) and prevent (mankind) from the Path of Allâh (Islâmic Monotheism); they have certainly strayed far away. (Tafsir Al-Qurtubî).

﴿إِنَّ ٱلَّذِينَ كَفَرُوا۟ وَظَلَمُوا۟ لَمْ يَكُنِ ٱللَّهُ لِيَغْفِرَ لَهُمْ وَلَا لِيَهْدِيَهُمْ طَرِيقًا﴾

168. Verily, those who disbelieve and did wrong (by concealing the truth about Prophet Muhammad (peace be upon him) and his message of true Islâmic Monotheism written in the Taurât (Torah) and the Injeel (Gospel) with them); Allâh will not forgive them, nor will He guide them to any way - (Tafsir Al-Qurtubî).

﴿إِلَّا طَرِيقَ جَهَنَّمَ خَٰلِدِينَ فِيهَآ أَبَدًا وَكَانَ ذَٰلِكَ عَلَى ٱللَّهِ يَسِيرًا﴾

169. Except the way of Hell, to dwell therein forever; and this is ever easy for Allâh.

﴿ يَٰٓأَيُّهَا ٱلنَّاسُ قَدْ جَآءَكُمُ ٱلرَّسُولُ بِٱلْحَقِّ مِن رَّبِّكُمْ فَـَٔامِنُواْ خَيْرًا لَّكُمْ ۚ وَإِن تَكْفُرُواْ فَإِنَّ لِلَّهِ مَا فِى ٱلسَّمَٰوَٰتِ وَٱلْأَرْضِ ۚ وَكَانَ ٱللَّهُ عَلِيمًا حَكِيمًا ﴿١٧٠﴾ ﴾

170. O mankind! Verily, there has come to you the Messenger (Muhammad (peace be upon him)) with the truth from your Lord. So believe in him, it is better for you. But if you disbelieve, then certainly to Allâh belongs all that is in the heavens and the earth. And Allâh is Ever All-Knowing, All-Wise.

Transliteration

166. Lakini Allahu yashhadu bima anzala ilayka anzalahu biAAilmihi waalmala-ikatu yashhadoona wakafa biAllahi shaheedan 167. Inna allatheena kafaroo wasaddoo AAan sabeeli Allahi qad dalloo dalalan baAAeedan 168. Inna allatheena kafaroo wathalamoo lam yakuni Allahu liyaghfira lahum wala liyahdiyahum tareeqan 169. Illa tareeqa jahannama khalideena feeha abadan wakana thalika AAala Allahi yaseeran 170. Ya ayyuha alnnasu qad jaakumu alrrasoolu bialhaqqi min rabbikum faaminoo khayran lakum wa-in takfuroo fa-inna lillahi ma fee alssamawati waal-ardi wakana Allahu AAaleeman hakeeman

Tafsir Ibn Kathir

(Verily, We have inspired you...) emphasized the Prophet's prophethood and refuted the idolators and People of the Scripture who denied him. Allah said,

(But Allah bears witness to that which He has sent down unto you,) meaning, even if they deny, defy and disbelieve in you, O Muhammad, Allah testifies that you are His Messenger to whom He sent down His Book, the Glorious Qur'an that,

(Falsehood cannot come to it from before it or behind it, (it is) sent down by the All-Wise, Worthy of all praise.) Allah then said,

(He has sent it down with His knowledge,) The knowledge of His that He willed His servants to have access to. Knowledge about the clear signs of guidance and truth, what Allah likes and is pleased with, what He dislikes and is displeased with, and knowledge of the Unseen, such as the past and the future. This also includes knowledge about His honorable attributes that no sent Messenger or illustrious angel can even know without Allah's leave. Similarly, Allah said,

(And they will never compass anything of His knowledge except that which He wills.) and,

(but they will never compass anything of His knowledge.) Allah's statement,

(and the angels bear witness.) to the truth of what you came with and what was revealed and sent down to you, along with Allah's testimony to the same,

(And Allah is All-Sufficient as a Witness.) Allah said,

(Verily, those who disbelieve and prevent (others) from the path of Allah, they have certainly strayed far away.) For they are disbelievers themselves and do not follow the truth. They strive hard to prevent people from following and embracing Allah's path. Therefore, they have defied the truth, deviated, and strayed far away from it. Allah also mentions His judgment against those who disbelieve in His Ayat, Book and Messenger, those who wrong themselves by their disbelief and hindering others from His path, committing sins and violating His prohibitions. Allah states that He will not forgive them;

(nor will He guide them to a way (that is, of good).)

(Except the way of Hell, to dwell therein forever...) and this is the exception. Allah then said,

(O mankind! Verily, there has come to you the Messenger with the truth from your Lord, so believe in him, it is better for you.) This Ayah means, Muhammad has come to you with guidance, the religion of truth and clear proof from Allah. Therefore, believe in what he has brought you and follow him, for this is better for you. Allah then said,

(But if you disbelieve, then certainly to Allah belongs all that is in the heavens and the earth.) Allah is far too rich than to need you or your faith, and no harm could ever affect Him because of your disbelief. Allah said in another Ayah,

(And Musa said: "If you disbelieve, you and all on earth together, then verily, Allah is Rich (Free of all needs), Owner of all praise.") Allah said here,

(And Allah is Ever All-Knowing,) He knows those who deserve to be guided, and He will guide them. He also knows those who deserve deviation, and He leads them to it,

(All-Wise) in His statements, actions, legislation and all that He decrees.

Surah: 4 Ayah: 171

﴿ يَٰأَهْلَ ٱلْكِتَٰبِ لَا تَغْلُوا۟ فِى دِينِكُمْ وَلَا تَقُولُوا۟ عَلَى ٱللَّهِ إِلَّا ٱلْحَقَّ إِنَّمَا ٱلْمَسِيحُ عِيسَى ٱبْنُ مَرْيَمَ رَسُولُ ٱللَّهِ وَكَلِمَتُهُۥٓ أَلْقَىٰهَآ إِلَىٰ مَرْيَمَ وَرُوحٌ مِّنْهُ فَـَٔامِنُوا۟ بِٱللَّهِ وَرُسُلِهِۦ وَلَا تَقُولُوا۟ ثَلَٰثَةٌ ٱنتَهُوا۟ خَيْرًا لَّكُمْ إِنَّمَا ٱللَّهُ إِلَٰهٌ وَٰحِدٌ سُبْحَٰنَهُۥٓ أَن يَكُونَ لَهُۥ وَلَدٌ لَّهُۥ مَا فِى ٱلسَّمَٰوَٰتِ وَمَا فِى ٱلْأَرْضِ وَكَفَىٰ بِٱللَّهِ وَكِيلًا ﴿١٧١﴾

171. O people of the Scripture! Do not exceed the limits in your religion, nor say of Allâh aught but the truth. The Messiah 'Isâ (Jesus), son of Maryam (Mary), was (no more than) a Messenger of Allâh and His Word, ("Be!" - and he was) which He bestowed on Maryam (Mary) and a spirit (Rûh) created by Him; so believe in Allâh and His Messengers. Say not: "Three (trinity)!" Cease! (it is) better for you.

For Allâh is (the only) One Ilâh (God), Glory be to Him (Far Exalted is He) above having a son. To Him belongs all that is in the heavens and all that is in the earth. And Allâh is All-Sufficient as a Disposer of affairs.

Transliteration

171. Ya ahla alkitabi la taghloo fee deenikum wala taqooloo AAala Allahi illa alhaqqa innama almaseehu AAeesa ibnu maryama rasoolu Allahi wakalimatuhu alqaha ila maryama waroohun minhu faaminoo biAllahi warusulihi wala taqooloo thalathatun intahoo khayran lakum innama Allahu ilahun wahidun subhanahu an yakoona lahu waladun lahu ma fee alssamawati wama fee al-ardi wakafa biAllahi wakeelan

Tafsir Ibn Kathir

Prohibiting the People of the Book From Going to Extremes in Religion

Allah forbids the People of the Scriptures from going to extremes in religion, which is a common trait of theirs, especially among the Christians. The Christians exaggerated over `Isa until they elevated him above the grade that Allah gave him. They elevated him from the rank of prophethood to being a god, whom they worshipped just as they worshipped Allah. They exaggerated even more in the case of those who they claim were his followers, claiming that they were inspired, thus following every word they uttered whether true or false, be it guidance or misguidance, truth or lies. This is why Allah said,

(They took their rabbis and their monks to be their lords besides Allah.) Imam Ahmad recorded that Ibn `Abbas said that `Umar said that the Messenger of Allah said,

«لَا تُطْرُونِي كَمَا أَطْرَتِ النَّصَارَى عِيسَى ابْنَ مَرْيَمَ. فَإِنَّمَا أَنَا عَبْدٌ فَقُولُوا: عَبْدُاللهِ وَرَسُولُه»

(Do not unduly praise me like the Christians exaggerated over `Isa, son of Maryam. Verily, I am only a servant, so say, `Allah's servant and His Messenger.') This is the wording of Al-Bukhari. Imam Ahmad recorded that Anas bin Malik said that a man once said, "O Muhammad! You are our master and the son of our master, our most righteous person and the son of our most righteous person..." The Messenger of Allah said,

«يَا أَيُّهَا النَّاسُ عَلَيْكُمْ بِقَوْلِكُمْ، وَلَا يَسْتَهْوِيَنَّكُمُ الشَّيْطَانُ، أَنَا مُحَمَّدُ بْنُ عَبْدِاللهِ، عَبْدُاللهِ وَرَسُولُهُ، وَاللهِ مَا أُحِبُّ أَنْ تَرْفَعُونِي فَوْقَ مَنْزِلَتِي الَّتِي أَنْزَلَنِي اللهُ عَزَّ وَجَل»

(O people! Say what you have to say, but do not allow Shaytan to trick you. I am Muhammad bin `Abdullah, Allah's servant and Messenger. By Allah! I do not like that you elevate me above the rank that Allah has granted me.) Allah's statement,

(nor say of Allah except the truth.) means, do not lie and claim that Allah has a wife or a son, Allah is far holier than what they attribute to Him. Allah is glorified, praised, and honored in His might, grandure and greatness, and there is no deity worthy of worship nor Lord but Him. Allah said;

(Al-Masih `Isa, son of Maryam, was (no more than) a Messenger of Allah and His Word, which He bestowed on Maryam and a spirit from (created by) Him;) `Isa is only one of Allah's servants and one of His creatures. Allah said to him, `Be', and he was, and He sent him as a Messenger. `Isa was a word from Allah that He bestowed on Maryam, meaning He created him with the word `Be' that He sent with Jibril to Maryam. Jibril blew the life of `Isa into Maryam by Allah's leave, and `Isa came to existence as a result. This incident was in place of the normal conception between man and woman that results in children. This is why `Isa was a word and a Ruh (spirit) created by Allah, as he had no father to conceive him. Rather, he came to existence through the word that Allah uttered, `Be,' and he was, through the life that Allah sent with Jibril. Allah said,

(Al-Masih (`Isa), son of Maryam, was no more than a Messenger; many were the Messengers that passed away before him. His mother (Maryam) was a Siddiqah. They both ate food.) And Allah said,

(Verily, the likeness of `Isa before Allah is the likeness of Adam. He created him from dust, then (He) said to him: "Be! - and he was.)

(And she who guarded her chastity, We breathed into her (garment) and We made her and her son (`Isa) a sign for all that exits.) (21:91)

(And Maryam, the daughter of `Imran who guarded her chastity,) and Allah said concerning the Messiah,

(He (`Isa) was not more than a servant. We granted Our favor to him.)

The Meaning of "His Word and a spirit from Him

`Abdur-Razzaq narrated that Ma`mar said that Qatadah said that the Ayah,

(And His Word, which He bestowed on Maryam and a spirit from (created by) Him;) means, He said,

(Be) and he was. Ibn Abi Hatim recorded that Ahmad bin Sinan Al-Wasiti said that he heard Shadh bin Yahya saying about Allah's statement,

(and His Word, which He bestowed on Maryam and a spirit from (created by) Him;) "`Isa was not the word. Rather, `Isa came to existence because of the word." Al-Bukhari recorded that `Ubadah bin As-Samit said that the Prophet said,

«مَنْ شَهِدَ أَنْ لَا إِلَهَ إِلَّا اللهُ، وَحْدَهُ لَا شَرِيكَ لَهُ، وَأَنَّ مُحَمَّدًا عَبْدُهُ وَرَسُولُهُ، وَأَنَّ عِيسَى عَبْدُاللهِ وَرَسُولُهُ وَكَلِمَتُهُ أَلْقَاهَا إِلَى مَرْيَمَ وَرُوحٌ مِنْهُ، وَأَنَّ الْجَنَّةَ حَقٌّ، وَالنَّارَ حَقٌّ، أَدْخَلَهُ اللهُ الْجَنَّةَ عَلَى مَا كَانَ مِنَ الْعَمَلِ»

(If anyone testifies that none has the right to be worshipped but Allah Alone Who has no partners, and that Muhammad is His servant and Messenger, and that `Isa is Allah's servant and Messenger and His Word which He bestowed on Maryam and a spirit created by Him, and that Paradise is true and Hell is true, then Allah will admit him into Paradise with the deeds which he performed.) In another narration, the Prophet said,

«مِنْ أَبْوَابِ الْجَنَّةِ الثَّمَانِيَّةِ يَدْخُلُ مِنْ أَيِّهَا شَاءَ»

(...through any of the eight doors of Paradise he wishes.) Muslim also recorded it. Therefore, `Ruh from Allah', in the Ayah and the Hadith is similar to Allah's statement,

(And has subjected to you all that is in the heavens and all that is in the earth; it is all from Him.) meaning, from His creation. `from Him' does not mean that it is a part of Him, as the Christians claim, may Allah's continued curses be upon them. Saying that something is from Allah, such as the spirit of Allah, the she-camel of Allah or the House of Allah, is meant to honor such items. Allah said,

(This is the she-camel of Allah...) and,

(and sanctify My House for those who circumambulate it.) An authentic Hadith states,

«فَأَدْخُلُ عَلَى رَبِّي فِي دَارِهِ»

(I will enter on my Lord in His Home) All these examples are meant to honor such items when they are attributed to Allah in this manner. Allah said,

(so believe in Allah and His Messengers.) believe that Allah is One and Alone and that He does not have a son or wife. Know and be certain that `Isa is the servant and Messenger of Allah. Allah said after that,

(Say not: "Three!") do not elevate `Isa and his mother to be gods with Allah. Allah is far holier than what they attribute to Him. In Surat Al-Ma'idah (chapter 5), Allah said,

(Surely, disbelievers are those who said: "Allah is the third of the three." But there is none who has the right to be worshipped but One God.) Allah said at the end of the same Surah,

(And (remember) when Allah will say (on the Day of Resurrection): "O `Isa, son of Maryam! Did you say unto men: `Worship me'") and in its beginning,

(Surely, in disbelief are they who say that Allah is the Messiah, son of Maryam.) The Christians, may Allah curse them, have no limit to their disbelief because of their ignorance, so their deviant statements and their misguidance grows. Some of them believe that `Isa is Allah, some believe that he is one in a trinity and some believe that he is the son of Allah. Their beliefs and creeds are numerous and contradict each other, prompting some people to say that if ten Christians meet, they would end up with eleven sects!

The Christian Sects

Sa`id bin Batriq, the Patriarch of Alexandria and a famous Christian scholar, mentioned in the year four hundred after the Hijrah, that a Christian Council convened during the reign of Constantine, who built the city that bears his name. In this Council, the Christians came up with what they called the Great Trust, which in reality is the Great Treachery. There were more than two thousand patriarchs in this Council, and they were in such disarray that they divided into many sects, where some sects had twenty, fifty or a hundred members, etc.! When the king saw that there were more than three hundred Patriarchs who had the same idea, he agreed with them and adopted their creed. Constantine who was a deviant philosopher -- gave his support to this sect for which, as an honor, churches were built and doctrines were taught to young children, who were baptized on this creed, and books were written about it. Meanwhile, the king oppressed all other sects. Another Council produced the sect known as the Jacobites, while the Nestorians were formed in a third Council. These three sects agreed that `Isa was divine, but disputed regarding the manner in which `Isa's divinity was related to his humanity; were they in unity or did Allah incarnate in `Isa! All three of these sects accuse each other of heresy and, we believe that all three of them are disbelievers. Allah said,

(Cease! (it is) better for you.) meaning, it will be better for you,

(For Allah is (the only) One God, hallowed be He above having a son.) and He is holier than such claim,

(To Him belongs all that is in the heavens and all that is in the earth. And Allah is All-Sufficient as a Disposer of affairs,) for all are creatures, property and servants under His control and disposal, and He is the Disposer of the affairs. Therefore, how can He have a wife or a son among them,

(He is the originator of the heavens and the earth. How can He have children.) and

(And they say: "The Most Gracious (Allah) has begotten a son. Indeed you have brought forth (said) a terrible evil thing.") Up to His saying,

(Alone.)

Surah: 4 Ayah: 172 & Ayah: 173

﴿ لَّن يَسْتَنكِفَ ٱلْمَسِيحُ أَن يَكُونَ عَبْدًا لِّلَّهِ وَلَا ٱلْمَلَٰٓئِكَةُ ٱلْمُقَرَّبُونَ ۚ وَمَن يَسْتَنكِفْ عَنْ عِبَادَتِهِۦ وَيَسْتَكْبِرْ فَسَيَحْشُرُهُمْ إِلَيْهِ جَمِيعًا ﴾ ﴿١٧٢﴾

172. The Messiah will never be proud to reject to be a slave to Allâh, nor the angels who are the near (to Allâh). And whosoever rejects His worship and is proud, then He will gather them all together unto Himself.

﴿ فَأَمَّا ٱلَّذِينَ ءَامَنُوا۟ وَعَمِلُوا۟ ٱلصَّٰلِحَٰتِ فَيُوَفِّيهِمْ أُجُورَهُمْ وَيَزِيدُهُم مِّن فَضْلِهِۦ ۖ وَأَمَّا ٱلَّذِينَ ٱسْتَنكَفُوا۟ وَٱسْتَكْبَرُوا۟ فَيُعَذِّبُهُمْ عَذَابًا أَلِيمًا وَلَا يَجِدُونَ لَهُم مِّن دُونِ ٱللَّهِ وَلِيًّا وَلَا نَصِيرًا ﴾ ﴿١٧٣﴾

173. So, as for those who believed (in the Oneness of Allâh - Islâmic Monotheism) and did deeds of righteousness, He will give them their (due) rewards - and more out of His Bounty. But as for those who refused His worship and were proud, He will punish them with a painful torment . And they will not find for themselves besides Allâh any protector or helper.

Transliteration

172. Lan yastankifa almaseehu an yakoona AAabdan lillahi wala almala-ikatu almuqarraboona waman yastankif AAan AAibadatihi wayastakbir fasayahshuruhum ilayhi jameeAAan   173. Faamma allatheena amanoo waAAamiloo alssalihati fayuwaffeehim ojoorahum wayazeeduhum min fadlihi waamma allatheena istankafoo waistakbaroo fayuAAaththibuhum AAathaban aleeman wala yajidoona lahum min dooni Allahi waliyyan wala naseeran

Tafsir Ibn Kathir

The Prophets and Angels Are Never too Proud to Worship Allah

Ibn Abi Hatim recorded that Ibn `Abbas said that, `proud', means insolent. Qatadah said that,

(Al-Masih will never be too proud to be a servant of Allah nor the angels who are near (to Allah).) (they) will never be arrogant, Allah then said,

(And whosoever rejects His worship and is proud, then He will gather them all together unto Himself.) on the Day of Resurrection. Then, Allah will judge between them with His just judgment that is never unjust or wrong.

(So, as for those who believed and did deeds of righteousness, He will give their (due) rewards, and more out of His bounty.) Allah will award them their full rewards for their righteous actions and will give them more of His bounty, kindness, ample mercy and favor.

(But as for those who refused His worship and were proud,) out of arrogance, they refused to obey and worship Him,

(He will punish them with a painful torment. And they will not find for themselves besides Allah any protector or helper.) In another Ayah, Allah said,

(Verily! Those who scorn My worship, they will surely enter Hell in humiliation,) degradation, disgrace and dishonor, for they were arrogant and rebellious.

Surah: 4 Ayah: 174 & Ayah: 175

﴿ يَٰٓأَيُّهَا ٱلنَّاسُ قَدْ جَآءَكُم بُرْهَٰنٌ مِّن رَّبِّكُمْ وَأَنزَلْنَآ إِلَيْكُمْ نُورًا مُّبِينًا ﴾

174. O mankind! Verily, there has come to you a convincing proof (Prophet Muhammad (peace be upon him)) from your Lord; and We sent down to you a manifest light (this Qur'ân).

﴿ فَأَمَّا ٱلَّذِينَ ءَامَنُواْ بِٱللَّهِ وَٱعْتَصَمُواْ بِهِۦ فَسَيُدْخِلُهُمْ فِى رَحْمَةٍ مِّنْهُ وَفَضْلٍ وَيَهْدِيهِمْ إِلَيْهِ صِرَٰطًا مُّسْتَقِيمًا ﴾

175. So, as for those who believed in Allâh and held fast to Him, He will admit them to His Mercy and Grace (i.e. Paradise), and guide them to Himself by the Straight Path.

Transliteration

174. Ya ayyuha alnnasu qad jaakum burhanun min rabbikum waanzalna ilaykum nooran mubeenan   175. Faamma allatheena amanoo biAllahi waiAAtasamoo bihi fasayudkhiluhum fee rahmatin minhu wafadlin wayahdeehim ilayhi siratan mustaqeeman

Tafsir Ibn Kathir

The Description of the Revelation that Came From Allah

Allah informs all people that a plain, unequivocal proof has come to them from Him. One that eradicates all possibility of having an excuse, or falling prey to evil doubts. Allah said,

(and We sent down to you a manifest light.) that directs to the Truth. Ibn Jurayj and others said, "It is the Qur'an."

(So, as for those who believed in Allah and held fast to (depend on) Him,) by worshipping Him and relying on Him for each and every thing. Ibn Jurayj said that this part of the Ayah means, "They believe in Allah and hold fast to the Qur'an."

(He will admit them to His mercy and grace,) meaning, He will grant them His mercy and admit them into Paradise, and will increase and multiply their rewards and their ranks, as a favor and bounty from Him.

(and guide them to Himself by a straight path.) and a clear way that has no wickedness in it or deviation. This, indeed, is the description of the believers in this life and the Hereafter, as they are on the straight and safe path in matters of action and creed. In the Hereafter, they are on the straight path of Allah that leads to the gardens of Paradise.

Surah: 4 Ayah: 176

﴿ يَسْتَفْتُونَكَ قُلِ ٱللَّهُ يُفْتِيكُمْ فِي ٱلْكَلَـٰلَةِ ۚ إِنِ ٱمْرُؤٌا۟ هَلَكَ لَيْسَ لَهُۥ وَلَدٌ وَلَهُۥٓ أُخْتٌ فَلَهَا نِصْفُ مَا تَرَكَ ۚ وَهُوَ يَرِثُهَآ إِن لَّمْ يَكُن لَّهَا وَلَدٌ ۚ فَإِن كَانَتَا ٱثْنَتَيْنِ فَلَهُمَا ٱلثُّلُثَانِ مِمَّا تَرَكَ ۚ وَإِن كَانُوٓا۟ إِخْوَةً رِّجَالًا وَنِسَآءً فَلِلذَّكَرِ مِثْلُ حَظِّ ٱلْأُنثَيَيْنِ ۗ يُبَيِّنُ ٱللَّهُ لَكُمْ أَن تَضِلُّوا۟ ۗ وَٱللَّهُ بِكُلِّ شَىْءٍ عَلِيمٌۢ ﴾ ۝

176. They ask you for a legal verdict. Say: "Allâh directs (thus) about Al-Kalâlah (those who leave neither descendants nor ascendants as heirs). If it is a man that dies leaving a sister, but no child, she shall have half the inheritance. If (such a deceased was) a woman, who left no child, her brother takes her inheritance. If there are two sisters, they shall have two-thirds of the inheritance; if there are brothers and sisters, the male will have twice the share of the female. (Thus) does Allâh make clear to you (His Law) lest you go astray. And Allâh is the All-Knower of everything."

Transliteration

176. Yastaftoonaka quli Allahu yufteekum fee alkalalati ini imruon halaka laysa lahu waladun walahu okhtun falaha nisfu ma taraka wahuwa yarithuha in lam yakun laha waladun fa-in kanata ithnatayni falahuma alththuluthani mimma taraka wa-in kanoo ikhwatan rijalan wanisaan falilththakari mithlu haththi alonthayayni yubayyinu Allahu lakum an tadilloo waAllahu bikulli shay-in AAaleemun

Tafsir Ibn Kathir

This is the Last Ayah Ever Revealed, the Ruling on Al-Kalalah

Al-Bukhari recorded that Al-Bara' said that the last Surah to be revealed was Surah Bara'ah (chapter 9) and the last Ayah to be revealed was, (They ask you for a legal verdict...) Imam Ahmad recorded that Jabir bin `Abdullah said, "The Messenger of Allah came visiting me when I was so ill that I fell unconscious. He performed ablution and poured the remaining water on me, or had it poured on me. When I regained consciousness, I said, `I will only leave inheritance through Kalalah, so what about the inheritance that I leave behind' Allah later revealed the Ayah about Fara'id (inheritance (4:11))."' The Two Sahihs and also the Group recorded it. In one of the wordings, Jabir said that the Ayah on inheritance was revealed;

(They ask you for a legal verdict. Say: "Allah directs (thus) about Al-Kalalah.) The wording of the Ayah indicates that the question was about the Kalalah, (Say: "Allah directs (thus)...) We mentioned the meaning of Kalalah before, that it means the crown that surrounds the head from all sides. This is why the scholars stated that Kalalah pertains to one who dies and leaves behind neither descendants, nor ascendants. Some said that the Kalalah pertains to one who has no offspring, as the Ayah states, (If it is a man that dies, leaving no child,) The meaning and ruling of Kalalah was somewhat confusing to the Leader of the Faithful `Umar bin Al-Khattab. It is recorded in the Two Sahihs that `Umar said, "There are three matters that I wished the Messenger of Allah had explained to us, so that we could abide by his explanation. (They are: the share in the inheritance of) the grandfather, the Kalalah and a certain type of Riba." Imam Ahmad recorded that Ma`dan bin Abi Talhah said that `Umar bin Al-Khattab said, "There is nothing that I asked the Messenger of Allah about its meaning more than the Kalalah, until he stabbed me with his finger in my chest and said,

《يَكْفِيكَ آيَةُ الصَّيْفِ الَّتِي فِي آخِرِ سُورَةِ النِّسَاءِ》

(The Ayah that is in the end of Surat An-Nisa' should suffice for you.)" Ahmad mentioned this short narration for this Hadith, Muslim recorded a longer form of it.

The Meaning of This Ayah

Allah said, (If it is a man that dies.) Allah said in another Ayah, (Everything will perish save His Face.) Therefore, everything and everyone dies and perishes except Allah, the Exalted and Most Honored. Allah said, (Whatsoever is on it (the earth) will perish. And the Face of your Lord full of majesty and honor will remain forever.) Allah said here, (leaving no child,) referring to the person who has neither children, nor parents. What testifies to this, is that Allah said afterwards, (Leaving a sister, she shall have half the inheritance.) Had there been a surviving ascendant, the sister would not have inherited anything, and there is a consensus on this point. Therefore, this Ayah is referring to the man who dies leaving behind neither descendants nor ascendants, as is apparent for those who contemplate its meaning. This is because when there is a surviving parent, the sister does not inherit anything, let alone half of the inheritance. Ibn Jarir and others mentioned that Ibn `Abbas and Ibn Az-Zubayr used to judge that if a person dies and leaves behind a daughter and a sister, the sister does not inherit anything. They would recite,

(If it is a man that dies, leaving a sister, but no child, she shall have half the inheritance.) They said that if one leaves behind a daughter, then he has left behind a child. Therefore the sister does not get anything. The majority of scholars disagreed with them, saying the daughter gets one half and the sister the other half, relying on other evidence. This Ayah (4:176 above) gives the sister half of the inheritance in the case that it specifies. As for giving the sister half in other cases, Al-Bukhari recorded that Sulayman said that Ibrahim reported to Al-Aswad that he said, "During the time of the Messenger of Allah , Mu`adh bin Jabal gave a judgment that the daughter gets one half and the sister the other half." Al-Bukhari recorded that Huzayl bin Shurahbil said, "Abu Musa Al-Ash`ari was asked about the case when there was a daughter, grand-daughter and sister to inherit. He said, `The daughter gets one-half and the sister one-half.' Go and ask Ibn Mas`ud, although I think he is going to agree with me.' So Ibn Mas`ud was asked and was told about Abu Musa's answer, and Ibn Mas`ud commented, `I would have deviated then and would not have become among those who are rightly guided. I will give a judgment similar to the judgment given by the Prophet . The daughter gets one-half, the grand-daughter gets one-sixth, and these two shares will add up to two-thirds. Whatever is left will be for the sister.' We went back to Abu Musa and conveyed to him Ibn Mas`ud's answer and he said, `Do not ask me (for legal verdicts) as long as this scholar is still among you.'" Allah then said,

(... and he will be her heir if she has no children.) This Ayah means, the brother inherits all of that his sister leaves behind if she has no surviving offspring or parents. If she has a surviving parent, her brother would not inherit anything. If there is someone who gets a fixed share in the inheritance, such as a husband or half brother from the mother's side, they take their share and the rest goes to the brother. It is recorded in the Two Sahihs that Ibn `Abbas said that the Messenger of Allah said,

«أَلْحِقُوا الْفَرَائِضَ بِأَهْلِهَا، فَمَا أَبْقَتِ الْفَرَائِضُ فَلِأَوْلَى رَجُلٍ ذَكَرٍ»

(Give the Farai'd to its people, and whatever is left is the share of the nearest male relative.) Allah said,

(If there are two sisters, they shall have two-thirds of the inheritance;) meaning, if the person who dies in Kalalah has two sisters, they get two-thirds of the inheritance. More than two sisters share in the two-thirds. From this Ayah, the scholars took the ruling regarding the two daughters, or more, that they share in the two-thirds, just as the share of the sisters (two or more) was taken from the Ayah about the daughters, (if (there are) only daughters, two or more, their share is two thirds of the inheritance.) (4:11). Allah said,

(if there are brothers and sisters, the male will have twice the share of the female.) This is the share that the male relatives (sons, grandsons, brothers) regularly get, that is, twice as much as the female gets. Allah said, ((Thus) does Allah make clear to you...) His Law and set limits, clarifying His legislation,

(Lest you go astray.) from the truth after this explanation,

(And Allah is the All-Knower of everything.) Allah has perfect knowledge in the consequences of everything and in the benefit that each matter carries for His servants. He also knows what each of the relatives deserves from the inheritance, according to the degree of relation he or she has with the deceased. Ibn Jarir recorded that Tariq bin Shihab said that `Umar gathered the Companions of the Messenger of Allah once and said, "I will give a ruling concerning the Kalalah that even women will talk about it in their bedrooms." A snake then appeared in the house and the gathering had to disperse. `Umar commented, `Had Allah willed this (`Umar's verdict regarding the Kalalah) to happen, it would have happened." The chain of narration for this story is authentic. Al-Hakim, Abu `Abdullah An-Naysaburi recorded that `Umar bin Al-Khattab said, `Had I asked the Messenger of Allah regarding three things, it would have been better for me than red camels. (They are:)

who should be the Khalifah after him; about a people who said, `We agree to pay Zakah, but not to you (meaning to the Khalifah),' if we are allowed to fight them; and about the Kalalah." Al-Hakim said, "Its chain is Sahih according to the Two Shaykhs, and they did not recorded it." Ibn Jarir also said that it was reported that `Umar said, "I feel shy to change a ruling that Abu Bakr issued. Abu Bakr used to say that the Kalalah is the person who has no descendants or ascendants." Abu Bakr's saying is what the majority of scholars among the Companions, their followers and the earlier and later Imams agree with. This is also the ruling that the Qur'an indicates. For Allah stated that He has explained and made plain the ruling of the Kalalah, when He said,

((Thus) does Allah makes clear to you (His Law) lest you go astray. And Allah is the All-Knower of everything.) And Allah knows best.

INTRODUCTION TO CHAPTER (SURAH) 5: AL-MAIDAH (THE TABLE, THE TABLE SPREAD)

Ibn kathir's Introduction

The Virtues of Surat Al-Ma'idah; When It was Revealed

At-Tirmidhi recorded that `Abdullah bin `Amr said, "The last Surahs to be revealed were Surat Al-Ma'idah and Surat Al-Fath (chapter 48)." At-Tirmidhi commented, "This Hadith is Hasan, Gharib." and it was also reported that Ibn `Abbas said that the last Surah to be revealed was,

(When there comes the help of Allah and the Conquest,) Al-Hakim collected a narration similar to that of At-Tirmidhi in his Mustadrak, and he said, "It is Sahih according to the criteria of the Two Shaykhs and they did not record it." Al-Hakim narrated that Jubayr bin Nufayr said, "I performed Hajj once and visited `A'ishah and she said to me, `O Jubayr! Do you read (or memorize) Al-Ma'idah ' I answered `Yes.' She said, `It was the last Surah to be revealed. Therefore, whatever permissible matters you find in it, then consider (treat) them permissible. And whatever impermissible matters you find in it, then consider (treat) them impermissible.'" Al-Hakim said, "It is Sahih according to the criteria of the Two Shaykhs and they did not record it. " Imam Ahmad recorded that `Abdur-Rahman bin Mahdi related that Mu`awiyah bin Salih added this statement in the last Hadith, "I (Jubayr) also asked `A'ishah about the Messenger of Allah's conduct and she answered by saying, `The Qur'an.'" An-Nasa'i also recorded it.

CHAPTER (SURAH) 5: AL-MAIDAH (THE TABLE, THE TABLE SPREAD), VERSES 001-081

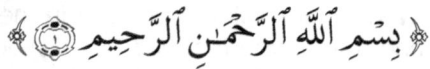

In the Name of Allâh, the Most Gracious, the Most Merciful.

Surah: 5 Ayah: 1 & Ayah: 2

﴿ يَٰٓأَيُّهَا ٱلَّذِينَ ءَامَنُوٓاْ أَوْفُواْ بِٱلْعُقُودِ ۚ أُحِلَّتْ لَكُم بَهِيمَةُ ٱلْأَنْعَٰمِ إِلَّا مَا يُتْلَىٰ عَلَيْكُمْ غَيْرَ مُحِلِّي ٱلصَّيْدِ وَأَنتُمْ حُرُمٌ ۗ إِنَّ ٱللَّهَ يَحْكُمُ مَا يُرِيدُ ۝ ﴾

1. O you who believe! Fulfill (your) obligations. Lawful to you (for food) are all the beasts of cattle except that which will be announced to you (herein), game (also) being unlawful when you assume Ihrâm for Hajj or 'Umrah (pilgrimage). Verily, Allâh commands that which He wills.

﴿ يَٰٓأَيُّهَا ٱلَّذِينَ ءَامَنُواْ لَا تُحِلُّواْ شَعَٰٓئِرَ ٱللَّهِ وَلَا ٱلشَّهْرَ ٱلْحَرَامَ وَلَا ٱلْهَدْىَ وَلَا ٱلْقَلَٰٓئِدَ وَلَآ ءَآمِّينَ ٱلْبَيْتَ ٱلْحَرَامَ يَبْتَغُونَ فَضْلًا مِّن رَّبِّهِمْ وَرِضْوَٰنًا ۚ وَإِذَا حَلَلْتُمْ فَٱصْطَادُواْ ۚ وَلَا يَجْرِمَنَّكُمْ شَنَـَٔانُ قَوْمٍ أَن صَدُّوكُمْ عَنِ ٱلْمَسْجِدِ ٱلْحَرَامِ أَن تَعْتَدُواْ ۘ وَتَعَاوَنُواْ عَلَى ٱلْبِرِّ وَٱلتَّقْوَىٰ ۖ وَلَا تَعَاوَنُواْ عَلَى ٱلْإِثْمِ وَٱلْعُدْوَٰنِ ۚ وَٱتَّقُواْ ٱللَّهَ ۖ إِنَّ ٱللَّهَ شَدِيدُ ٱلْعِقَابِ ۝ ﴾

2. O you who believe! Violate not the sanctity of the Symbols of Allâh, nor of the Sacred Month, nor of the animals brought for sacrifice, nor the garlanded people or animals, and others nor the people coming to the Sacred House (Makkah), seeking the bounty and good pleasure of their Lord. But when you finish the Ihrâm (of Hajj or 'Umrah), you may hunt, and let not the hatred of some people in (once) stopping you from Al-Masjid-al-Harâm (at Makkah) lead you to transgression (and hostility on your part). Help you one another in Al-Birr and At-Taqwa (virtue, righteousness and piety); but do not help one another in sin and transgression. And fear Allâh. Verily, Allâh is Severe in punishment.

Transliteration

1. Ya ayyuha allatheena amanoo awfoo bialAAuqoodi ohillat lakum baheematu al-anAAami illa ma yutla AAalaykum ghayra muhillee alssaydi waantum hurumun inna Allaha yahkumu ma yureedu 2. Ya ayyuha allatheena amanoo la tuhilloo shaAAa-ira Allahi wala alshshahra alharama wala alhadya wala alqala-ida wala ammeena albayta alharama yabtaghoona fadlan min rabbihim waridwanan wa-itha halaltum faistadoo wala yajrimannakum shanaanu qawmin an saddookum AAani almasjidi alharami an taAAtadoo wataAAawanoo AAala albirri waalttaqwa wala taAAawanoo AAala al-ithmi waalAAudwani waittaqoo Allaha inna Allaha shadeedu alAAiqabi

Tafsir Ibn Kathir

Ibn Abi Hatim recorded that a man came to `Abdullah bin Mas`ud and said to him, "Advise me." He said, "When you hear Allah's statement,

(O you who believe!) then pay full attention, for it is a righteous matter that He is ordaining or an evil thing that He is forbidding." Khaythamah said, "Everything in the Qur'an that reads,

(O you who believe!) reads in the Tawrah, `O you who are in need.'" Allah said,

(Fulfill (your) obligations.) Ibn `Abbas, Mujahid and others said that `obligations' here means treaties. Ibn Jarir mentioned that there is a consensus for this view. Ibn Jarir also said that it means treaties, such as the alliances that they used to conduct. `Ali bin Abi Talhah reported that Ibn `Abbas commented:

(O you who believe! Fulfill (your) obligations.) "Refers to the covenants, meaning, what Allah permitted, prohibited, ordained and set limits for in the Qur'an. Therefore, do not commit treachery or break the covenants. Allah emphasized this command when He said,

(And those who break the covenant of Allah, after its ratification, and sever that which Allah has commanded to be joined,) until,

(unhappy (evil) home (i.e. Hell).)" Ad-Dahhak said that,

(Fulfill your obligations.) "Refers to what Allah has permitted and what He has prohibited. Allah has taken the covenant from those who proclaim their faith in the Prophet and the Book to fulfill the obligations that He has ordered for them in the permissible and the impermissible."

Explaining the Lawful and the Unlawful Beasts

Allah said,

(Lawful to you (for food) are all the beasts of cattle) camels, cows and sheep, as Al-Hasan, Qatadah and several others stated. Ibn Jarir said that this Tafsir conforms to the meaning of (`beasts of cattle') that the Arabs had. We should mention that Ibn `Umar, Ibn `Abbas and others relied on this Ayah as evidence to allow eating the meat of the fetus if it is found dead in the belly of its slaughtered mother. There is a Hadith to the same effect collected in the Sunan of Abu Dawud, At-Tirmidhi and Ibn Majah and narrated by Abu Sa`id who said, "We asked, `O Messenger of Allah! When we slaughter a camel, cow or sheep, we sometimes find a fetus in its belly, should we discard it or eat its meat' He said,

«كُلُوهُ إِنْ شِئْتُمْ فَإِنَّ ذَكَاتَهُ ذَكَاةُ أُمِّهِ»

(Eat it if you want, because its slaughter was fulfilled when its mother was slaughtered.)" At-Tirmidhi said, "This Hadith is Hasan." Abu Dawud recorded that Jabir bin `Abdullah said that the Messenger of Allah said,

«ذَكَاةُ الْجَنِينِ ذَكَاةُ أُمِّهِ»

(Proper slaughter of the fetus is fulfilled with the slaughter of its mother.) Only Abu Dawud collected this narration. Allah's statement,

(except that which will be announced to you (herein),) `Ali bin Abi Talhah reported that Ibn `Abbas said that it refers to, "The flesh of dead animals, blood and the meat of swine." Qatadah said, "The meat of dead animals and animals slaughtered without Allah's Name being pronounced at the time of slaughtering." It appears, and Allah knows best, that the Ayah refers to Allah's other statement,

(Forbidden to you (for food) are: Al-Maytah (the dead animals), blood, the flesh of swine, and what has been slaughtered as a sacrifice for others than Allah, and that which has been killed by strangling, or by a violent blow, or by a headlong fall, or by the goring of horns - and that which has been (partly) eaten by a wild animal.)(5:3), for although the animals mentioned in this Ayah are types of permissible cattle (except for swine), they become impermissible under the circumstances that the Ayah (5:3) specifies. This is why Allah said afterwards,

(Unless you are able to slaughter it (before its death) and that which is sacrificed (slaughtered) on An-Nusub (stone altars)) as the latter type is not permissible, because it can no longer be slaughtered properly. Hence, Allah's statement,

(Lawful to you are all the beasts of cattle except that which will be announced to you,) means, except the specific circumstances that prohibit some of these which will be announced to you. Allah said,

(game (also) being unlawful when you assume Ihram.) Some scholars said that the general meaning of `cattle' includes domesticated cattle, such as camels, cows and sheep, and wild cattle, such as gazzelle, wild cattle and wild donkeys. Allah made the exceptions mentioned above (dead animals blood, flesh of swine etc.), and prohibited hunting wild beasts while in the state of Ihram. It was also reported that the meaning here is, "We have allowed for you all types of cattle in all circumstances, except what We excluded herewith for the one hunting game while in the state of Ihram." Allah said,

(But if one is forced by necessity, without willful disobedience, and not transgressing, then, Allah is Oft-Forgiving, Most Merciful.) This Ayah means, "We allowed eating the meat of dead animals, when one is forced by necessity, under the condition that one is not transgressing the limits or overstepping them." Here, Allah states, "Just as We allowed the meat of cattle in all conditions and circumstances, then do not hunt game when in the state of Ihram, for this is the decision of Allah, Who is the Most Wise in all that He commands and forbids." So Allah said;

(Verily, Allah commands that which He wills.)

The Necessity of Observing the Sanctity of the Sacred Area and the Sacred Months

Allah continues,

(O you who believe! Violate not the sanctity of Sha'a'ir Allah (the symbols of Allah),) Ibn `Abbas said, "Sha`a'ir Allah means the rituals of Hajj." Mujahid said, "As-Safa and Al-Marwah, and the sacrificial animal are the symbols of Allah." It was also stated that Sha`a'ir Allah is what He prohibited. Therefore, it means, do not violate what Allah prohibited. Allah said afterwards,

(nor of the Sacred Month,) for you are required to respect and honor the Sacred Month and to refrain from what Allah forbade during it, such as fighting. This also lays emphasis on avoiding sins during that time. As Allah said;

(They ask you concerning fighting in the Sacred Month. Say, "Fighting therein is a great (transgression).") and,

(Verily, the number of months with Allah is twelve months (in a year).) Al-Bukhari recorded in his Sahih that Abu Bakrah said that the Messenger of Allah said during the Farewell Hajj,

«إِنَّ الزَّمَانَ قَدِ اسْتَدَارَ كَهَيْئَتِهِ يَوْمَ خَلَقَ اللهُ السَّمَواتِ وَالْأَرْضَ السَّنَةُ اثْنَا عَشَرَ شَهْرًا، مِنْهَا أَرْبَعَةٌ حُرُمٌ، ثَلَاثٌ مُتَوَالِيَاتٌ: ذُو الْقَعْدَةِ وَذُو الْحِجَّةِ وَالْمُحَرَّمُ، وَرَجَبُ مُضَرَ الَّذِي بَيْنَ جُمَادَى وَشَعْبَانَ»

(The division of time has returned as it was when Allah created the Heavens and the earth. The year is twelve months, four of which are sacred: Three are in succession, (they are:) Dhul-Qa'dah, Dhul-Hijjah and Muharram, and (the fourth is) Rajab of (the tribe of) Mudar which comes between Jumada (Ath-Thaniyah) and Sha'ban.) This Hadith testifies to the continued sanctity of these months until the end of time.

Taking the Hady to the Sacred House of Allah, Al-Ka`bah

Allah's statement,

(nor of the Hady brought for sacrifice, nor the garlands,) means, do not abandon the practice of bringing the Hady (sacrificial animals) to the Sacred House, as this ritual is a form of honoring the symbols of Allah. Do not abandon the practice of garlanding these animals on their necks, so that they are distinguished from other cattle. This way, it will be known that these animals are intended to be offered as Hady at the Ka`bah, and thus those who might intend some harm to them would refrain from doing so. Those who see the Hady might be encouraged to imitate this ritual, and indeed, he who calls to a type of guidance, will earn rewards equal to the rewards of those who follow his lead, without decrease in their own rewards. When the Messenger of Allah intended to perform Hajj, he spent the night at Dhul-Hulayfah, which is also called Wadi Al-`Aqiq. In the morning, the Prophet made rounds with his wives, who were nine at that time, performed Ghusl (bath), applied some perfume and performed a two Rak`ah prayer. He then garlanded the Hady and announced aloud his intention to perform Hajj and `Umrah. The Prophet's Hady at the time

Chapter 5: Al-Maidah (The Table, The Table Spread), Verses 001-081

consisted of plenty of camels, more than sixty, and they were among the best animals, the healthiest and most physically acceptable, just as Allah's statement proclaims,

(Thus it is, and whosoever honors the symbols of Allah, then it is truly, from the piety of the hearts.) Muqatil bin Hayyan said that Allah's statement,

(nor the garlands) means, "Do not breach their sanctity." During the time of Jahiliyyah, the people used to garland themselves with animal hair and pelts when they left their areas in months other than the Sacred Months. The idolators of the Sacred House Area used to garland themselves with the tree-stems of the Sacred Area, so that they were granted safe passage." This statement was collected by Ibn Abi Hatim, who also recorded that Ibn `Abbas said, "There are two Ayat in this Surah (Al-Ma'idah) that were abrogated, the Ayah about the garlands (5:2), and

(So if they come to you (O Muhammad), either judge between them, or turn away from them.)"

The Necessity of Preserving the Sanctity and Safety of those who Intend to Travel to the Sacred House

Allah said,

(nor the people coming to the Sacred House (Makkah), seeking the bounty and good pleasure of their Lord.) The Ayah commands: Do not fight people who are heading towards the Sacred House of Allah, which if anyone enters it, he must be granted safe refuge. Likewise, those who are heading towards the Sacred House seeking the bounty and good pleasure of Allah, must not be stopped, prevented, or frightened away from entering the Sacred House. Mujahid, `Ata', Abu Al-`Aliyah, Mutarrif bin `Abdullah, `Abdullah bin `Ubayd bin `Umayr, Ar-Rabi` bin Anas, Muqatil bin Hayyan, Qatadah and several others said that,

(seeking the bounty of their Lord.) refers to trading. A similar discussion preceded concerning the Ayah;

(There is no sin on you if you seek the bounty of your Lord (during pilgrimage by trading).) Allah said;

(and pleasure.) Ibn `Abbas said that the word `pleasure' in the Ayah refers to, "seeking Allah's pleasure by their Hajj." `Ikrimah, As-Suddi and Ibn Jarir mentioned that this Ayah was revealed concerning Al-Hutam bin Hind Al-Bakri, who had raided the cattle belonging to the people of Al-Madinah. The following year, he wanted to perform `Umrah to the House of Allah and some of the Companions wanted to attack him on his way to the House. Allah revealed,

(nor the people coming to the Sacred House (Makkah), seeking the bounty and good pleasure of their Lord.)

Hunting Game is Permissible After Ihram Ends

Allah said,

(But when you finish the Ihram, then hunt,) When you end your Ihram, it is permitted for you to hunt game, which was prohibited for you during Ihram. Although this Ayah contains a command that takes effect after the end of a state of prohibition (during Ihram in this case), the Ayah, in fact, brings back the ruling that was previously in effect. If the previous ruling was an obligation, the new command will uphold that obligation, and such is the case with recommended and permissible matters. There are many Ayat that deny that the ruling in such cases is always an obligation. Such is also the case against those who say that it is always merely allowed. What we mentioned here is the correct opinion that employs the available evidence, and Allah knows best.

Justice is Always Necessary

Allah said,

(and let not the hatred of some people in (once) stopping you from Al-Masjid Al-Haram (at Makkah) lead you to transgression (and hostility on your part).) The meaning of this Ayah is apparent, as it commands: Let not the hatred for some people, who prevented you from reaching the Sacred House in the year of Hudaybiyyah, make you transgress Allah's Law and commit injustice against them in retaliation. Rather, rule as Allah has commanded you, being just with every one. We will explain a similar Ayah later on,

(And let not the enmity and hatred of others make you avoid justice. Be just: that is nearer to piety,) which commands: do not be driven by your hatred for some people into abandoning justice, for justice is ordained for everyone, in all situations. Ibn Abi Hatim recorded that Zayd bin Aslam said, "The Messenger of Allah and his Companions were in the area of Al-Hudaybiyyah when the idolators prevented them from visiting the House, and that was especially hard on them. Later on, some idolators passed by them from the east intending to perform `Umrah. So the Companions of the Prophet said, `Let us prevent those (from `Umrah) just as their fellow idolators prevented us.' Thereafter, Allah sent down this Ayah." Ibn Abbas and others said that "Shana'an" refers to enmity and hate. Allah said next,

(Help you one another in Al-Birr and At-Taqwa; but do not help one another in sin and transgression.) Allah commands His believing servants to help one another perform righteous, good deeds, which is the meaning of `Al-Birr', and to avoid sins, which is the meaning of `At-Taqwa'. Allah forbids His servants from helping one another in sin, `Ithm' and committing the prohibitions. Ibn Jarir said that, "Ithm means abandoning what Allah has ordained, while transgression means overstepping the limits that Allah set in your religion, along with overstepping what Allah has ordered concerning yourselves and others." Imam Ahmad recorded that Anas bin Malik said that the Messenger of Allah said,

«انْصُرْ أَخَاكَ ظَالِمًا أَوْ مَظْلُومًا»

(Support your brother whether he was unjust or the victim of injustice.) He was asked, "O Messenger of Allah! We know about helping him when he suffers injustice, so what about helping him when he commits injustice" He said,

«تَحْجُزُهُ وَتَمْنَعُهُ مِنَ الظُّلْمِ فَذَاكَ نَصْرُهُ»

(Prevent and stop him from committing injustice, and this represents giving support to him.) Al-Bukhari recorded this Hadith through Hushaym. Ahmad recorded that one of the Companions of the Prophet narrated the Hadith,

«الْمُؤْمِنُ الَّذِي يُخَالِطُ النَّاسَ وَيَصْبِرُ عَلَى أَذَاهُمْ أَعْظَمُ أَجْرًا مِنَ الَّذِي لَا يُخَالِطُ النَّاسَ وَلَا يَصْبِرُ عَلَى أَذَاهُمْ»

(The believer who mingles with people and is patient with their annoyance, earns more reward than the believer who does not mingle with people and does not observe patience with their annoyance.) Muslim recorded a Hadith that states,

«مَنْ دَعَا إِلَى هُدًى كَانَ لَهُ مِنَ الْأَجْرِ مِثْلُ أُجُورِ مَنِ اتَّبَعَهُ إِلَى يَوْمِ الْقِيَامَةِ لَا يَنْقُصُ ذَلِكَ مِنْ أُجُورِهِمْ شَيْئًا، وَمَنْ دَعَا إِلَى ضَلَالَةٍ كَانَ عَلَيْهِ مِنَ الْإِثْمِ مِثْلُ آثَامِ مَنِ اتَّبَعَهُ إِلَى يَوْمِ الْقِيَامَةِ، لَا يَنْقُصُ ذَلِكَ مِنْ آثَامِهِمْ شَيْئًا»

(He who calls to a guidance, will earn a reward similar to the rewards of those who accept his call, until the Day of Resurrection, without decreasing their rewards. Whoever calls to a heresy, will carry a burden similar to the burdens of those who accept his call, until the Day of Resurrection, without decreasing their own burdens.)

Surah: 5 Ayah: 3

﴿ حُرِّمَتْ عَلَيْكُمُ ٱلْمَيْتَةُ وَٱلدَّمُ وَلَحْمُ ٱلْخِنزِيرِ وَمَآ أُهِلَّ لِغَيْرِ ٱللَّهِ بِهِۦ وَٱلْمُنْخَنِقَةُ وَٱلْمَوْقُوذَةُ وَٱلْمُتَرَدِّيَةُ وَٱلنَّطِيحَةُ وَمَآ أَكَلَ ٱلسَّبُعُ إِلَّا مَا ذَكَّيْتُمْ وَمَا ذُبِحَ عَلَى ٱلنُّصُبِ وَأَن تَسْتَقْسِمُواْ بِٱلْأَزْلَٰمِ ذَٰلِكُمْ فِسْقٌ ٱلْيَوْمَ يَئِسَ ٱلَّذِينَ كَفَرُواْ مِن دِينِكُمْ فَلَا تَخْشَوْهُمْ وَٱخْشَوْنِ ٱلْيَوْمَ أَكْمَلْتُ لَكُمْ دِينَكُمْ وَأَتْمَمْتُ عَلَيْكُمْ نِعْمَتِى

$$\text{وَرَضِيتُ لَكُمُ ٱلْإِسْلَـٰمَ دِينًا ۚ فَمَنِ ٱضْطُرَّ فِى مَخْمَصَةٍ غَيْرَ مُتَجَانِفٍ لِّإِثْمٍ فَإِنَّ ٱللَّهَ غَفُورٌ رَّحِيمٌ ﴿٣﴾}$$

3. Forbidden to you (for food) are: Al-Maitah (the dead animals - cattle-beast not slaughtered), blood, the flesh of swine, and that on which Allâh's Name has not been mentioned while slaughtering, (that which has been slaughtered as a sacrifice for others than Allâh, or has been slaughtered for idols) and that which has been killed by strangling, or by a violent blow, or by a headlong fall, or by the goring of horns - and that which has been (partly) eaten by a wild animal - unless you are able to slaughter it (before its death) - and that which is sacrificed (slaughtered) on An-Nusub (stone altars). (Forbidden) also is to use arrows seeking luck or decision; (all) that is Fisqun (disobedience of Allâh and sin). This day, those who disbelieved have given up all hope of your religion; so fear them not, but fear Me. This day, I have perfected your religion for you, completed My Favor upon you, and have chosen for you Islâm as your religion. But as for him who is forced by severe hunger, with no inclination to sin (such can eat these above-mentioned meats), then surely, Allâh is Oft-Forgiving, Most Merciful.

Transliteration

3. Hurrimat AAalaykumu almaytatu waalddamu walahmu alkhinzeeri wama ohilla lighayri Allahi bihi waalmunkhaniqatu waalmawqoothatu waalmutaraddiyatu waalnnateehatu wama akala alssabuAAu illa ma thakkaytum wama thubiha AAala alnnusubi waan tastaqsimoo bial-azlami thalikum fisqun alyawma ya-isa allatheena kafaroo min deenikum fala takhshawhum waikhshawni alyawma akmaltu lakum deenakum waatmamtu AAalaykum niAAmatee waradeetu lakumu al-islama deenan famani idturra fee makhmasatin ghayra mutajanifin li-ithmin fa-inna Allaha ghafoorun raheemun

Tafsir Ibn Kathir

The Animals that are Unlawful to Eat

Allah informs His servants that He forbids consuming the mentioned types of foods, such as the Maytah, which is the animal that dies before being properly slaughtered or hunted. Allah forbids this type of food due to the harm it causes, because of the blood that becomes clogged in the veins of the dead animal. Therefore, the Maytah is harmful, religiously and physically, and this is why Allah has prohibited it. The only exception to this ruling is fish, for fish is allowed, even when dead, by slaughtering or otherwise. Malik in his Muwatta, also Abu Dawud, At-Tirmidhi, An-Nasa'i and Ibn Majah in their Sunan, Ibn Khuzaymah and Ibn Hibban in their Sahihs, all recorded that Abu Hurayrah said that the Messenger of Allah was asked about seawater. He said,

$$\text{«هُوَ الطَّهُورُ مَاؤُهُ الْحِلُّ مَيْتَتُهُ»}$$

(Its water is pure and its dead are permissible.) The same ruling applies to locusts, as proven in a Hadith that we will mention later. Allah's statement,

Chapter 5: Al-Ma'idah (The Table, The Table Spread), Verses 001-081

(blood...) This refers to flowing blood, according to Ibn `Abbas and Sa`id bin Jubayr, and it is similar to Allah's other statement,

(Blood poured forth...) Ibn Abi Hatim recorded that Ibn `Abbas was asked about the spleen and he said, "Eat it." They said, "It is blood." He said, "You are only prohibited blood that was poured forth." Abu `Abdullah, Muhammad bin Idris Ash-Shafi`i recorded that Ibn `Umar said that the Messenger of Allah said,

«أُحِلَّ لَنَا مَيْتَتَانِ وَدَمَانِ، فَأَمَّا الْمَيْتَتَانِ فَالسَّمَكُ وَالْجَرَادُ، وَأَمَّا الدَّمَانِ فَالْكَبِدُ وَالطِّحَال»

(We were allowed two dead animals and two (kinds of) blood. As for the two dead animals, they are fish and locust. As for the two bloods, they are liver and spleen.) Imam Ahmad bin Hanbal, Ibn Majah, Ad-Daraqutni and Al-Bayhaqi also recorded this Hadith through `Abdur-Rahman bin Zayd bin Aslam, who is a weak narrator. Allah's statement,

(the flesh of swine...) includes domesticated and wild swine, and also refers to the whole animal, including its fat, for this is what the Arabs mean by Lahm or `flesh'. Muslim recorded that Buraydah bin Al-Husayb Al-Aslami said that the Messenger of Allah said,

«مَنْ لَعِبَ بِالنَّرْدَشِيرِ، فَكَأَنَّمَا صَبَغَ يَدَهُ فِي لَحْمِ الْخِنْزِيرِ وَدَمِهِ»

(He who plays Nardshir (a game with dice that involves gambling) is just like the one who puts his hand in the flesh and blood of swine.) If this is the case with merely touching the flesh and blood of swine, so what about eating and feeding on it This Hadith is a proof that Lahm means the entire body of the animal, including its fat. In is recorded in the Two Sahihs that the Messenger of Allah said,

«إِنَّ اللهَ حَرَّمَ بَيْعَ الْخَمْرِ وَالْمَيْتَةِ وَالْخِنْزِيرِ وَالْأَصْنَام»

(Allah made the trade of alcohol, dead animals, pigs and idols illegal.) The people asked, "O Allah's Messenger! What about the fat of dead animals, for it was used for greasing the boats and the hides; and people use it for lanterns" He said,

«لَا، هُوَ حَرَام»

(No, it is illegal.) In the Sahih of Al-Bukhari, Abu Sufyan narrated that he said to Heraclius, Emperor of Rome, "He (Muhammad) prohibited us from eating dead animals and blood." Allah said,

(And that which has been slaughtered as a sacrifice for other than Allah.) Therefore, the animals on which a name other than Allah was mentioned upon slaughtering it, is impermissible, because Allah made it necessary to mention His Glorious Name upon slaughtering the animals, which He created. Whoever does not do so, mentioning other than Allah's Name, such as the name of an idol, a false deity or a monument, when slaughtering, he makes this meat unlawful, according to the consensus. Allah's statement,

(and that which has been killed by strangling...) either intentionally or by mistake, such as when an animal moves while restrained and dies by strangulation because of its struggling, this animal is also unlawful to eat.

(or by a violent blow...) This refers to the animal that is hit with a heavy object until it dies. Ibn `Abbas and several others said it is the animal that is hit with a staff until it dies. Qatadah said, "The people of Jahiliyyah used to strike the animal with sticks and when it died, they would eat it." It is recorded in the Sahih that `Adi bin Hatim said, "I asked, `O Allah's Messenger! I use the Mi`rad for hunting and catch game with it.' He replied,

«إِذَا رَمَيْتَ بِالْمِعْرَاضِ فَخَزَقَ فَكُلْهُ، وَإِنْ أَصَابَ بَعَرْضِهِ فَإِنَّمَا هُوَ وَقِيذٌ فَلَا تَأْكُلْه»

(If the game is hit by its sharp edge, eat it. But, if it is hit by its broad side, do not eat it, for it has been beaten to death.) Therefore, the Prophet made a distinction between killing the animal with the sharp edge of an arrow or a hunting stick, and rendered it lawful, and what is killed by the broad side of an object, and rendered it unlawful because it was beaten to death. There is a consensus among the scholars of Fiqh on this subject. rAs for the animal that falls headlong from a high place and dies as a result, it is also prohibited. `Ali bin Abi Talhah reported that Ibn `Abbas said that an animal that dies by a headlong fall, "Is that which falls from a mountain." Qatadah said that it is the animal that falls in a well. As-Suddi said that it is the animal that falls from a mountain or in a well. As for the animal that dies by being gorged by another animal, it is also prohibited, even if the horn opens a flesh wound and it bleeds to death from its neck. Allah's statement,

(and that which has been (partly) eaten by a wild animal,) refers to the animal that was attacked by a lion, leopard, tiger, wolf or dog, then the wild beast eats a part of it and it dies because of that. This type is also prohibited, even if the animal bled to death from its neck. There is also a consensus on this ruling. During the time of Jahiliyyah, the people used to eat the sheep, camel, or cow that were partly eaten by a wild animal. Allah prohibited this practice for the believers. Allah's statement,

(unless you are able to slaughter it,) before it dies, due to the causes mentioned above. This part of the Ayah is connected to, (and that which has been killed by strangling, or by a violent blow, or by a headlong fall, or by the goring of horns - and that which has been (partly) eaten by a wild animal.) `Ali bin Abi Talhah reported that Ibn `Abbas commented on Allah's statement,

(unless you are able to slaughter it,) "Unless you are able to slaughter the animal in the cases mentioned in the Ayah while it is still alive, then eat it, for it was properly slaughtered." Similar was reported from Sa`id bin Jubayr, Al-Hasan Al-Basri and As-Suddi. Ibn Jarir recorded that `Ali, may Allah be pleased with him, said, "If you are able to slaughter the animal that has been hit by a violent blow, or by a headlong fall, or by the gorging of horns while it still moves a foot or a leg, then eat from its meat." Similar was reported from Tawus, Al-Hasan, Qatadah, `Ubayd bin `Umayr, Ad-Dahhak and several others, that if the animal that is being slaughtered still moves, thus demonstrating that it is still alive while slaughtering, then it is lawful. The Two Sahihs recorded that Rafi` bin Khadij said, "I asked, `O Allah's Messenger! We fear that we may meet our enemy tomorrow and we have no knives, could we slaughter the animals with reeds' The Prophet said,

«مَا أَنْهَرَ الدَّمَ، وَذُكِرَ اسْمُ اللهِ عَلَيْهِ، فَكُلُوهُ، لَيْسَ السِّنَّ وَالظُّفُرَ، وَسَأُحَدِّثُكُمْ عَنْ ذلِكَ: أَمَّا السِّنُّ فَعَظْمٌ، وَأَمَّا الظُّفُرُ فَمُدَى الْحَبَشَة»

(You can use what makes blood flow and you can eat what is slaughtered with the Name of Allah. But do not use teeth or claws (in slaughtering). I will tell you why, as for teeth, they are bones, and claws are used by Ethiopians for slaughtering.)" Allah said next,

(and that which is sacrificed on An-Nusub.) Nusub were stone altars that were erected around the Ka`bah, as Mujahid and Ibn Jurayj stated. Ibn Jurayj said, "There were three hundred and sixty Nusub (around the Ka`bah) that the Arabs used to slaughter in front of, during the time of Jahiliyyah. They used to sprinkle the animals that came to the Ka`bah with the blood of slaughtered animals, whose meat they cut to pieces and placed on the altars." Allah forbade this practice for the believers. He also forbade them from eating the meat of animals that were slaughtered in the vicinity of the Nusub, even if Allah's Name was mentioned on these animals when they were slaughtered, because it is a type of Shirk that Allah and His Messenger have forbidden.

The Prohibition of Using Al-Azlam for Decision Making

Allah said,

((Forbidden) also is to make decisions with Al-Azlam) The Ayah commands, "O believers! You are forbidden to use Al-Azlam (arrows) for decision making," which was a practice of the Arabs during the time of Jahiliyyah. They would use three arrows, one with the word `Do' written on it, another that says `Do not', while the third does not say anything. Some of them would write on the first arrow, `My Lord commanded me,' and, `My Lord forbade me,' on the second arrow and they would not write anything on the third arrow. If the blank arrow was picked, the person would keep trying until the arrow that says do or do not was picked, and the person would implement the command that he picked. Ibn `Abbas said that the Azlam were arrows that they used to seek decisions through. Muhammad bin Ishaq and others said that the major idol of the tribe of Quraysh was Hubal, which was erected on the tip of a well inside the Ka`bah, where gifts were presented and where the treasure of the Ka`bah was kept. There, they also had seven arrows that they would use to seek a decision concerning matters of dispute. Whatever the chosen arrow would tell them, they would abide by it! Al-Bukhari recorded that when the Prophet entered Al-Ka`bah (after Makkah was conquered), he found pictures of Ibrahim and Isma`il in it holding the Azlam in their hands. The Prophet commented,

«قَاتَلَهُمُ اللهُ لَقَدْ عَلِمُوا أَنَّهُمَا لَمْ يَسْتَقْسِمَا بِهَا أَبَدًا»

(May Allah fight them (the idolaters)! They know that they never used the Azlam to make decisions.) Mujahid commented on Allah's statement,

((Forbidden) also is to make decisions with Al-Azlam,) "These were arrows that the Arabs used, and dice that the Persians and Romans used in gambling." This statement by Mujahid, that these arrows were used in gambling, is doubtful unless we say that they used the arrows for gambling sometimes and for decisions other times, and Allah knows best. We should also state that Allah mentioned Azlam and gambling in His statement before the end of the Surah (5:90, 91),

(O you who believe! Intoxicants (all kinds of alcoholic drinks), and gambling, and Al-Ansab, and Al-Azlam are an abomination of Shaytan's handiwork. So avoid that in order that you may be successful. Shaytan wants only to excite enmity and hatred between you with intoxicants (alcoholic drinks) and gambling, and hinder you from the remembrance of Allah and from the Salah (the prayer). So, will you not then abstain) In this Ayah, Allah said,

((Forbidden) also is to make decisions with Al-Azlam, (all) that is Fisq.) meaning, all these practices constitute disobedience, sin, misguidance, ignorance and, above all, Shirk. Allah has commanded the believers to seek decisions from Him when they want to do something, by first worshipping Him and then asking Him for the best decision concerning the matter they seek. Imam Ahmad, Al-Bukhari and the collectors of Sunan recorded that Jabir bin `Abdullah said, "The Prophet used to teach us how to make Istikharah (asking Allah to guide one to the right action), in all matters, as he taught us the Surahs of the Qur'an. He said,

«إِذَا هَمَّ أَحَدُكُمْ بِالْأَمْرِ فَلْيَرْكَعْ رَكْعَتَيْنِ مِنْ غَيْرِ الْفَرِيضَةِ، ثُمَّ لْيَقُلْ: اللَّهُمَّ إِنِّي أَسْتَخِيرُكَ بِعِلْمِكَ، وَأَسْتَقْدِرُكَ بِقُدْرَتِكَ، وَأَسْأَلُكَ مِنْ فَضْلِكَ الْعَظِيمِ، فَإِنَّكَ

تَقْدِرُ وَلَا أَقْدِرُ وَتَعْلَمُ وَلَا أَعْلَمُ، وَأَنْتَ عَلَّامُ الْغُيُوبِ، اللَّهُمَّ إِنْ كُنْتَ تَعْلَمُ أَنَّ هَذَا الْأَمْرَ ويسميه باسمه خَيْرٌ لِي فِي دِينِي وَدُنْيَايَ وَمَعَاشِي وَعَاقِبَةِ أَمْرِي أَوْ قَالَ: عَاجِلِ أَمْرِي وَآجِلِهِ فَاقْدُرْهُ لِي، وَيَسِّرْهُ لِي، ثُمَّ بَارِكْ لِي فِيهِ، اللَّهُمَّ وَإِنْ كُنْتَ تَعْلَمُ أَنَّهُ شَرٌّ لِي فِي دِينِي وَدُنْيَايَ وَمَعَاشِي وَعَاقِبَةِ أَمْرِي، فَاصْرِفْنِي عَنْهُ، وَاصْرِفْهُ عَنِّي، وَاقْدُرْ لِيَ الْخَيْرَ حَيْثُ كَانَ، ثُمَّ رَضِّنِي بِهِ»

(If anyone of you thinks of doing any matter, he should offer a two Rak'ah prayer, other than the compulsory, and say (after the prayer) `O Allah! I ask guidance from Your knowledge, from Your ability and I ask for Your great bounty, for You are capable and I am not, You know and I do not, and You know the Unseen. O Allah! If You know that this matter (and one should mention the matter or deed here) is good for my religion, my livelihood and the Hereafter (or he said, `for my present and later needs') then ordain it for me, make it easy for me to have, and then bless it for me. O Allah! And if You know that this is harmful to me in my religion and livelihood and for the Hereafter then keep it away from me and let me be away from it. And ordain whatever is good for me, and make me satisfied with it.') This is the wording collected by Ahmad, and At-Tirmidhi said, "Hasan Sahih Gharib."

Shaytan and the Disbelievers Do Not Hope that Muslims Will Ever Follow Them

Allah said,

(This day, those who disbelieved have given up all hope of your religion;) `Ali bin Abi Talhah reported that Ibn `Abbas said that the Ayah means, "They gave up hope that Muslims would revert to their religion." This is similar to the saying of `Ata' bin Abi Rabah, As-Suddi and Muqatil bin Hayyan. This meaning is supported by a Hadith recorded in the Sahih that states,

«إِنَّ الشَّيْطَانَ قَدْ يَئِسَ أَنْ يَعْبُدَهُ الْمُصَلُّونَ فِي جَزِيرَةِ الْعَرَبِ، وَلكِنْ بِالتَّحْرِيشِ بَيْنَهُمْ»

(Verily, Shaytan has given up hope that those who pray in the Arabian Peninsula, will worship him. But he will still stir trouble among them.) It is also possible that the Ayah negates the possibility that the disbelievers and Shaytan will ever be like Muslims, since Muslims have various qualities that contradict Shirk and its people. This is why Allah commanded His believing servants to observe patience, to be steadfast in defying and contradicting the disbelievers, and to fear none but Allah. Allah said,

(So fear them not, but fear Me.) meaning, 'do not fear them when you contradict them. Rather, fear Me and I will give you victory over them, I will eradicate them, and make you prevail over them, I will please your hearts and raise you above them in this life and the Hereafter.

Islam Has Been Perfected For Muslims

Allah said,

(This day, I have perfected your religion for you, completed My favor upon you, and have chosen for you Islam as your religion.) This, indeed, is the biggest favor from Allah to this Ummah, for He has completed their religion for them, and they, thus, do not need any other religion or any other Prophet except Muhammad . This is why Allah made Muhammad the Final Prophet and sent him to all humans and Jinn. Therefore, the permissible is what he allows, the impermissible is what he prohibits, the Law is what he legislates and everything that he conveys is true and authentic and does not contain lies or contradictions. Allah said;

(And the Word of your Lord has been fulfilled in truth and in justice,) meaning, it is true in what it conveys and just in what it commands and forbids. When Allah completed the religion for Muslims, His favor became complete for them as well. Allah said,

(This day, I have perfected your religion for you, completed My favor upon you, and have chosen for you Islam as your religion.) meaning, accept Islam for yourselves, for it is the religion that Allah likes and which He chose for you, and it is that with which He sent the best of the honorable Messengers and the most glorious of His Books. Ibn Jarir recorded that Harun bin `Antarah said that his father said, "When the Ayah, (This day, I have perfected your religion for you...) was revealed, during the great day of Hajj (the Day of `Arafah, the ninth day of Dhul-Hijjah) `Umar cried. The Prophet said, `What makes you cry' He said, `What made me cry is that our religion is being perfected for us. Now it is perfect, nothing is perfect, but it is bound to deteriorate.' The Prophet said,

《«صَدَقْتَ»》

(You have said the truth.)" What supports the meaning of this Hadith is the authentic Hadith,

《«إِنَّ الْإِسْلَامَ بَدَأَ غَرِيبًا، وَسَيَعُودُ غَرِيبًا، فَطُوبَى لِلْغُرَبَاءِ»》

(Islam was strange in its beginning and will return strange once more. Therefore, Tuba for the strangers.) Imam Ahmad recorded that Tariq bin Shihab said, "A Jewish man said to `Umar bin Al-Khattab, `O Leader of the Believers! There is a verse in your Book, which is read by all of you (Muslims), and had it been revealed to us, we would have taken that day (on which it was revealed) as a day of celebration.' `Umar bin Al-Khattab asked, `Which is that verse' The Jew replied, (This day, I have perfected your religion for you, completed My favor upon you...) `Umar replied, `By Allah! I know when and where this verse was revealed to Allah's Messenger . It was the evening on the Day of `Arafah on a Friday.'" Al-Bukhari recorded this Hadith through Al-Hasan bin As-Sabbah from Ja`far bin `Awn. Muslim, At-Tirmidhi and An-Nasa'i also recorded this Hadith. In the narration collected by Al-Bukhari in the book of Tafsir, through Tariq, he said, "The Jews said to `Umar, `By Allah! There is a verse that is read by all of you (Muslims), and had it been revealed to us, we would have taken that day (on which it was revealed) as a day of celebration.' `Umar said, `By Allah! I know when and where this verse was revealed and where the Messenger of Allah was at that time. It was the day of `Arafah, and I was at `Arafah, by Allah." Sufyan (one of the narrators) doubted if Friday was mentioned in this narration. Sufyan's confusion was either because he was unsure if his teacher included this statement in the Hadith or not. Otherwise, if it was because he doubted that the particular day during the Farewell Hajj was a Friday, it would be a mistake that could not and should not have come from someone like Sufyan Ath-Thawri. The fact that it was a Friday, is agreed on by the scholars of Sirah and Fiqh. There are numerous Hadiths that support this fact that are definitely authentic and of the Mutawatir type. This Hadith was also reported from `Umar through various chains of narration.

Permitting the Dead Animals in Conditions of Necessity

Allah said,

(But as for him who is forced by severe hunger, with no inclination to sin (such can eat these above mentioned animals), then surely, Allah is Oft-Forgiving, Most Merciful.) Therefore, when one is forced to take any of the impermissible things that Allah mentioned to meet a necessity, he is allowed and Allah is Oft-Forgiving, Most Merciful with him. Allah is well aware of His servant's needs during dire straits, and He will forgive and pardon His servant in this case. In the Musnad and the Sahih of Ibn Hibban, it is recorded that Ibn `Umar said that Messenger of Allah said,

«إِنَّ اللهَ يُحِبُّ أَنْ تُؤْتَى رُخْصَتُهُ كَمَا يَكْرَهُ أَنْ تُؤْتَى مَعْصِيَتُهُ»

(Allah likes that His Rukhsah (allowance) be used, just as He dislikes that disobedience to Him is committed.) We should mention here that it is not necessary for one to wait three days before eating the meat of dead animals, as many unlettered Muslims mistakenly think. Rather, one can eat such meat when the dire need arises. Imam Ahmad recorded that Abu Waqid Al-Laythi said that the Companions asked, "O Messenger of Allah! We live in a land where famine often strikes us. Therefore, when are we allowed to eat the meat of dead animals" The Prophet replied,

«إِذَا لَمْ تَصْطَبِحُوا، وَلَمْ تَغْتَبِقُوا، وَلَمْ تَحْتَفِئُوا بَقْلًا فَشَأْنُكُمْ بِهَا»

(When you neither find food for lunch and dinner nor have any produce to eat, then eat from it.) Only Imam Ahmad collected this narration and its chain meets the criteria of the Two Sahihs. Allah said,

(with no inclination to sin,) meaning, one does not incline to commit what Allah has prohibited. Allah has allowed one when necessity arises to eat from what He otherwise prohibits, under the condition that his heart does not incline to eat what Allah prohibited. Allah said in Surat Al-Baqarah,

(But if one is forced by necessity without willful disobedience nor transgressing due limits, then there is no sin on him. Truly, Allah is Oft-Forgiving, Most Merciful.) Some scholars used this Ayah as evidence that those who travel for the purpose of committing an act of disobedience are not allowed to use any of the legal concessions of travel, because these concessions are not earned through sin, and Allah knows best.

Surah: 5 Ayah: 4

﴿ يَسْـَٔلُونَكَ مَاذَآ أُحِلَّ لَهُمْ ۖ قُلْ أُحِلَّ لَكُمُ ٱلطَّيِّبَـٰتُ ۙ وَمَا عَلَّمْتُم مِّنَ ٱلْجَوَارِحِ مُكَلِّبِينَ تُعَلِّمُونَهُنَّ مِمَّا عَلَّمَكُمُ ٱللَّهُ ۖ فَكُلُوا۟ مِمَّآ أَمْسَكْنَ عَلَيْكُمْ وَٱذْكُرُوا۟ ٱسْمَ ٱللَّهِ عَلَيْهِ ۖ وَٱتَّقُوا۟ ٱللَّهَ ۚ إِنَّ ٱللَّهَ سَرِيعُ ٱلْحِسَابِ ﴾

4. They ask you (O Muhammad (peace be upon him)) what is lawful for them (as food). Say: "Lawful unto you are At-Tayyibât (all kind of Halâl (lawful-good) foods which Allâh has made lawful (meat of slaughtered eatable animals, milk products, fats, vegetables and fruits)). And those beasts and birds of prey which you have trained as hounds, training and teaching them (to catch) in the manner as directed to you by Allâh; so eat of what they catch for you, but pronounce the Name of Allâh over it, and fear Allâh. Verily, Allâh is Swift in reckoning."

Transliteration

4. Yas-aloonaka matha ohilla lahum qul ohilla lakumu alttayyibatu wama AAallamtum mina aljawarihi mukallibeena tuAAallimoonahunna mimma AAallamakumu Allahu fakuloo mimma amsakna AAalaykum waothkuroo isma Allahi AAalayhi waittaqoo Allaha inna Allaha sareeAAu alhisabi

Tafsir Ibn Kathir

Clarifying the Lawful

In the previous Ayah Allah mentioned the prohibited types of food, the impure and unclean things, harmful for those who eat them, either to their bodies, religion or both, except out of necessity,

(while He has explained to you in detail what is forbidden to you, except under compulsion of necessity) After that, Allah said,

Chapter 5: Al-Maidah (The Table, The Table Spread), Verses 001-081

(They ask you what is lawful for them. Say, "Lawful unto you are At-Tayyibat...") In Surat Al-A`raf Allah describes Muhammad allowing the good things and prohibiting the filthy things. Muqatil said, "At-Tayyibat includes everything Muslims are allowed and the various types of legally earned provision." Az-Zuhri was once asked about drinking urine for medicinal purposes and he said that it is not a type of Tayyibat." Ibn Abi Hatim also narrated this statement. Using Jawarih to Hunt Game is Permissible Allah said,

(And those Jawarih (beasts and birds of prey) which you have trained as hounds...) That is, lawful for you are the animals slaughtered in Allah's Name, and the good things for sustenance. (The game you catch) with the Jawarih are also lawful for you. This refers to trained dogs and falcons, as is the opinion of the majority of the Companions, their followers, and the Imams. `Ali bin Abi Talhah reported that Ibn `Abbas said that,

(And those Jawarih (beasts and birds of prey) which you have trained as hounds...) refers to trained hunting dogs, falcons and all types of birds and beasts that are trained to hunt, including dogs, wild cats, falcons, and so forth. Ibn Abi Hatim collected this and said, "Similar was reported from Khaythamah, Tawus, Mujahid, Makhul and Yahya bin Abi Kathir." Ibn Jarir recorded that Ibn `Umar said, "You are permitted the animal that the trained birds, such as falcons, hunt for you if you catch it (before it eats from it). Otherwise, do not eat from it." I say, the majority of scholars say that hunting with trained birds is just like hunting with trained dogs, because bird's of prey catch the game with their claws, just like dogs. Therefore, there is no difference between the two. Ibn Jarir recorded that `Adi bin Hatim said that he asked the Messenger of Allah about the game that the falcon hunts and the Messenger said,

«مَا أَمْسَكَ عَلَيْكَ فَكُلْ»

(Whatever it catches for you, eat from it.) These carnivores that are trained to catch game are called Jawarih in Arabic, a word that is derived from Jarh, meaning, what one earns. The Arabs would say, "So-and-so has Jaraha something good for his family," meaning, he has earned them something good. The Arabs would say, "So-and-so does not have a Jarih for him," meaning, a caretaker. Allah also said,

(And He knows what you have done during the day...) meaning, the good or evil you have earned or committed. Allah's statement,

(trained as hounds,) those Jawarih that have been trained to hunt as hounds with their claws or talons. Therefore, if the game is killed by the weight of its blow, not with its claws, then we are not allowed to eat from the game. Allah said,

(training them in the manner as directed to you by Allah,) as when the beast is sent, it goes after the game, and when it catches it, it keeps it until its owner arrives and does not catch it to eat it itself. This is why Allah said here, (so eat of what they catch for you, but pronounce the Name of Allah over it,) When the beast is trained, and it catches the game for its owner who mentioned Allah's Name when he sent the beast after the game, then this game is allowed according to the consensus of scholars, even if it was killed. There are Hadiths in the Sunnah that support this statement. The Two Sahihs recorded that `Adi bin Hatim said, "I said, `O Allah's Messenger! I send hunting dogs and mention Allah's Name.' He replied,

«إِذَا أَرْسَلْتَ كَلْبَكَ الْمُعَلَّمَ وَذَكَرْتَ اسْمَ اللهِ فَكُلْ مَا أَمْسَكَ عَلَيْكَ»

(If, with mentioning Allah's Name, you let loose your tamed dog after a game and it catches it, you may eat what it catches.) I said, `Even if it kills the game' He replied,

«وَإِنْ قَتَلْنَ، مَا لَمْ يَشْرِكْهَا كَلْبٌ لَيْسَ مِنْهَا، فَإِنَّكَ إِنَّمَا سَمَّيْتَ عَلَى كَلْبِكَ وَلَمْ تُسَمِّ عَلَى غَيْرِهِ»

(Even if it kills the game, unless another dog joins the hunt, for you mentioned Allah's Name when sending your dog, but not the other dog.) I said, `I also use the Mi`rad and catch game with it.' He replied,

«إِذَا رَمَيْتَ بِالْمِعْرَاضِ فَخَزَقَ فَكُلْهُ، وَإِنْ أَصَابَهُ بِعَرْضٍ فَإِنَّهُ وَقِيذٌ فَلَا تَأْكُلْهُ»

(If the game is hit by its sharp edge, eat it, but if it is hit by its broad side, do not eat it, for it has been beaten to death.) In another narration, the Prophet said,

«وَإِذَا أَرْسَلْتَ كَلْبَكَ فَاذْكُرِ اسْمَ اللهِ، فَإِنْ أَمْسَكَ عَلَيْكَ، فَأَدْرَكْتَهُ حَيًّا فَاذْبَحْهُ، وَإِنْ أَدْرَكْتَهُ قَدْ قَتَلَ وَلَمْ يَأْكُلْ مِنْهُ فَكُلْهُ، فَإِنَّ أَخْذَ الْكَلْبِ ذَكَاتُهُ»

(If you send your hunting dog, then mention Allah's Name and whatever it catches for you and you find alive, slaughter it. If you catch the game dead and the dog did not eat from it, then eat from it, for the dog has caused its slaughter to be fulfilled.) In yet another narration of two Sahihs, the Prophet said,

«فَإِنْ أَكَلَ فَلَا تَأْكُلْ، فَإِنِّي أَخَافُ أَنْ يَكُونَ أَمْسَكَ عَلَى نَفْسِه»

(If the dog eats from the game, do not eat from it for I fear that it has caught it as prey for itself.)

Mention Allah's Name Upon Sending the Predators to Catch the Game

Allah said,

(so eat of what they catch for you, but pronounce the Name of Allah over it,) meaning, upon sending it. The Prophet said to `Adi bin Hatim,

»إِذَا أَرْسَلْتَ كَلْبَكَ الْمُعَلَّمَ، وَذَكَرْتَ اسْمَ اللهِ، فَكُلْ مَا أَمْسَكَ عَلَيْكَ«

(When you send your trained dog and mention Allah's Name, eat from what it catches for you.) It is recorded in the Two Sahihs that Abu Tha`labah related that the Prophet said,

»إِذَا أَرْسَلْتَ كَلْبَكَ فَاذْكُرِ اسْمَ اللهِ، وَإِذَا رَمَيْتَ بِسَهْمِكَ فَاذْكُرِ اسْمَ الله«

(If you send your hunting dog, mention Allah's Name over it. If you shoot an arrow, mention Allah's Name over it.) `Ali bin Abi Talhah reported that Ibn `Abbas commented,

[وَاذْكُرُواْ اسْمَ اللَّهِ عَلَيْهِ]

(but pronounce the Name of Allah over it,) "When you send a beast of prey, say, `In the Name of Allah!' If you forget, then there is no harm." It was also reported that this Ayah commands mentioning Allah's Name upon eating. It is recorded in the Two Sahihs that the Messenger of Allah taught his stepson `Umar bin Abu Salamah saying,

»سَمِّ اللهَ وَكُلْ بِيَمِينِكَ وَكُلْ مِمَّا يَلِيكَ«

(Mention Allah's Name, eat with your right hand and eat from the part of the plate that is in front of you.) Al-Bukhari recorded that `A'ishah said, "They asked, `O Allah's Messenger! Some people, - recently converted from disbelief - bring us some meats that we do not know if Allah's Name was mentioned over or not.' He replied,

»سَمُّوا اللهَ أَنْتُمْ وَكُلُوا«

(Mention Allah's Name on it and eat from it.)"

Surah: 5 Ayah: 5

﴿ ٱلْيَوْمَ أُحِلَّ لَكُمُ ٱلطَّيِّبَٰتُ ۖ وَطَعَامُ ٱلَّذِينَ أُوتُوا۟ ٱلْكِتَٰبَ حِلٌّ لَّكُمْ وَطَعَامُكُمْ حِلٌّ لَّهُمْ ۖ وَٱلْمُحْصَنَٰتُ مِنَ ٱلْمُؤْمِنَٰتِ وَٱلْمُحْصَنَٰتُ مِنَ ٱلَّذِينَ أُوتُوا۟ ٱلْكِتَٰبَ مِن

$$\text{قَبْلِكُمْ إِذَآ ءَاتَيْتُمُوهُنَّ أُجُورَهُنَّ مُحْصِنِينَ غَيْرَ مُسَـٰفِحِينَ وَلَا مُتَّخِذِىٓ أَخْدَانٍ ۗ وَمَن يَكْفُرْ بِٱلْإِيمَـٰنِ فَقَدْ حَبِطَ عَمَلُهُۥ وَهُوَ فِى ٱلْـَٔاخِرَةِ مِنَ ٱلْخَـٰسِرِينَ}$$

5. Made lawful to you this day are At-Tayyibât (all kinds of Halâl (lawful) foods, which Allâh has made lawful (meat of slaughtered eatable animals, milk products, fats, vegetables and fruits). The food (slaughtered cattle, eatable animals) of the people of the Scripture (Jews and Christians) is lawful to you and yours is lawful to them. (Lawful to you in marriage) are chaste women from the believers and chaste women from those who were given the Scripture (Jews and Christians) before your time when you have given their due Mahr (bridal-money given by the husband to his wife at the time of marriage), desiring chastity (i.e. taking them in legal wedlock) not committing illegal sexual intercourse, nor taking them as girl-friends. And whosoever disbelieves in Faith (i.e. in the Oneness of Allâh and in all the other Articles of Faith i.e. His (Allâh's), Angels, His Holy Books, His Messengers, the Day of Resurrection and Al-Qadar (Divine Preordainments)), then fruitless is his work; and in the Hereafter he will be among the losers.

Transliteration

5. Alyawma ohilla lakumu alttayyibatu wataAAamu allatheena ootoo alkitaba hillun lakum wataAAamukum hillun lahum waalmuhsanatu mina almu/minati waalmuhsanatu mina allatheena ootoo alkitaba min qablikum itha ataytumoohunna ojoorahunna muhsineena ghayra musafiheena wala muttakhithee akhdanin waman yakfur bial-eemani faqad habita AAamaluhu wahuwa fee al-akhirati mina alkhasireena

Tafsir Ibn Kathir

Permitting the Slaughtered Animals of the People of the Book

After Allah mentioned the filthy things that He prohibited for His believing servants and the good things that He allowed for them, He said next,

(Made lawful to you this day are At-Tayyibat.) Allah then mentioned the ruling concerning the slaughtered animals of the People of the Book, the Jews and Christians,

(The food of the People of the Scripture is lawful to you..) meaning, their slaughtered animals, as Ibn `Abbas, Abu Umamah, Mujahid, Sa`id bin Jubayr, `Ikrimah, `Ata', Al-Hasan, Makhul, Ibrahim An-Nakha`i, As-Suddi and Muqatil bin Hayyan stated. This ruling, that the slaughtered animals of the People of the Book are permissible for Muslims, is agreed on by the scholars, because the People of the Book believe that slaughtering for other than Allah is prohibited. They mention Allah's Name upon slaughtering their animals, even though they have deviant beliefs about Allah that do not befit His majesty. It is recorded in the Sahih that `Abdullah bin Mughaffal said, "While we were attacking the fort of Khaybar, a person threw a leather bag containing fat, and I ran to take it and said, `I will not give anyone anything from this container today.' But when I turned I saw the Prophet (standing behind) while smiling." The scholars rely on this Hadith as evidence that we are allowed to eat what we need of foods from the booty before it is divided. The scholars of the Hanafi, the Shafi`i and the Hanbali Madhhabs rely on this Hadith to allow eating parts of the slaughtered animals of the Jews that they prohibit for themselves, such as the fat. They used this Hadith as evidence against the scholars of the Maliki Madhhab who disagreed with this ruling. A better proof is the Hadith recorded in the Sahih that the people of Khaybar gave the Prophet a gift of a roasted leg of sheep, which they poisoned. The Prophet used to like eating the leg of the sheep and he took a bite from it, but it told the Prophet that it was poisoned, so he discarded that bite. The bite that the Prophet took effected the palate of his mouth, while Bishr bin Al-Bara' bin Ma`rur died from eating from that sheep. The Prophet had the Jewish woman, Zaynab, who poisoned the sheep, killed. Therefore, the Prophet and his Companions wanted to eat from that sheep and did not ask the Jews if they removed what the Jews believed was prohibited for them, such as its fat. Allah's statement,

(and your food is lawful to them.) means, you are allowed to feed them from your slaughtered animals. Therefore, this part of the Ayah is not to inform the People of the Scriptures that they are allowed to eat our food -- unless we consider it information for us about the ruling that they have -- i. e, that they are allowed all types of foods over which Allah's Name was mentioned, whether slaughtered according to their religion or otherwise. The first explanation is more plausible. So it means: you are allowed to feed them from your slaughtered animals just as you are allowed to eat from theirs, as equal compensation and fair treatment. The Prophet gave his robe to `Abdullah bin Ubayy bin Salul, who was wrapped with it when he died. They say that he did that because `Abdullah had given his robe to Al-`Abbas when Al-`Abbas came to Al-Madinah. As for the Hadith,

«لَا تَصْحَبْ إِلَّا مُؤْمِنًا، وَلَا يَأْكُلْ طَعَامَكَ إِلَّا تَقِيٌّ»

(Do not befriend but a believer, nor should other than a Taqi (pious person) eat your food.), This is to encourage such behavior, and Allah knows best.

The Permission to Marry Chaste Women From the People of the Scriptures

Allah said,

((Lawful to you in marriage) are chaste women from the believers) The Ayah states: you are allowed to marry free, chaste believing women. This Ayah is talking about women who do not commit fornication, as evident by the word `chaste'. Allah said in another Ayah,

(Desiring chastity not committing illegal sexual intercourse, nor taking them as boyfriends (lovers).) (4:25) `Abdullah Ibn `Umar used to advise against marrying Christian women saying, "I do not know of a worse case of Shirk than her saying that `Isa is her lord, while Allah said,

(And do not marry idolatresses till they believe.)" Ibn Abi Hatim recorded that Abu Malik Al-Ghifari said that Ibn `Abbas said that when this Ayah was revealed,

(And do not marry idolatresses till they believe,) the people did not marry the pagan women. When the following Ayah was revealed,

((Lawful to you in marriage) are chaste women from the believers and chaste women from those who were given the Scripture before your time) they married women from the People of the Book. " Some of the Companions married Christian women and did not see any problem in this, relying on the honorable Ayah,

((Lawful to you in marriage) are chaste women from those who were given the Scripture before your time) Therefore, they made this Ayah an exception to the Ayah in Surat Al-Baqarah,

(And do not marry the idolatresses till they believe,) considering the latter Ayah to include the People of the Book in its general meaning. Otherwise, there is no contradiction here, since the People of the Book were mentioned alone when mentioning the rest of the idolators. Allah said,

(Those who disbelieve from among the People of the Scripture and the idolators, were not going to leave (their disbelief) until there came to them clear evidence.) and,

(And say to those who were given the Scripture and to those who are illiterates: "Do you (also) submit yourselves" If they do, they are rightly guided.) Allah said next,

(When you have given them their due), This refers to the Mahr, so just as these women are chaste and honorable, then give them their Mahr with a good heart. We should mention here that Jabir bin `Abdullah, `Amir Ash-Sha`bi, Ibrahim An-Nakha`i and Al-Hasan Al-Basri stated that when a man marries a woman and she commits illegal sexual intercourse before the marriage is consummated, the marriage is annulled. In this case, she gives back the Mahr that he paid her. Allah said,

(Desiring chastity, not illegal sexual intercourse, nor taking them as girl-friends (or lovers).) And just as women must be chaste and avoid illegal sexual activity, such is the case with men, who must also be chaste and honorable. Therefore, Allah said,

(...not illegal sexual intercourse') as adulterous people do, those who do not avoid sin, nor reject adultery with whomever offers it to them.

(nor taking them as girl-friends (or lovers),) meaning those who have mistresses and girlfriends who commit illegal sexual intercourse with them, as we mentioned in the explanation of Surat An-Nisa'.

Surah: 5 Ayah: 6

﴿ يَٰٓأَيُّهَا ٱلَّذِينَ ءَامَنُوٓاْ إِذَا قُمْتُمْ إِلَى ٱلصَّلَوٰةِ فَٱغْسِلُواْ وُجُوهَكُمْ وَأَيْدِيَكُمْ إِلَى ٱلْمَرَافِقِ وَٱمْسَحُواْ بِرُءُوسِكُمْ وَأَرْجُلَكُمْ إِلَى ٱلْكَعْبَيْنِ ۚ وَإِن كُنتُمْ جُنُبًا فَٱطَّهَّرُواْ ۚ وَإِن كُنتُم مَّرْضَىٰٓ أَوْ عَلَىٰ سَفَرٍ أَوْ جَآءَ أَحَدٌ مِّنكُم مِّنَ ٱلْغَآئِطِ أَوْ

Chapter 5: Al-Maidah (The Table, The Table Spread), Verses 001-081

لَمَسْتُمُ ٱلنِّسَآءَ فَلَمْ تَجِدُواْ مَآءً فَتَيَمَّمُواْ صَعِيدًا طَيِّبًا فَٱمْسَحُواْ بِوُجُوهِكُمْ وَأَيْدِيكُم مِّنْهُ مَا يُرِيدُ ٱللَّهُ لِيَجْعَلَ عَلَيْكُم مِّنْ حَرَجٍ وَلَٰكِن يُرِيدُ لِيُطَهِّرَكُمْ وَلِيُتِمَّ نِعْمَتَهُۥ عَلَيْكُمْ لَعَلَّكُمْ تَشْكُرُونَ ۝

6. O you who believe! When you intend to offer As-Salât (the prayer), wash your faces and your hands (forearms) up to the elbows, rub (by passing wet hands over) your heads, and (wash) your feet up to ankles. If you are in a state of Janâba (i.e. aftwer a sexual discharge), purify yourself (bathe your whole body). But if you are ill or on a journe, or any of you comes after answering the call of nature, or you have been in contact with women (i.e. sexual intercourse) , and you find no water, then perform Tayammum with clean earth and rub therewith your faces and hands. Allâh does not want to place you in difficulty, but He wants to purify you, and to complete His Favor on you that you may be thankful.

Transliteration

6. Ya ayyuha allatheena amanoo itha qumtum ila alssalati faighsiloo wujoohakum waaydiyakum ila almarafiqi waimsahoo biruoosikum waarjulakum ila alkaAAbayni wa-in kuntum junuban faittaharoo wa-in kuntum marda aw AAala safarin aw jaa ahadun minkum mina algha-iti aw lamastumu alnnisaa falam tajidoo maan fatayammamoo saAAeedan tayyiban faimsahoo biwujoohikum waaydeekum minhu ma yureedu Allahu liyajAAala AAalaykum min harajin walakin yureedu liyutahhirakum waliyutimma niAAmatahu AAalaykum laAAallakum tashkuroona

Tafsir Ibn Kathir

The Order to Perform Wudu'

Allah said,

(When you stand for (intend to offer) the Salah,) Allah commanded performing Wudu' for the prayer. This is a command of obligation in the case of impurity, and in the case of purity, it is merely a recommendation. It was said that in the beginning of Islam, Muslims had to perform Wudu' for every prayer, but later on, this ruling was abrogated. Imam Ahmad bin Hanbal recorded that Sulayman bin Buraydah said that his father said, "The Prophet used to perform Wudu' before every prayer. On the Day of Victory, he performed Wudu' and wiped on his Khuffs and prayed the five prayers with one Wudu'. `Umar said to him, `O Messenger of Allah! You did something new that you never did before.' The Prophet said,

«إني عمدا فعلته يا عمر»

(`I did that intentionally O `Umar!)'" Muslim and the collectors of the Sunan also recorded this Hadith. At-Tirmidhi said,"Hasan Sahih." Ibn Jarir recorded that Al-Fadl bin Al-Mubashshir said, "I saw Jabir bin `Abdullah perform several prayers with only one Wudu'. When he would answer the call of nature, he performed Wudu' and wiped the top of his Khuffs with his wet hand. I said, `O Abu `Abdullah! Do you do this according to your own opinion' He said, `Rather, I saw the Prophet do the same thing. So, I do what I saw the Messenger of Allah doing.'" Ibn Majah also recorded this Hadith. Ahmad recorded that `Ubaydullah bin `Abdullah bin `Umar was asked; "Did you see `Abdullah bin `Umar perform Wudu' for every prayer, whether he was in a state of purity or not," So he replied, "Asma' bint Zayd bin Al-Khattab told him that `Abdullah bin Hanzalah bin Abi `Amir Al-Ghasil told her that the Messenger of Allah was earlier commanded to perform Wudu' for every prayer, whether he needed it or not. When that became hard on him, he was commanded to use Siwak for every prayer, and to perform Wudu' when Hadath (impurity) occurs. `Abdullah (Ibn `Umar) thought that he was able to do that (perform Wudu' for every prayer) and he kept doing that until he died." Abu Dawud also collected this narration. This practice by Ibn `Umar demonstrates that it is encouraged, not obligatory, to perform Wudu' for every prayer, and this is also the opinion of the majority of scholars. Abu Dawud recorded that `Abdullah bin `Abbas said that when the Messenger of Allah once left the area where he answered the call of nature, he was brought something to eat. They said, "Should we bring you your water for Wudu" He said,

《إِنَّمَا أُمِرْتُ بِالْوُضُوءِ إِذَا قُمْتُ إِلَى الصَّلَاةِ》

(I was commanded to perform Wudu' when I stand up for prayer.) At-Tirmidhi and An-Nasa'i also recorded this Hadith and At-Tirmidhi said, "This Hadith is Hasan." Muslim recorded that Ibn `Abbas said, "We were with the Prophet when he went to answer the call of nature and when he came back, he was brought some food. He was asked, `O Messenger of Allah! Do you want to perform Wudu" He said,

《لِمَ؟ أُصَلِّي فَأَتَوَضَّأَ》

(`Why? Am I about to pray so that I have to make Wudu'.?)'"

The Intention and Mentioning Allah's Name for Wudu'

Allah said;

(then wash your faces...) The obligation for the intention before Wudu' is proven by this Ayah;

(When you stand (intend) to offer the Salah then wash your faces...) This is because it is just like the Arabs saying; "When you see the leader, then stand." Meaning stand for him. And the Two Sahihs recorded the Hadith,

《الْأَعْمَالُ بِالنِّيَّاتِ وَإِنَّمَا لِكُلِّ امْرِئٍ مَا نَوَى》

(Actions are judged by their intentions, and each person will earn what he intended.) It is also recommended before washing the face that one mentions Allah's Name for the Wudu'. A Hadith that was narrated by several Companions states that the Prophet said,

«لَا وُضُوءَ لِمَنْ لَمْ يَذْكُرِ اسْمَ اللهِ عَلَيْهِ»

(There is no Wudu' for he who does not mention Allah's Name over it.) It is also recommended that one washes his hands before he puts his hands in the vessel of water, especially after one wakes up from sleep, for the Two Sahihs recorded that Abu Hurayrah said that the Messenger of Allah said,

«إِذَا اسْتَيْقَظَ أَحَدُكُمْ مِنْ نَوْمِهِ فَلَا يُدْخِلْ يَدَهُ فِي الْإِنَاءِ قَبْلَ أَنْ يَغْسِلَهَا ثَلَاثًا، فَإِنَّ أَحَدَكُمْ لَا يَدْرِي أَيْنَ بَاتَتْ يَدُه»

(If one of you wakes up from his sleep, let him not put his hand in the pot until he washes it thrice, for one of you does not know where his hand spent the night.) The face according to the scholars of Fiqh starts where the hair line on the head starts, regardless of one's lack or abundance of hair, until the end of the cheeks and chin, and from ear to ear.

Passing the Fingers through the Beard While Performing Wudu'

Imam Ahmad recorded that Abu Wa'il said, "I saw `Uthman when he was performing Wudu'... When he washed his face, he passed his fingers through his beard three times. He said, `I saw the Messenger of Allah do what you saw me doing.'" At-Tirmidhi and Ibn Majah also recorded this Hadith. At-Tirmidhi said "Hasan Sahih." while Al-Bukhari graded it Hasan.

How to Perform Wudu'

Imam Ahmad recorded that Ibn `Abbas once performed Wudu' and took a handful of water and rinsed his mouth and nose with it. He took another handful of water and joined both hands and washed his face. He took another handful of water and washed his right hand, and another handful and washed his left hand with it. He next wiped his head. Next, he took a handful of water and sprinkled it on his right foot and washed it and took another handful of water and washed his left foot. When he finished, he said, "This is how I saw the Messenger of Allah (performing Wudu')." Al-Bukhari also recorded it. Allah said,

(and your hands (forearms) up to (Ila) the elbows...) meaning, including the elbows. Allah said in another Ayah (using Ila),

(And devour not their substance to (Ila) your substance (by adding or including it in your property). Surely, this is a great sin.) It is recommended that those who perform Wudu' should wash a part of the upper arm with the elbow. Al-Bukhari and Muslim recorded that Abu Hurayrah said that the Messenger of Allah said,

«إِنَّ أُمَّتِي يُدْعَوْنَ يَوْمَ الْقِيَامَةِ غُرًّا مُحَجَّلِينَ مِنْ آثَارِ الْوُضُوءِ، فَمَنِ اسْتَطَاعَ مِنْكُمْ أَنْ يُطِيلَ غُرَّتَهُ فَلْيَفْعَل»

(On the Day of Resurrection, my Ummah will be called "those with the radiant appendages" because of the traces of Wudu'. Therefore, whoever can increase the area of his radiance should do so.) Muslim recorded that Abu Hurayrah said, "I heard my intimate friend (the Messenger) saying,

«تَبْلُغُ الْحِلْيَةُ مِنَ الْمُؤْمِنِ حَيْثُ يَبْلُغُ الْوَضُوء»

(The radiance of the believer reaches the areas that the water of (his) Wudu' reaches.)" Allah said next,

(Rub your heads.) It is recorded in the Two Sahihs that Malik bin `Amr bin Yahya Al-Mazini said that his father said that a man said to `Abdullah bin Zayd bin `Asim, the grandfather of `Amr bin Yahya and one of the Companions of the Messenger , "Can you show me how the Messenger of Allah used to perform Wudu'" `Abdullah bin Zayd said, "Yes." He then asked for a pot of water. He poured from it on his hands and washed them twice, then he rinsed his mouth and washed his nose (with water) thrice (by putting water in it and blowing it out). He washed his face thrice and after that he washed his forearms up to the elbows twice. He then passed his wet hands over his head from its front to its back and vice versa, beginning from the front and taking them to the back of his head up to the nape of the neck and then brought them to the front again from where he had started. He next washed his feet. A similar description of the Wudu' of the Messenger of Allah was performed by `Ali in the Hadith by `Abdu Khayr. Abu Dawud recorded that Mu`awiyah and Al-Miqdad bin Ma`dikarib narrated similar descriptions of the Wudu' of the Messenger of Allah . These Hadiths indicate that it is necessary to wipe the entire head. `Abdur-Razzaq recorded that Humran bin Aban said, "I saw `Uthman bin `Affan performing Wudu', and he poured water over his hands and washed them thrice, and then rinsed his mouth and washed his nose (by putting water in it, and then blowing it out). Then he washed his face thrice, and then his right forearm up to the elbows thrice, and washed the left forearm thrice. Then he passed his wet hands over his head, then he washed his right foot thrice, and next his left foot thrice. After that `Uthman said, `I saw the Prophet performing Wudu' like this, and said,

«مَنْ تَوَضَّأَ نَحْوَ وُضُوئِي هَذَا، ثُمَّ صَلَّى رَكْعَتَيْنِ لَا يُحَدِّثُ فِيهِمَا نَفْسَهُ، غُفِرَ لَهُ مَا تَقَدَّمَ مِنْ ذَنْبِه»

(If anyone performs Wudu' like that of mine and offers a two-Rak`ah prayer during which he does not think of anything else, then his past sins will be forgiven.)"' Al-Bukhari and Muslim also recorded this Hadith in the Two Sahihs. In his Sunan, Abu

Dawud also recorded it from `Uthman, under the description of Wudu', and in it, that he wiped his head one time.

The Necessity of Washing the Feet

Allah said,

(and your feet up to ankles.) Ibn Abi Hatim recorded that Ibn `Abbas stated that the Ayah refers to washing (the feet). `Abdullah bin Mas`ud, `Urwah, `Ata', `Ikrimah, Al-Hasan, Mujahid, Ibrahim, Ad-Dahhak, As-Suddi, Muqatil bin Hayyan, Az-Zuhri and Ibrahim At-Taymi said similarly. This clearly indicates the necessity of washing the feet, just as the Salaf have said, and not only wiping over the top of the bare foot.

The Hadiths that Indicate the Necessity of Washing the Feet

We mentioned the Hadiths by the two Leaders of the Faithful, `Uthman and `Ali, and also by Ibn `Abbas, Mu`awiyah, `Abdullah bin Zayd bin `Asim and Al-Miqdad bin Ma`dikarib, that the Messenger of Allah washed his feet for Wudu', either once, twice or thrice. It is recorded in the Two Sahihs that `Abdullah bin `Amr said, "The Messenger of Allah was once late during a trip we were taking, and he caught up with us when the time remaining for the `Asr prayer was short. We were still performing Wudu' (in a rush) and we were wiping our feet. He shouted at the top of his voice,

«أَسْبِغُوا الْوُضُوءَ وَيْلٌ لِلْأَعْقَابِ مِنَ النَّارِ»

(Perform Wudu' thoroughly. Save your heels from the Fire.)" The same narration was also collected in the Two Sahihs from Abu Hurayrah. Muslim recorded that `A'ishah said that the Prophet said,

«أَسْبِغُوا الْوُضُوءَ وَيْلٌ لِلْأَعْقَابِ مِنَ النَّارِ»

(Perform Wudu' thoroughly. Save your heels from the Fire.) `Abdullah bin Al-Harith bin Jaz' said that he heard the Messenger of Allah saying,

«وَيْلٌ لِلْأَعْقَابِ وَبُطُونِ الْأَقْدَامِ مِنَ النَّارِ»

(Save your heels and the bottom of the feet from the Fire.) It was recorded by Al-Bayhaqi and Al-Hakim, and this chain is Sahih. Muslim recorded that `Umar bin Al-Khattab said that a man once performed Wudu' and left a dry spot the size of a fingernail on his foot. The Prophet saw that and he said to him,

«ارْجِعْ فَأَحْسِنْ وُضُوءَكَ»

(Go back and perform proper Wudu'.) Al-Hafiz Abu Bakr Al-Bayhaqi also recorded that Anas bin Malik said that a man came to the Prophet , after he performed Wudu' and left a dry spot the size of a fingernail on his foot. The Messenger of Allah said to him,

«ارْجِعْ فَأَحْسِنْ وُضُوءَكَ»

(Go back and perform proper Wudu'.) Imam Ahmad recorded that some of the wives of the Prophet said that the Prophet saw a man praying, but noticed a dry spot on his foot, the size of a Dirham. The Messenger of Allah ordered that man to perform Wudu' again. This Hadith was also collected by Abu Dawud from Baqiyyah, who added in his narration, "And (the Prophet ordered him) to repeat the prayer." This Hadith has a strong, reasonably good chain of narrators. Allah knows best.

The Necessity of Washing Between the Fingers

In the Hadith that Humran narrated, `Uthman washed between his fingers when he was describing the Wudu' of the Prophet . The collectors of the Sunan recorded that Laqit bin Sabrah said, "I said, `O Messenger of Allah! Tell me about Wudu'.' The Messenger replied,

«أَسْبِغِ الْوُضُوءَ، وَخَلِّلْ بَيْنَ الْأَصَابِعِ، وَبَالِغْ فِي الِاسْتِنْشَاقِ إِلَّا أَنْ تَكُونَ صَائِمًا»

(Perform Wudu' thoroughly, wash between the fingers and exaggerate in rinsing your nose, unless you are fasting.)"

Wiping Over the Khuffs is an Established Sunnah

Imam Ahmad bin Hanbal recorded that Aws bin Abi Aws said, "I saw the Messenger of Allah perform Wudu' and wipe over his Khuffs. He then stood up for prayer." Abu Dawud recorded this Hadith by Aws bin Abi Aws, who said in this narration, "I saw the Messenger of Allah , after he answered the call of nature, perform Wudu' and wipe over his Khuffs and feet." Imam Ahmad recorded that Jarir bin `Abdullah Al-Bajali said, "I embraced Islam after Surat Al-Ma'idah was revealed and I saw the Messenger of Allah wipe after I became Muslim." It is recorded in the Two Sahihs that Hammam said, "Jarir answered the call of nature and then performed Wudu' and wiped over his Khuffs. He was asked, `Do you do this' He said, `Yes. I saw the Messenger of Allah , after he answered the call of nature, perform Wudu' and wipe on his Khuffs.'" Al-A`mash commented that Ibrahim said, "They liked this Hadith because Jarir embraced Islam after Surat Al-Ma'idah was revealed." This is the wording collected by Muslim. The subject of the Messenger of Allah wiping over his Khuffs, instead of washing the feet, if he had worn his Khuffs while having Wudu', reaches the Mutawatir grade of narration, and they describe this practice by his words and actions.

Performing Tayammum with Clean earth When There is no Water and When One is Ill

Allah said,

(But if you are ill or on a journey or any of you comes from the Gha'it (toilet), or you have touched women and you find no water, then perform Tayammum with clean earth and rub therewith your faces and hands.) We discussed all of this in Surat An-Nisa', and thus we do not need to repeat it here. We also mentioned the reason behind revealing this Ayah. Yet, Al-Bukhari mentioned an honorable Hadith here specifically about the Tafsir of this noble Ayah. He recorded that `A'ishah said, "Upon returning to Al-Madinah, a necklace of mine was broken (and lost) in Al-Bayda' area. Allah's Messenger stayed there and went to sleep with his head on my lap. Abu Bakr (`A'ishah's father) came and hit me on my flank with his hand saying, `You have detained the people because of a necklace' So I wished I were dead because (I could not move) the Messenger was sleeping on my lap and because of the pain Abu Bakr caused me. Allah's Messenger got up when dawn broke and there was no water. So Allah revealed,

(O you who believe! When you stand (intend) to offer As-Salah (the prayer), then wash your faces) iuntil the end of the Ayah. Usayd bin Al-Hudayr said, `O the family of Abu Bakr! Allah has blessed the people because of you. Therefore, you are only a blessing for the people." Allah said,

(Allah does not want to place you in difficulty,) This is why He made things easy and lenient for you. This is why He allowed you to use Tayammum when you are ill and when you do not find water, to make things comfortable for you and as mercy for you. Allah made Tayammum in place of Wudu', and Allah made it the same as ablution with water for the one who it is legitimate for, except for certain things, as we mentioned before. For example; Tayammum only involves one strike with the hand on the sand and wiping the face and hands. Allah said,

(but He wants to purify you, and to complete His favor on you that you may be thankful.) for His bounties on you, such as His easy, kind, merciful, comfortable and lenient legislation.

Supplicating to Allah after Wudu'

The Sunnah encourages supplicating to Allah after Wudu' and states that those who do so are among those who seek to purify themselves, as the Ayah above states. Imam Ahmad, Muslim and the collectors of Sunan narrated that `Uqbah bin `Amir said, "We were on watch, guarding camels, and when my turn to guard came, I took the camels back at night. I found that the Messenger of Allah was giving a speech to the people. I heard these words from that speech:

«مَا مِنْ مُسْلِمٍ يَتَوَضَّأُ فَيُحْسِنُ وُضُوءَهُ، ثُمَّ يَقُومُ فَيُصَلِّي رَكْعَتَيْنِ مُقْبِلًا عَلَيْهِمَا بِقَلْبِهِ وَوَجْهِهِ، إِلَّا وَجَبَتْ لَهُ الْجَنَّة»

(Any Muslim who performs Wudu' properly, then stands up and prays a two Rak'ah prayer with full attention in his heart and face, will earn Paradise.) I said, `What a good statement this is!' A person who was close by said, `The statement he said before it is even better.' When I looked, I found that it was `Umar, who said, `I saw that you just came. The Prophet said,

«مَا مِنْكُمْ مِنْ أَحَدٍ يَتَوَضَّأُ فَيُبْلِغُ أَوْفَيُسْبِغُ الْوُضُوءَ، يَقُولُ: أَشْهَدُ أَنْ لَا إِلَهَ إِلَّا اللهُ وَأَنَّ مُحَمَّدًا عَبْدُهُ وَرَسُولُهُ، إِلَّا فُتِحَتْ لَهُ أَبْوَابُ الْجَنَّةِ الثَّمَانِيَةِ، يَدْخُلُ مِنْ أَيِّهَا شَاءَ»

(When any of you performs Wudu' properly and says, `I bear witness that there is no deity worthy of worship except Allah and that Muhammad is His servant and Messenger', the eight doors of Paradise will be opened for him so that he can enter from any door he wishes.)" This is the wording collected by Muslim.

The Virtue of Wudu'

Malik recorded that Abu Hurayrah said that the Messenger of Allah said,

«إِذَا تَوَضَّأَ الْعَبْدُ الْمُسْلِمُ أَوِ الْمُؤْمِنُ فَغَسَلَ وَجْهَهُ، خَرَجَ مِنْ وَجْهِهِ، كُلُّ خَطِيئَةٍ نَظَرَ إِلَيْهَا بِعَيْنَيْهِ مَعَ الْمَاءِ أَوْ مَعَ آخِرِ قَطْرِ الْمَاءِ، فَإِذَا غَسَلَ يَدَيْهِ خَرَجَ مِنْ يَدَيْهِ كُلُّ خَطِيئَةٍ بَطَشَتْهَا يَدَاهُ مَعَ الْمَاءِ أَوْ مَعَ آخِرِ قَطْرِ الْمَاءِ، فَإِذَا غَسَلَ رِجْلَيْهِ خَرَجَتْ كُلُّ خَطِيئَةٍ مَشَتْهَا رِجْلَاهُ مَعَ الْمَاءِ أَوْ مَعَ آخِرِ قَطْرِ الْمَاءِ، حَتَّى يَخْرُجَ نَقِيًّا مِنَ الذُّنُوبِ»

(When the Muslim or the believing servant performs Wudu' and washes his face, every sin that he looked at with his eyes will depart from his face with the water, or with the last drop of water. When he washes his hands, every sin that his hands committed will depart from his hands with the water, or with the last drop of water. When he washes his feet, every sin to which his feet took him will depart with the water, or with the last drop of water. Until, he ends up sinless.) Muslim also recorded it.

Muslim recorded that Abu Malik Al-Ash`ari said that the Messenger of Allah said,

Chapter 5: Al-Maidah (The Table, The Table Spread), Verses 001-081

«الطُّهُورُ شَطْرُ الْإِيمَانِ، وَالْحَمْدُ لِلَّهِ تَمْلَأُ الْمِيزَانَ، وَسُبْحَانَ اللَّهِ وَاللَّهُ أَكْبَرُ تَمْلَأُ مَا بَيْنَ السَّمَاءِ وَالْأَرْضِ، وَالصَّوْمُ جُنَّةٌ، وَالصَّبْرُ ضِيَاءٌ، وَالصَّدَقَةُ بُرْهَانٌ، وَالْقُرْآنُ حُجَّةٌ لَكَ أَوْ عَلَيْكَ، كُلُّ النَّاسِ يَغْدُو، فَبَائِعٌ نَفْسَهُ فَمُعْتِقُهَا أَوْ مُوبِقُهَا»

(Purity is half of faith and Al-Hamdu Lillah (all the thanks are due to Allah) fills the Mizan (the Scale). And Subhan Allah and Allahu Akbar (all praise is due to Allah, and Allah is the Most Great) fills what is between the heaven and earth. As-Sawm (the fast) is a Junnah (a shield), Sabr (patience) is a light, Sadaqah (charity) is evidence (of faith) and the Qur'an is proof for, or against you. Every person goes out in the morning and ends up selling himself, he either frees his soul or destroys it.)

Muslim recorded that Ibn `Umar said that the Messenger of Allah said,

«لَا يَقْبَلُ اللَّهُ صَدَقَةً مِنْ غُلُولٍ، وَلَا صَلَاةً بِغَيْرِ طُهُورٍ»

(Allah does not accept charity from one who commits Ghulul, or prayer without purity.)

Surah: 5 Ayah: 7, Ayah: 8, Ayah: 9, Ayah: 10 & Ayah: 11

﴿ وَاذْكُرُوا۟ نِعْمَةَ ٱللَّهِ عَلَيْكُمْ وَمِيثَٰقَهُ ٱلَّذِى وَاثَقَكُم بِهِۦٓ إِذْ قُلْتُمْ سَمِعْنَا وَأَطَعْنَا ۖ وَٱتَّقُوا۟ ٱللَّهَ ۚ إِنَّ ٱللَّهَ عَلِيمٌۢ بِذَاتِ ٱلصُّدُورِ ۝ ﴾

7. And remember Allâh's Favor to you and His Covenant with which He bound you when you said: "We hear and we obey." And fear Allâh. Verily, Allâh is All-Knower of that which is in (the secrets of your) breasts.

﴿ يَٰٓأَيُّهَا ٱلَّذِينَ ءَامَنُوا۟ كُونُوا۟ قَوَّٰمِينَ لِلَّهِ شُهَدَآءَ بِٱلْقِسْطِ ۖ وَلَا يَجْرِمَنَّكُمْ شَنَـَٔانُ قَوْمٍ عَلَىٰٓ أَلَّا تَعْدِلُوا۟ ۚ ٱعْدِلُوا۟ هُوَ أَقْرَبُ لِلتَّقْوَىٰ ۖ وَٱتَّقُوا۟ ٱللَّهَ ۚ إِنَّ ٱللَّهَ خَبِيرٌۢ بِمَا تَعْمَلُونَ ۝ ﴾

8. O you who believe! Stand out firmly for Allâh as just witnesses; and let not the enmity and hatred of others make you avoid justice. Be just: that is nearer to piety; and fear Allâh. Verily, Allâh is Well-Acquainted with what you do.

﴿ وَعَدَ ٱللَّهُ ٱلَّذِينَ ءَامَنُوا۟ وَعَمِلُوا۟ ٱلصَّٰلِحَٰتِ ۙ لَهُم مَّغْفِرَةٌ وَأَجْرٌ عَظِيمٌ ۝ ﴾

9. Allâh has promised those who believe (in the Oneness of Allâh - Islâmic Monotheism) and do deeds of righteousness, that for them there is forgiveness and a great reward (i.e. Paradise).

﴿ وَٱلَّذِينَ كَفَرُواْ وَكَذَّبُواْ بِـَٔايَٰتِنَآ أُوْلَٰٓئِكَ أَصْحَٰبُ ٱلْجَحِيمِ ۝ ﴾

10. They who disbelieve and deny our Ayât (proofs, evidences, verses, lessons, signs, revelations, etc.) are those who will be the dwellers of the Hell-fire.

﴿ يَٰٓأَيُّهَا ٱلَّذِينَ ءَامَنُواْ ٱذْكُرُواْ نِعْمَتَ ٱللَّهِ عَلَيْكُمْ إِذْ هَمَّ قَوْمٌ أَن يَبْسُطُوٓاْ إِلَيْكُمْ أَيْدِيَهُمْ فَكَفَّ أَيْدِيَهُمْ عَنكُمْ وَٱتَّقُواْ ٱللَّهَ وَعَلَى ٱللَّهِ فَلْيَتَوَكَّلِ ٱلْمُؤْمِنُونَ ۝ ﴾

11. O you who believe! Remember the Favor of Allâh unto you when some people desired (made a plan) to stretch out their hands against you, but (Allâh) held back their hands from you. So fear Allâh. And in Allâh let believers put their trust.

Transliteration

7. Waothkuroo niAAmata Allahi AAalaykum wameethaqahu allathee wathaqakum bihi ith qultum samiAAna waataAAna waittaqoo Allaha inna Allaha AAaleemun bithati alssudoori 8. Ya ayyuha allatheena amanoo koonoo qawwameena lillahi shuhadaa bialqisti wala yajrimannakum shanaanu qawmin AAala alla taAAdiloo iAAdiloo huwa aqrabu lilttaqwa waittaqoo Allaha inna Allaha khabeerun bima taAAmaloona 9. WaAAada Allahu allatheena amanoo waAAamiloo alssalihati lahum maghfiratun waajrun AAatheemun 10. Waallatheena kafaroo wakaththaboo bi-ayatina ola-ika as-habu aljaheemi 11. Ya ayyuha allatheena amanoo othkuroo niAAmata Allahi AAalaykum ith hamma qawmun an yabsutoo ilaykum aydiyahum fakaffa aydiyahum AAankum waittaqoo Allaha waAAala Allahi falyatawakkali almu/minoona

Tafsir Ibn Kathir

Reminding the Believers of the Bounty of the Message and Islam

Allah reminds His believing servants of His bounty by legislating this glorious religion and sending them this honorable Messenger. He also reminds them of the covenant and pledges that He took from them to follow the Messenger , support and aid him, implement his Law and convey it on his behalf, while accepting it themselves. Allah said,

(And remember Allah's favor upon you and His covenant with which He bound you when you said, "We hear and we obey.") This is the pledge that they used to give to the Messenger of Allah when they embraced Islam. They used to say, "We gave our pledge of obedience to the Messenger of Allah to hear and obey, in times when we are active and otherwise, even if we were passed on for rights, and not to dispute leadership with its rightful people." Allah also said,

(And what is the matter with you that you believe not in Allah! While the Messenger invites you to believe in your Lord; and He has indeed taken your covenant, if you are real believers.) It was also said that this Ayah (5:7) reminds the Jews of the pledges and promises Allah took from them to follow Muhammad and adhere to his Law, as `Ali bin Abi Talhah reported that Ibn `Abbas stated. Allah then said,

(And have Taqwa of Allah.) in all times and situations. Allah says that He knows the secrets and thoughts that the hearts conceal,

(Verily, Allah is All-Knower of the secrets of (your) breasts.)

The Necessity of Observing Justice

Allah said,

(O you who believe! Stand out firmly for Allah...) meaning, in truth for the sake of Allah, not for the sake of people or for fame,

(as just witnesses) observing justice and not transgression. It is recorded in the Two Sahihs that An-Nu`man bin Bashir said, "My father gave me a gift, but `Amrah bint Rawahah, my mother, said that she would not agree to it unless he made Allah's Messenger as a witness to it. So, my father went to Allah's Messenger to ask him to be a witness to his giving me the gift. Allah's Messenger asked,

«أَكَلَّ وَلَدِكَ نَحَلْتَ مِثْلَهُ؟»

(`Have you given the like of it to everyone of your offspring') He replied in the negative. Allah's Messenger said,

«اتَّقُوا اللَّهَ وَاعْدِلُوا فِي أَوْلَادِكُمْ»

(Have Taqwa of Allah and treat your children equally.) And said;

«إِنِّي لَا أَشْهَدُ عَلَى جَوْرٍ»

(I shall not be witness to injustice.) My father then returned and took back his gift." Allah said;

(and let not the enmity and hatred of others make you avoid justice.) The Ayah commands: Do not be carried away by your hatred for some people to avoid observing justice with them. Rather, be just with every one, whether a friend or an enemy. This is why Allah said,

(Be just: that is nearer to Taqwa) this is better than if you abandon justice in this case. Although Allah said that observing justice is `nearer to Taqwa', there is not any other course of action to take, therefore `nearer' here means `is'. Allah said in another Ayah,

(The dwellers of Paradise will, on that Day, have the best abode, and have the fairer of places for repose.) Some of the female Companions said to `Umar, "You are more rough and crude than the Messenger of Allah ," meaning, you are rough, not that the Prophet is rough at all. Allah said next,

(and have Taqwa of Allah. Verily, Allah is WellAcquainted with what you do.) and consequently, He will reward or punish you according to your actions, whether good or evil. Hence Allah's statement afterwards,

(Allah has promised those who believe and do deeds of righteousness, that for them there is forgiveness) for their sins,

(and a great reward.) which is Paradise, that is part of Allah's mercy for His servants. They will not earn Paradise on account of their good actions, but rather on account of His mercy and favor, even though they will qualify to earn this mercy on account of their good actions. Allah has made these actions the cause and path that lead to His mercy, favor, pardon and acceptance. Therefore, all this is from Allah Alone and all thanks are due to Him. Allah said next,

(And they who disbelieve and deny our Ayat are those who will be the dwellers of the Hell-fire.) This only demonstrates Allah's perfect justice, wisdom and judgment, He is never wrong, for He is the Most Wise, Most Just and Most Able.

Among Allah's Favors is that He Prevented the Disbelievers from Fighting the Muslims

Allah said,

(O you who believe! Remember the favor of Allah unto you when some people desired (made a plan) to stretch out their hands against you, but (Allah) withheld their hands from you.) `Abdur-Razzaq recorded that Jabir said, "The Prophet once stayed at an area and the people spread out seeking shade under various trees. The Prophet hung his weapon on a tree, and a bedouin man came and took possession of the Prophet's weapon and held it aloft. He came towards the Prophet and said, `Who can protect you from me' He replied, `Allah, the Exalted, Most Honored.' The bedouin man repeated his question twice or thrice, each time the Prophet answering him by saying, `Allah.' The bedouin man then lowered the sword, and the Prophet called his Companions and told them what had happened while the bedouin was sitting next to him, for the Prophet did not punish him.' Ma`mar said that Qatadah used to mention that some Arabs wanted to have the Prophet killed, so they sent that bedouin. Qatadah would then mention this Ayah,

(Remember the favor of Allah unto you when some people desired (made a plan) to stretch out their hands against you...) The story of this bedouin man, whose name is Ghawrath bin Al-Harith, is mentioned in the Sahih. Muhammad bin Ishaq bin Yasar, Mujahid and `Ikrimah said that this Ayah was revealed about Bani An-Nadir, who plotted to drop a stone on the head of the Messenger when he came to them for help to pay the blood money of two persons whom Muslims killed. The Jews left the execution of this plot to `Amr bin Jihash bin Ka`b and ordered him to throw a stone on the Prophet from above, when he came to them and sat under the wall. Allah told His Prophet about their plot, and he went back to Al-Madinah and his Companions followed him later on. Allah sent down this Ayah concerning this matter. Allah's statement,

(And in Allah let the believers put their trust.) and those who do so, then Allah shall suffice for them and shall protect them from the evil plots of the people. Thereafter, Allah commanded His Messenger to expel Bani An-Nadir, and he laid siege to their area and forced them to evacuate Al-Madinah.

Surah: 5 Ayah: 12, Ayah: 13 & Ayah: 14

﴿ ۞ وَلَقَدْ أَخَذَ ٱللَّهُ مِيثَٰقَ بَنِىٓ إِسْرَٰٓءِيلَ وَبَعَثْنَا مِنْهُمُ ٱثْنَىْ عَشَرَ نَقِيبًا ۖ وَقَالَ ٱللَّهُ إِنِّى مَعَكُمْ ۖ لَئِنْ أَقَمْتُمُ ٱلصَّلَوٰةَ وَءَاتَيْتُمُ ٱلزَّكَوٰةَ وَءَامَنتُم بِرُسُلِى وَعَزَّرْتُمُوهُمْ وَأَقْرَضْتُمُ ٱللَّهَ قَرْضًا حَسَنًا لَّأُكَفِّرَنَّ عَنكُمْ سَيِّـَٔاتِكُمْ وَلَأُدْخِلَنَّكُمْ جَنَّٰتٍ تَجْرِى مِن تَحْتِهَا ٱلْأَنْهَٰرُ ۚ فَمَن كَفَرَ بَعْدَ ذَٰلِكَ مِنكُمْ فَقَدْ ضَلَّ سَوَآءَ ٱلسَّبِيلِ ﴿١٢﴾

12. Indeed Allâh took the covenant from the Children of Israel (Jews), and We appointed twelve leaders among them. And Allâh said: "I am with you if you perform As-Salât (Iqâmat-as-Salât) and give Zakât and believe in My Messengers; honor and assist them, and lend a good loan to Allâh, verily, I will expiate your sins and admit you to Gardens under which rivers flow (in Paradise). But if any of you after this, disbelieved, he has indeed gone astray from the Straight Path."

﴿ فَبِمَا نَقْضِهِم مِّيثَٰقَهُمْ لَعَنَّٰهُمْ وَجَعَلْنَا قُلُوبَهُمْ قَٰسِيَةً ۖ يُحَرِّفُونَ ٱلْكَلِمَ عَن مَّوَاضِعِهِۦ ۙ وَنَسُوا۟ حَظًّا مِّمَّا ذُكِّرُوا۟ بِهِۦ ۚ وَلَا تَزَالُ تَطَّلِعُ عَلَىٰ خَآئِنَةٍ مِّنْهُمْ إِلَّا قَلِيلًا مِّنْهُمْ ۖ فَٱعْفُ عَنْهُمْ وَٱصْفَحْ ۚ إِنَّ ٱللَّهَ يُحِبُّ ٱلْمُحْسِنِينَ ﴿١٣﴾

13. So because of their breach of their covenant, We cursed them and made their hearts grow hard. They change the words from their (right) places and have abandoned a good part of the Message that was sent to them. And you will not cease to discover deceit in them, except a few of them. But forgive them, and overlook (their misdeeds). Verily, Allâh loves Al-Muhsinûn (good-doers - see V.2:112).

﴿ وَمِنَ ٱلَّذِينَ قَالُوٓاْ إِنَّا نَصَٰرَىٰٓ أَخَذۡنَا مِيثَٰقَهُمۡ فَنَسُواْ حَظًّا مِّمَّا ذُكِّرُواْ بِهِۦ فَأَغۡرَيۡنَا بَيۡنَهُمُ ٱلۡعَدَاوَةَ وَٱلۡبَغۡضَآءَ إِلَىٰ يَوۡمِ ٱلۡقِيَٰمَةِۚ وَسَوۡفَ يُنَبِّئُهُمُ ٱللَّهُ بِمَا كَانُواْ يَصۡنَعُونَ ۝ ﴾

14. And from those who call themselves Christians, We took their covenant, but they have abandoned a good part of the Message that was sent to them. So We planted amongst them enmity and hatred till the Day of Resurrection (when they discarded Allâh's Book, disobeyed Allâh's Messengers and His Orders and transgressed beyond bounds in Allâh's disobedience); and Allâh will inform them of what they used to do.

Transliteration

12. Walaqad akhatha Allahu meethaqa banee isra-eela wabaAAathna minhumu ithnay AAashara naqeeban waqala Allahu innee maAAakum la-in aqamtumu alssalata waataytumu alzzakata waamantum birusulee waAAazzartumoohum waaqradtumu Allaha qardan hasanan laokaffiranna AAankum sayyi-atikum walaodkhilannakum jannatin tajree min tahtiha al-anharu faman kafara baAAda thalika minkum faqad dalla sawaa alssabeeli   13. Fabima naqdihim meethaqahum laAAannahum wajaAAalna quloobahum qasiyatan yuharrifoona alkalima AAan mawadiAAihi wanasoo haththan mimma thukkiroo bihi wala tazalu tattaliAAu AAala kha-inatin minhum illa qaleelan minhum faoAAfu AAanhum waisfah inna Allaha yuhibbu almuhsineena   14. Wamina allatheena qaloo inna nasara akhathna meethaqahum fanasoo haththan mimma thukkiroo bihi faaghrayna baynahumu alAAadawata waalbaghdaa ila yawmi alqiyamati wasawfa yunabbi-ohumu Allahu bima kanoo yasnaAAoona

Tafsir Ibn Kathir

Cursing the People of the Book for Breaking the Covenant

Allah commanded His believing servants to fullfil the promises and pledges that He took from them and which they gave His servant and Messenger, Muhammad, peace be upon him. Allah also commanded them to stand for the truth and give correct testimony. He also reminded them of the obvious and subtle favors of the truth and guidance that He granted them. Next, Allah informed them of the pledges and promises that He took from the People of the Book, who were before them, the Jews and Christians. When they broke these promises and covenants, Allah cursed them as a consequence and expelled them from His grace and mercy. He also sealed their hearts from receiving guidance and the religion of truth, beneficial knowledge and righteous actions. Allah said,

(Indeed Allah took the covenant from the Children of Israel and We appointed twelve leaders among them.) These twelve people were leaders who gave the pledge to Allah to listen and obey Allah, His Messenger and His Book on behalf of their tribes. Muhammad bin Ishaq and Ibn `Abbas said that this occurred when Musa went to fight the mighty enemy (in Palestine), and Allah commanded him to choose a leader from every tribe.

The Leaders of Ansar on the Night of `Aqabah

Likewise, when the Messenger of Allah took the pledge from the Ansar in the `Aqabah area, there were twelve leaders from the Ansar. There were three men from the tribe of Aws: Usayd bin Al-Hudayr, Sa`d bin Khaythamah and Rifa`ah bin `Abdul-Mundhir, or Abu Al-Haytham bin At-Tayhan. There were nine people from the tribe of Khazraj: Abu Umamah As`ad bin Zurarah, Sa`d bin Ar-Rabi`, `Abdullah bin Rawahah, Rafi` bin Malik bin Al-`Ajlan, Al-Bara' bin Ma`rur, `Ubadah bin As-Samit, Sa`d bin `Ubadah, `Abdullah bin `Amr bin Haram and Al-Mundhir bin `Umar bin Khunays. Ka`b bin Malik mentioned these men in his poem, as recorded by Ibn Ishaq.On that night, these men were the leaders or representatives of their tribes by the command of the Prophet . They gave the pledge and promise of allegiance and obedience to the Prophet on behalf of their people. Allah said,

(And Allah said, "I am with you...) with My protection, support and aid,

(if you perform the Salah and give the Zakah and believe in My Messengers;) concerning what they bring you of the revelation,

(honor and assist them...) and support them on the truth,

(and lend to Allah a good loan...) by spending in His cause, seeking to please Him.

(verily, I will remit your sins) and errors, I will erase them, cover them, and will not punish you for them,

(and admit you to Gardens under which rivers flow (in Paradise).) thus, protecting you from what you fear and granting you what you seek.

Breaking the Covenant

Allah said,

(But if any of you after this, disbelieved, he has indeed gone astray from the straight way.) Therefore, those who break this covenant, even though they pledged and vowed to keep it, yet, they broke it and denied it ever existed, they have avoided the clear path and deviated from the path of guidance to the path of misguidance. Allah then mentioned the punishment that befell those who broke His covenant and the pledge they gave Him,

(So because of their breach of their covenant, We cursed them...) Allah states, because of their breaking the promise that We took from them, We cursed them, deviated them away from the truth, and expelled them from guidance,

(and made their hearts grow hard...) and they do not heed any word of advice that they hear, because of the hardness of their hearts.

(They change the words from their (right) places...) Since their comprehension became corrupt, they behaved treacherously with Allah's Ayat, altering His Book from its apparent meanings which He sent down, and distorting its indications. They attributed to Allah what He did not say, and we seek refuge with Allah from such behavior.

(and have abandoned a good part of the Message that was sent to them.) by not implementing it and by ignoring it. Allah said next,

(And you will not cease to discover deceit in them,) such as their plots and treachery against you, O Muhammad, and your Companions. Mujahid said that this Ayah refers to their plot to kill the Messenger of Allah .

(But forgive them, and overlook (their misdeeds).) This, indeed, is the ultimate victory and triumph. Some of the Salaf said, "You would never treat those who disobey Allah with you better than obeying Allah with them." This way, their hearts will gather around the truth and Allah might lead them to the right guidance. This is why Allah said,

(Verily, Allah loves the doers of good.) Therefore, forgive those who err against you. Qatadah said that this Ayah was abrogated with Allah's statement,

(Fight against those who believe not in Allah, nor in the Last Day).

The Christians Also Broke their Covenant with Allah and the Repercussion of this Behavior

Allah said, (And from those who call themselves Christians, We took their covenant,) Meaning: `From those who call themselves Christians and followers of `Isa, son of Maryam, while in fact they are not as they claim. We took from them the covenant and pledges that they would follow the Prophet , aid him, honor him and follow his footsteps.' And that they would believe in every Prophet whom Allah sends to the people of the earth. They imitated the Jews and broke the promises and the pledges. This is why Allah said,

(but they have abandoned a good part of the Message that was sent to them. So We planted amongst them enmity and hatred till the Day of Resurrection;) Meaning: `We planted enmity and hatred between them, and they will remain like this until the Day of Resurrection.' Indeed, the numerous Christian sects have always been enemies and adversaries of each other, accusing each other of heresy and cursing each other. Each sect among them excommunicates the other sects and does not allow them entrance to their places of worship. The Monarchist sect accuses the Jacobite sect of heresy, and such is the case with the Nestorians and the Arians. Each sect among them will continue to accuse the other of disbelief and heresy in this life and on the Day when the Witnesses will come forth. Allah then said,

(and Allah will inform them of what they used to do.) warning and threatening the Christians because of their lies against Allah and His Messenger and their false claims about Allah, hallowed be He above what they say about Him. The Christians attribute a companion and a son to Allah, while He is the One and Only, the All-Sufficient, Who neither begets nor was He begotten, and there is none like unto Him.

Surah: 5 Ayah: 15 & Ayah: 16

﴿ يَـٰٓأَهْلَ ٱلْكِتَـٰبِ قَدْ جَآءَكُمْ رَسُولُنَا يُبَيِّنُ لَكُمْ كَثِيرًا مِّمَّا كُنتُمْ تُخْفُونَ مِنَ ٱلْكِتَـٰبِ وَيَعْفُوا۟ عَن كَثِيرٍ ۚ قَدْ جَآءَكُم مِّنَ ٱللَّهِ نُورٌ وَكِتَـٰبٌ مُّبِينٌ ۝ ﴾

15. O people of the Scripture (Jews and Christians)! Now has come to you Our Messenger (Muhammad (peace be upon him)) explaining to you much of that which you used to hide from the Scripture and passing over (i.e. leaving out without explaining) much. Indeed, there has come to you from Allâh a light (Prophet Muhammad (peace be upon him)) and a plain Book (this Qur'ân).

﴿ يَهْدِى بِهِ ٱللَّهُ مَنِ ٱتَّبَعَ رِضْوَٰنَهُۥ سُبُلَ ٱلسَّلَـٰمِ وَيُخْرِجُهُم مِّنَ ٱلظُّلُمَـٰتِ إِلَى ٱلنُّورِ بِإِذْنِهِۦ وَيَهْدِيهِمْ إِلَىٰ صِرَٰطٍ مُّسْتَقِيمٍ ۝ ﴾

16. Wherewith Allâh guides all those who seek His Good Pleasure to ways of peace, and He brings them out of darkness by His Will unto light and guides them to a Straight Way (Islâmic Monotheism).

Transliteration

15. Ya ahla alkitabi qad jaakum rasooluna yubayyinu lakum katheeran mimma kuntum tukhfoona mina alkitabi wayaAAfoo AAan katheerin qad jaakum mina Allahi noorun wakitabun mubeenun   16. Yahdee bihi Allahu mani ittabaAAa ridwanahu subula alssalami wayukhrijuhum mina alththulumati ila alnnoori bi-ithnihi wayahdeehim ila siratin mustaqeemin

Tafsir Ibn Kathir

Explaining the Truth Through the Messenger and the Qur'an

Allah states that He sent His Messenger Muhammad with the guidance and the religion of truth to all the people of the earth, the Arabs and non-Arabs, lettered and unlettered. Allah also states that He sent Muhammad with clear evidences and the distinction between truth and falsehood. Allah said,

(O People of the Scripture! Now has come to you Our Messenger explaining to you much of that which you used to hide from the Scripture and passing over much.) So the Prophet explained where they altered, distorted, changed and lied about Allah. He also ignored much of what they changed, since it would not bring about any benefit if it was explained. In his Mustadrak, Al-Hakim recorded that Ibn `Abbas said, "He who disbelieves in stoning (the adulterer to death) will have inadvertently disbelieved in the Qur'an, for Allah said,

(O People of the Scripture! Now has come to you Our Messenger explaining to you much of that which you used to hide from the Scripture) and stoning was among the things that they used to hide." Al-Hakim said, "Its chain is Sahih, and they did not record it." Allah next mentions the Glorious Qur'an that He sent down to His honorable Prophet,

(Indeed, there has come to you from Allah a light and a plain Book. Wherewith Allah guides all those who seek His pleasure to ways of peace.) meaning, ways of safety and righteousness,

(and He brings them out of darkness by His permission unto light and guides them to a straight path.) He thus saves them from destruction and explains to them the best, most clear path. Therefore, He protects them from what they fear, and brings about the best of what they long for, all the while ridding them of misguidance and directing them to the best, most righteous state of being.

Surah: 5 Ayah: 17 & Ayah: 18

﴿ لَّقَدْ كَفَرَ ٱلَّذِينَ قَالُوٓا۟ إِنَّ ٱللَّهَ هُوَ ٱلْمَسِيحُ ٱبْنُ مَرْيَمَ ۚ قُلْ فَمَن يَمْلِكُ مِنَ ٱللَّهِ شَيْـًٔا إِنْ أَرَادَ أَن يُهْلِكَ ٱلْمَسِيحَ ٱبْنَ مَرْيَمَ وَأُمَّهُۥ وَمَن فِى ٱلْأَرْضِ جَمِيعًا ۗ وَلِلَّهِ مُلْكُ ٱلسَّمَـٰوَٰتِ وَٱلْأَرْضِ وَمَا بَيْنَهُمَا ۚ يَخْلُقُ مَا يَشَآءُ ۚ وَٱللَّهُ عَلَىٰ كُلِّ شَىْءٍ قَدِيرٌ ﴾ ۱۷

17. Surely, in disbelief are they who say that Allâh is the Messiah, son of Maryam (Mary). Say (O Muhammad (peace be upon him)) "Who then has the least power against Allâh, if He were to destroy the Messiah, son of Maryam (Mary), his mother, and all those who are on the earth together?" And to Allâh belongs the dominion of the heavens and the earth, and all that is between them. He creates what He wills. And Allâh is Able to do all things.

﴿ وَقَالَتِ ٱلْيَهُودُ وَٱلنَّصَـٰرَىٰ نَحْنُ أَبْنَـٰٓؤُا۟ ٱللَّهِ وَأَحِبَّـٰٓؤُهُۥ ۚ قُلْ فَلِمَ يُعَذِّبُكُم بِذُنُوبِكُم ۖ بَلْ أَنتُم بَشَرٌ مِّمَّنْ خَلَقَ ۚ يَغْفِرُ لِمَن يَشَآءُ وَيُعَذِّبُ مَن يَشَآءُ ۚ وَلِلَّهِ مُلْكُ ٱلسَّمَـٰوَٰتِ وَٱلْأَرْضِ وَمَا بَيْنَهُمَا ۖ وَإِلَيْهِ ٱلْمَصِيرُ ﴾ ۱۸

18. And (both) the Jews and the Christians say: "We are the children of Allâh and His loved ones." Say: "Why then does He punish you for your sins?" Nay, you are but human beings, of those He has created, He forgives whom He wills and He punishes whom He wills. And to Allâh belongs the dominion of the heavens and the earth and all that is between them; and to Him is the return (of all).

Transliteration

17. Laqad kafara allatheena qaloo inna Allaha huwa almaseehu ibnu maryama qul faman yamliku mina Allahi shay-an in arada an yuhlika almaseeha ibna maryama waommahu waman fee al-ardi jameeAAan walillahi mulku alssamawati waal-ardi

Chapter 5: Al-Maidah (The Table, The Table Spread), Verses 001-081

wama baynahuma yakhluqu ma yashao waAllahu AAala kulli shay-in qadeerun 18. Waqalati alyahoodu waalnnasara nahnu abnao Allahi waahibbaohu qul falima yuAAaththibukum bithunoobikum bal antum basharun mimman khalaqa yaghfiru liman yashao wayuAAaththibu man yashao walillahi mulku alssamawati waal-ardi wama baynahuma wa-ilayhi almaseeru

Tafsir Ibn Kathir

The Polytheism and Disbelief of the Christians

Allah states that the Christians are disbelievers because of their claim that `Isa, son of Maryam, one of Allah's servants and creatures, is Allah. Allah is holier than what they attribute to Him. Allah then reminds them of His perfect ability over everything and that everything is under His complete control and power,

(Say: "Who then has the least power against Allah, if He were to destroy the Messiah, son of Maryam, his mother, and all those who are on the earth together") Therefore, if Allah wills to do that, who would be able to stop Him or prevent Him from doing it Allah then said,

(And to Allah belongs the dominion of the heavens and the earth, and all that is between them. He creates what He wills.) All things in existence are Allah's property and creation and He is able to do everything. He is never asked about what He does with His power, domain, justice and greatness so this refutes the Christian creed, may Allah's continued curses be upon them until the Day of Resurrection.

Refuting the People of the Book's Claim that they are Allah's Children

Allah then refutes the Christians' and Jews' false claims and lies,

(And the Jews and the Christians say, "We are the children of Allah and His loved ones.") They claim: "We are the followers of Allah's Prophets, who are His children, whom He takes care of. He also loves us." The People of the Book claim in their Book that Allah said to His servant Isra'il, "You are my firstborn." But they explained this statement in an improper manner and altered its meaning. Some of the People of the Book who later became Muslims refuted this false statement saying, "This statement only indicates honor and respect, as is common in their speech at that time." The Christians claim that `Isa said to them, "I will go back to my father and your father," meaning, my Lord and your Lord. It is a fact that the Christians did not claim that they too are Allah's sons as they claimed about `Isa. Rather this statement by `Isa only meant to indicate a closeness with Allah. This is why when they said that they are Allah's children and loved ones, Allah refuted their claim,

(Say, "Why then does He punish you for your sins") meaning, if you were truly as you claim, Allah's children and loved ones, then why did He prepare the Fire because of your disbelief, lies and false claims

(Nay, you are but human beings, of those He has created,) Allah states: you are just like the rest of the children of Adam, and Allah is the Lord of all His creation,

(He forgives whom He wills and punishes whom He wills.) Allah does what He wills, there is none who can escape His judgement, and He is swift in reckoning.

(And to Allah belongs the dominion of the heavens and the earth and all that is between them;) Therefore, everything is Allah's property and under His power and control,

(and to Him is the return.) In the end, the return will be to Allah and He will judge between His servants as He will, and He is the Most Just Who is never wrong in His judgment.

Surah: 5 Ayah: 19

﴿ يَـٰٓأَهۡلَ ٱلۡكِتَـٰبِ قَدۡ جَآءَكُمۡ رَسُولُنَا يُبَيِّنُ لَكُمۡ عَلَىٰ فَتۡرَةٖ مِّنَ ٱلرُّسُلِ أَن تَقُولُواْ مَا جَآءَنَا مِنۢ بَشِيرٖ وَلَا نَذِيرٖۖ فَقَدۡ جَآءَكُم بَشِيرٞ وَنَذِيرٞۗ وَٱللَّهُ عَلَىٰ كُلِّ شَيۡءٖ قَدِيرٞ ﴾

19. O people of the Scripture (Jews and Christians)! Now has come to you Our Messenger (Muhammad (peace be upon him)) making (things) clear unto you, after a break in (the series of) Messengers, lest you say: "There came unto us no bringer of glad tidings and no warner." But now has come unto you a bringer of glad tidings and a warner. And Allâh is Able to do all things.

Transliteration

19. Ya ahla alkitabi qad jaakum rasooluna yubayyinu lakum AAala fatratin mina alrrusuli an taqooloo ma jaana min basheerin wala natheerin faqad jaakum basheerun wanatheerun waAllahu AAala kulli shay-in qadeerun

Tafsir Ibn Kathir

Allah is addressing the People of the Book -- the Jews and the Christians, saying that He has sent His Messenger Muhammad to them, the Final Prophet, after whom there will be no Prophet or Messenger. Rather, He is the Final Messenger who came after a long time passed between him and `Isa, son of Maryam peace be upon them. There is a difference of opinion about the length of time between `Isa and Muhammad. Abu `Uthman An-Nahdi and Qatadah were reported to have said that this period was six hundred years. Al-Bukhari also recorded this opinion from Salman Al-Farisi. Qatadah said that this period was five hundred and sixty years, while Ma`mar said that it is five hundred and forty years. Some said that this period is six hundred and twenty years. There is no contradiction here if we consider the fact that those who said that this period was six hundred years were talking about solar years, while the second refers to lunar years, since there is a difference of about three years between every one hundred lunar and solar years. As in Allah's statement,

(And they stayed in their Cave three hundred years, adding nine.) meaning, nine more lunar years to substitute for the difference between lunar and solar years, thus agreeing with the three hundred years that the People of the Book knew about. We should assert again that the time period we mentioned here was between `Isa, the last Prophet to the Children of Israel, and Muhammad, the Last Prophet and

Messenger among the children of Adam. In the Sahih collected by Al-Bukhari, Abu Hurayrah said that the Messenger of Allah said,

«إِنَّ أَوْلَى النَّاسِ بِابْنِ مَرْيَمَ لَأَنَا، لَيْسَ بَيْنِي وَبَيْنَهُ نَبِيٌّ»

(I, among all people, have the most right to the son of Maryam, for there was no Prophet between Him and I.) This Hadith refutes the opinion of Al-Quda`i and others, that there was a Prophet after `Isa called Khalid bin Sinan. Allah sent Muhammad after a period of time during which there was no Prophet, clear path, or unchanged religions. Idol worshipping, fire worshipping and cross worshipping flourished during this time. Therefore, the bounty of sending Muhammad was the perfect bounty at a time when he was needed the most. Evil had filled the earth by then, and tyranny and ignorance had touched all the servants, except a few of those who remained loyal to the true teachings of previous Prophets, such as some Jewish rabbis, Christian priests and Sabian monks. Imam Ahmad recorded that `Iyad bin Himar Al-Mujash`i said that the Prophet gave a speech one day and said,

«وَإِنَّ رَبِّي أَمَرَنِي أَنْ أُعَلِّمَكُمْ مَا جَهِلْتُمْ مِمَّا عَلَّمَنِي فِي يَوْمِي هَذَا، كُلُّ مَالٍ نَحَلْتُهُ عِبَادِي حَلَالٌ، وَإِنِّي خَلَقْتُ عِبَادِي حُنَفَاءَ كُلَّهُمْ، وَإِنَّ الشَّيَاطِينَ أَتَتْهُمْ فَأَضَلَّتْهُمْ عَنْ دِينِهِمْ، وَحَرَّمَتْ عَلَيْهِمْ مَا أَحْلَلْتُ لَهُمْ، وَأَمَرَتْهُمْ أَنْ يُشْرِكُوا بِي مَا لَمْ أُنْزِلْ بِهِ سُلْطَانًا، ثُمَّ إِنَّ اللهَ عَزَّ وَجَلَّ نَظَرَ إِلَى أَهْلِ الْأَرْضِ فَمَقَتَهُمْ عَرَبَهُمْ وَعَجَمَهُمْ، إِلَّا بَقَايَا مِنْ بَنِي إِسْرَائِيلَ، وَقَالَ: إِنَّمَا بَعَثْتُكَ لِأَبْتَلِيَكَ وَأَبْتَلِيَ بِكَ، وَأَنْزَلْتُ عَلَيْكَ كِتَابًا لَا يَغْسِلُهُ الْمَاءُ، تَقْرَأُهُ نَائِمًا وَيَقْظَانًا، ثُمَّ إِنَّ اللهَ أَمَرَنِي أَنْ أُحَرِّقَ قُرَيْشًا فَقُلْتُ: يَارَبِّ إِذَنْ يَثْلَغُوا رَأْسِي، فَيَدَعُوهُ خُبْزَةً، فَقَالَ: اسْتَخْرِجْهُمْ كَمَا اسْتَخْرَجُوكَ، واغْزُهُمْ نُعْزِكَ، وَأَنْفِقْ عَلَيْهِمْ فَسَنُنْفِقَ عَلَيْكَ، وَابْعَثْ جَيْشًا نَبْعَثْ خَمْسًا أَمْثَالَهُ، وَقَاتِلْ بِمَنْ أَطَاعَكَ مَنْ عَصَاكَ، وَأَهْلُ الْجَنَّةِ ثَلَاثَةٌ: ذُو سُلْطَانٍ مُقْسِطٌ مُوَفَّقٌ مُتَصَدِّقٌ، وَرَجُلٌ رَحِيمٌ رَقِيقُ الْقَلْبِ بِكُلِّ ذِي قُرْبَى وَمُسْلِمٍ، وَرَجُلٌ عَفِيفٌ فَقِيرٌ ذُو عِيَالٍ (مُتَصَدِّقٌ). وَأَهْلُ النَّارِ خَمْسَةٌ: الضَّعِيفُ الَّذِي لَا دِينَ لَهُ، وَالَّذِينَ هُمْ فِيكُمْ تَبَعٌ أَوْ تَبَعًا شَكَّ

يَحْيِي لَا يَبْتَغُونَ أَهْلًا وَلَا مَالًا، وَالْخَائِنُ الَّذِي لَا يَخْفَى لَهُ طَمَعٌ وَإِنْ دَقَّ إِلَّا خَانَهُ، وَرَجُلٌ لَا يُصْبِحُ وَلَا يُمْسِي إِلَّا وَهُوَ يُخَادِعُكَ عَنْ أَهْلِكَ وَمَالِكَ وَذَكَرَ الْبَخِيلَ أَوِ الْكَذَّابَ وَالشِّنْظِيرَ: الْفَاحِشَ»

(My Lord has commanded me to teach you what you have no knowledge of and of which He taught me this day, `All the wealth that I gave to My servants is permissible. I created all My servants Hunafa (monotheists). But, the devils came to them and deviated them from their religion, prohibited for them what I allowed and commanded them to associate others with Me (in worship), which I gave no permission for.' Then Allah looked at the people of the earth and disliked them all, the Arabs and non-Arabs among them, except a few from among the Children of Israel. Allah said (to me), `I only sent you to test you and to test with you. I sent to you a Book that cannot be washed by water (it is eternal), and you will read it while asleep and while awake.' Allah has also Commanded me to burn (destroy) Quraysh. So I said, `O Lord! They will smash my head and leave it like a piece of bread.' He said, `I will drive them out as they drove you out, and when you invade them We will help you. Spend on them (your companions) and We will spend on you, send an army and We will send five armies like it (in its support). Fight with those who obey you, against those who disobey you. And the inhabitants of Paradise are three: a just, prosperous, and charitable ruler; A merciful man who has a kind heart toward every relative and every Muslim; a forgiving, poor man with dependants (who is charitable). And the inhabitants of the Fire are five: the weak one with no religion; those who follow after you not for family reasons nor wealth; and the treacherous who does not hide his treachery, acting treacherous in even the most insignificant matters; and a person who comes every morning and every evening, is cheating your family or your wealth.') And he mentioned the stingy, or the liar, and the foulmouthed person." Therefore, the Hadith states that Allah looked at the people of the earth and disliked them all, both the Arabs and non-Arabs among them, except a few among the Children of Israel, or a few among the People of the Book as Muslim recorded. The religion was distorted and changed for the people of the earth until Allah sent Muhammad , and Allah, thus, guided the creatures and took them away from the darkness to the light and placed them on a clear path and a glorious Law. Allah said,

(lest you say, "There came unto us no bringer of glad tidings and no warner.") meaning, so that you, who changed the true religion, do not make it an excuse and say, "No Messenger came to us bringing glad tidings and warning against evil." There has come to you a bringer of good news and a warner, Muhammad .

(And Allah is able to do all things.) Ibn Jarir said this part of the Ayah means, "I am able to punish those who disobey Me and to reward those who obey Me."

Surah: 5 Ayah: 20, Ayah: 21, Ayah: 22, Ayah: 23, Ayah: 24, Ayah: 25, Ayah: 26

﴿ وَإِذْ قَالَ مُوسَىٰ لِقَوْمِهِۦ يَٰقَوْمِ ٱذْكُرُوا۟ نِعْمَةَ ٱللَّهِ عَلَيْكُمْ إِذْ جَعَلَ فِيكُمْ أَنۢبِيَآءَ وَجَعَلَكُم مُّلُوكًا وَءَاتَىٰكُم مَّا لَمْ يُؤْتِ أَحَدًا مِّنَ ٱلْعَٰلَمِينَ ۝ ﴾

20. And (remember) when Mûsâ (Moses) said to his people: "O my people! Remember the Favor of Allâh to you, when He made Prophets among you, made you kings and gave you what He had not given to any other among the 'Alamîn (mankind and jinn, in the past)."

﴿ يَٰقَوْمِ ٱدْخُلُوا۟ ٱلْأَرْضَ ٱلْمُقَدَّسَةَ ٱلَّتِى كَتَبَ ٱللَّهُ لَكُمْ وَلَا تَرْتَدُّوا۟ عَلَىٰٓ أَدْبَارِكُمْ فَتَنقَلِبُوا۟ خَٰسِرِينَ ۝ ﴾

21. "O my people! Enter the holy land (Palestine) which Allâh has assigned to you and turn not back (in flight); for then you will be returned as losers."

﴿ قَالُوا۟ يَٰمُوسَىٰٓ إِنَّ فِيهَا قَوْمًا جَبَّارِينَ وَإِنَّا لَن نَّدْخُلَهَا حَتَّىٰ يَخْرُجُوا۟ مِنْهَا فَإِن يَخْرُجُوا۟ مِنْهَا فَإِنَّا دَٰخِلُونَ ۝ ﴾

22. They said: "O Mûsâ (Moses)! In it (this holy land) are a people of great strength, and we shall never enter it, till they leave it; when they leave, then we will enter."

﴿ قَالَ رَجُلَانِ مِنَ ٱلَّذِينَ يَخَافُونَ أَنْعَمَ ٱللَّهُ عَلَيْهِمَا ٱدْخُلُوا۟ عَلَيْهِمُ ٱلْبَابَ فَإِذَا دَخَلْتُمُوهُ فَإِنَّكُمْ غَٰلِبُونَ وَعَلَى ٱللَّهِ فَتَوَكَّلُوٓا۟ إِن كُنتُم مُّؤْمِنِينَ ۝ ﴾

23. Two men of those who feared (Allâh and) on whom Allâh had bestowed His Grace (they were Yûsha' (Joshua) and Kâlab (Caleb)) said: "Assault them through the gate; for when you are in, victory will be yours; and put your trust in Allâh if you are believers indeed."

﴿ قَالُوا۟ يَٰمُوسَىٰٓ إِنَّا لَن نَّدْخُلَهَآ أَبَدًا مَّا دَامُوا۟ فِيهَا فَٱذْهَبْ أَنتَ وَرَبُّكَ فَقَٰتِلَآ إِنَّا هَٰهُنَا قَٰعِدُونَ ۝ ﴾

24. They said: "O Mûsâ (Moses)! We shall never enter it as long as they are there. So go you and your Lord and fight you two, we are sitting right here."

﴿ قَالَ رَبِّ إِنِّى لَآ أَمْلِكُ إِلَّا نَفْسِى وَأَخِى ۖ فَٱفْرُقْ بَيْنَنَا وَبَيْنَ ٱلْقَوْمِ ٱلْفَـٰسِقِينَ ﴾

25. He (Mûsâ (Moses)) said: "O my Lord! I have power only over myself and my brother, so separate us from the people who are the Fâsiqûn (rebellious and disobedient to Allâh)!"

﴿ قَالَ فَإِنَّهَا مُحَرَّمَةٌ عَلَيْهِمْ أَرْبَعِينَ سَنَةً ۚ يَتِيهُونَ فِى ٱلْأَرْضِ ۚ فَلَا تَأْسَ عَلَى ٱلْقَوْمِ ٱلْفَـٰسِقِينَ ﴾

26. (Allâh) said: "Therefore it (this holy land) is forbidden to them for forty years; in distraction they will wander through the land. So be not sorrowful over the people who are the Fâsiqûn (rebellious and disobedient to Allâh)."

Transliteration

20. Wa-ith qala moosa liqawmihi ya qawmi othkuroo niAAmata Allahi AAalaykum ith jaAAala feekum anbiyaa wajaAAalakum mulookan waatakum ma lam yu/ti ahadan mina alAAalameena   21. Ya qawmi odkhuloo al-arda almuqaddasata allatee kataba Allahu lakum wala tartaddoo AAala adbarikum fatanqaliboo khasireena 22. Qaloo ya moosa inna feeha qawman jabbareena wa-inna lan nadkhulaha hatta yakhrujoo minha fa-in yakhrujoo minha fa-inna dakhiloona   23. Qala rajulani mina allatheena yakhafoona anAAama Allahu AAalayhima odkhuloo AAalayhimu albaba fa-itha dakhaltumoohu fa-innakum ghaliboona waAAala Allahi fatawakkaloo in kuntum mu/mineena 24. Qaloo ya moosa inna lan nadkhulaha abadan ma damoo feeha fa-ithhab anta warabbuka faqatila inna hahuna qaAAidoona   25. Qala rabbi innee la amliku illa nafsee waakhee faofruq baynana wabayna alqawmi alfasiqeena 26. Qala fa-innaha muharramatun AAalayhim arbaAAeena sanatan yateehoona fee al-ardi fala ta/sa AAala alqawmi alfasiqeena

Tafsir Ibn Kathir

Musa Reminds His People of Allah's Favors on Them; The Jews Refuse to Enter the Holy Land

Allah states that His servant, Messenger, to whom He spoke directly, Musa, the son of `Imran, reminded his people that among the favors Allah granted them, is that He will give them all of the good of this life and the Hereafter, if they remain on the righteous and straight path. Allah said,

(And (remember) when Musa said to his people: "O my people! Remember the favor of Allah to you, when He made Prophets among you,) for whenever a Prophet died, another rose among them, from the time of their father Ibrahim and thereafter. There were many Prophets among the Children of Israel calling to Allah and warning against His torment, until `Isa was sent as the final Prophet from the Children of Israel. Allah then sent down the revelation to the Final Prophet and Messenger, Muhammad, the

Chapter 5: Al-Maidah (The Table, The Table Spread), Verses 001-081

son of `Abdullah, from the offspring of Isma`il, the son of Ibrahim, peace be upon them. Muhammad is the most honorable Prophet of all times. Allah said next,

(made you kings) `Abdur-Razzaq recorded that Ibn `Abbas commented: "Having a servant, a wife and a house." In his Mustadrak, Al-Hakim recorded that Ibn `Abbas said, "A wife and a servant, and, a

(and gave you what He had not given to any other among the nations (`Alamin).) means, during their time." Al-Hakim said, "Sahih according to the criteria of the Two Sahihs, but they did not collect it." Qatadah said, "They were the first people to take servants." A Hadith states,

«مَنْ أَصْبَحَ مِنْكُمْ مُعَافًى فِي جَسَدِهِ، آمِنًا فِي سِرْبِهِ، عِنْدَهُ قُوتُ يَوْمِهِ، فَكَأَنَّمَا حِيزَتْ لَهُ الدُّنْيَا بِحَذَافِيرِهَا»

(He among you who wakes up while healthy in body, safe in his family and having the provision for that very day, is as if the world and all that was in it were collected for him.) Allah's statement,

(and gave you what He had not given to any other among the nations (Al-`Alamin).) means, during your time, as we stated. The Children of Israel were the most honorable among the people of their time, compared to the Greek, Copts and the rest of mankind. Allah said in another Ayah,

(And indeed We gave the Children of Israel the Scripture, and the understanding of the Scripture and its laws, and the Prophethood; and provided them with good things, and preferred them above the nations (Al-`Alamin).) Allah said,

(They said: "O Musa! Make for us a god as they have gods." He said: "Verily, you are an ignorant people." (Musa added:) "Verily, these people will be destroyed for that which they are engaged in (idol worship)." And all that they are doing is in vain. He said: "Shall I seek for you a god other than Allah, while He has given you superiority over the nations.") Therefore, they were the best among the people of their time. The Muslim Ummah is more respected and honored before Allah, and has a more perfect legislative code and system of life, it has the most honorable Prophet, the larger kingdom, more provisions, wealth and children, a larger domain and more lasting glory than the Children of Israel. Allah said,

(Thus We have made you, a just (the best) nation, that you be witnesses over mankind.) We mentioned the Mutawatir Hadiths about the honor of this Ummah and its status and honor with Allah, when we explained Allah's statement in Surah Al-`Imran (3),

(You are the best of peoples ever raised up for mankind...) Allah states next that Musa encouraged the Children of Israel to perform Jihad and enter Jerusalem, which was under their control during the time of their father Ya`qub. Ya`qub and his children later moved with his children and household to Egypt during the time of Prophet Yusuf. His offspring remained in Egypt until their exodus with Musa. They found a mighty, strong people in Jerusalem who had previously taken it over. Musa, Allah's Messenger, ordered the Children of Israel to enter Jerusalem and fight their enemy, and he promised them victory and triumph over the mighty people if they did so. They declined, rebelled and defied his order and were punished for forty years by being lost, wandering in the land uncertain of where they should go. This was their punishment for defying Allah's command. Allah said that Musa ordered them to enter the Holy Land,

(which Allah has assigned to you) meaning, which Allah has promised to you by the words of your father Isra'il, that it is the inheritance of those among you who believe.

(and turn not back) in flight from Jihad.

(". ..for then you will be returned as losers." They said, "O Musa! In it are a people of great strength, and we shall never enter it, till they leave it; when they leave, then we will enter.") Their excuse was this, in this very town you commanded us to enter and fight its people, there is a mighty, strong, vicious people who have tremendous physique and physical ability. We are unable to stand against these people or fight them. Therefore, they said, we are incapable of entering this city as long as they are still in it, but if they leave it, we will enter it. Otherwise, we cannot stand against them.

The Speeches of Yuwsha' (Joshua) and Kalib (Caleb)

Allah said,

(Two men of those who feared (Allah and) on whom Allah had bestowed His grace said...) When the Children of Israel declined to obey Allah and follow His Messenger Musa, two righteous men among them, on whom Allah had bestowed a great bounty and who were afraid of Allah and His punishment, encouraged them to go forward. It was also said that the Ayah reads in a way that means that these men were respected and honored by their people. These two men were Yuwsha`, the son of Nun, and Kalib, the son of Yufna, as Ibn `Abbas, Mujahid, `Ikrimah, `Atiyyah, As-Suddi, Ar-Rabi` bin Anas and several other Salaf and latter scholars stated. These two men said to their people,

("Assault them through the gate, for when you are in, victory will be yours. And put your trust in Allah if you are believers indeed.") Therefore, they said, if you rely on and trust in Allah, follow His command and obey His Messenger, then Allah will give you victory over your enemies and will give you triumph and dominance over them. Thus, you will conquer the city that Allah has promised you. This advice did not benefit them in the least,

(They said, "O Musa! We shall never enter it as long as they are there. So go, you and your Lord, and fight you two, we are sitting right here.") This is how they declined to join Jihad, defied their Messenger, and refused to fight their enemy.

Chapter 5: Al-Maidah (The Table, The Table Spread), Verses 001-081

The Righteous Response of the Companions During the Battle of Badr

Compare this to the better response the Companions gave to the Messenger of Allah during the battle of Badr, when he asked for their advice about fighting the Quraysh army that came to protect the caravan led by Abu Sufyan. When the Muslim army missed the caravan and the Quraysh army, between nine hundred and one thousand strong, helmeted and drawing closer, Abu Bakr stood up and said something good. Several more Muhajirin also spoke, all the while the Messenger of Allah saying,

«أشيروا علي أيها المسلمون»

(Advise me, O Muslims!) inquiring of what the Ansar, the majority then, had to say. Sa`d bin Mu`adh said, "It looks like you mean us, O Messenger of Allah! By He Who has sent you with the Truth! If you seek to cross this sea and went in it, we will follow you and none among us will remain behind. We would not hate for you to lead us to meet our enemy tomorrow. We are patient in war, vicious in battle. May Allah allow you to witness from our efforts what comforts your eyes. Therefore, march forward with the blessing of Allah." The Messenger of Allah () was pleased with the words of Sa`d and was encouraged to march on. Abu Bakr bin Marduwyah recorded that Anas said that when the Messenger of Allah went to Badr, he asked the Muslims for their opinion, and `Umar gave his. The Prophet again asked the Muslims for their opinion and the Ansar said, "O Ansar! It is you whom the Prophet wants to hear." They said, "We will never say as the Children of Israel said to Musa,

(So go, you and your Lord, and fight you two, we are sitting right here.) By He Who has sent you with the Truth! If you took the camels to Bark Al-Ghimad (near Makkah) we shall follow you." Imam Ahmad, An-Nasa'i and Ibn Hibban also recorded this Hadith. In the Book of Al-Maghazi and At-Tafsir, Al-Bukhari recorded that `Abdullah bin Mas`ud said, "On the day of Badr, Al-Miqdad said, `O Messenger of Allah! We will never say to you what the Children of Israel said to Musa,

(So go, you and your Lord, and fight you two, we are sitting right here.) Rather, march on and we will be with you.' The Messenger of Allah was satisfied after hearing this statement."

Musa Supplicates to Allah Against the Jews

Musa said,

("O my Lord! I have power only over myself and my brother, so separate us from the rebellious people!") When the Children of Israel refused to fight, Musa became very angry with them and supplicated to Allah against them,

(O my Lord! I have power only over myself and my brother') meaning, only I and my brother Harun among them will obey, implement Allah's command and accept the call,

(So Ifruq us from the rebellious people!) Al-`Awfi reported that Ibn `Abbas said, "Meaning, judge between us and them." `Ali bin Abi Talhah reported similarly from him. Ad-Dahhak said that the Ayah means, "Judge and decide between us and them." Other scholars said that the Ayah means, "Separate between us and them."

Forbidding the Jews from Entering the Holy Land for Forty Years

Allah said,

(Therefore it is forbidden to them for forty years; in distraction they will wander through the land.) When Musa supplicated against the Jews for refusing to fight in Jihad, Allah forbade them from entering the land for forty years. They wandered about lost in the land of At-Tih, unable to find their way out. During this time, tremendous miracles occurred, such as the clouds that shaded them and the manna and quails Allah sent down for them. Allah brought forth water springs from solid rock, and the other miracles that He aided Musa bin `Imran with. During this time, the Tawrah was revealed and the Law was established for the Children of Israel and the Tabernacle of the Covenant was erected.

Conquering Jerusalem

Allah's statement,

(for forty years;) defines,

(in distraction they will wander through the land.) When these years ended, Yuwsha` bin Nun led those who remained among them and the second generation, and laid siege to Jerusalem, conquering it on a Friday afternoon. When the sun was about to set and Yuwsha` feared that the Sabbath would begin, he said (to the sun), "You are commanded and I am commanded, as well. O Allah! Make it stop setting for me." Allah made the sun stop setting until Yuwsha` bin Nun conquered Jerusalem. Next, Allah commanded Yuwsha` to order the Children of Israel to enter Jerusalem from its gate while bowing and saying Hittah, meaning, `remove our sins.' Yet, they changed what they were commanded and entered it while dragging themselves on their behinds and saying, `Habbah (a seed) in Sha`rah (a hair)." We mentioned all of this in the Tafsir of Surat Al-Baqarah. Ibn Abi Hatim recorded that Ibn `Abbas commented,

(Therefore it is forbidden to them for forty years; in distraction they will wander through the land.) "They wandered in the land for forty years, during which Musa and Harun died, as well as everyone above forty years of age. When the forty years ended, Yuwsha` son of Nun assumed their leadership and later conquered Jerusalem. When Yuwsha` was reminded that the day was Friday and the sun was about to set, while they were still attacking Jerusalem, he feared that the Sabbath might begin. Therefore, he said to the sun, `I am commanded and you are commanded.' Allah made the sun stop setting and the Jews conquered Jerusalem and found wealth unseen before. They wanted to let the fire consume the booty, but the fire would not do that. Yuwsha` said, `Some of you have committed theft from the booty.' So he summoned the twelve leaders of the twelve tribes and took the pledge from them. Then, the hand of one of them became stuck to the hand of Yuwsha` and Yuwsha` said, `You committed the theft, so bring it forth.' So, that man brought a cow's head made of gold with two eyes made of precious stones and a set of teeth made of pearls. When Yuwsha` added it to the booty, the fire consumed it, as they were prohibited to keep the booty." There is evidence supporting all of this in the Sahih.

Allah Comforts Musa

Conforting Musa, Allah said

(So do not greive for the rebellious people.) Allah said: Do not feel sorrow or sadness over My judgment against them, for they deserve such judgment. This story chastises the Jews, exposes their defiance of Allah and His Messenger, and their refusal to obey the order for Jihad. They were weak and could not bear the thought of fighting their enemy, being patient, and enduring this way. This occurred although they had the Messenger of Allah and the one whom He spoke to among them, the best of Allah's creation that time. Their Prophet promised them triumph and victory against their enemies. They also witnessed the torment and punishment of drowning with which Allah punished their enemy Fir`awn and his soldiers, so that their eyes were pleased and comforted. All this did not happen too long ago, yet they refused to perform Jihad against people who had less than a tenth of the power and strength than the people of Egypt had. Therefore, the evil works of the Jews were exposed to everyone, and the exposure was such an enormous one that the night, or the tail, can never cover its tracks. They were also blinded by their ignorance and transgression. Thus, they became hated by Allah, and they became His enemies. Yet, they claim that they are Allah's children and His loved ones! May Allah curse their faces that were transformed to the shape of swine and apes, and may Allah's curse accompany them to the raging Fire. May Allah make them abide in the Fire for eternity, and He did; all thanks are due to Him.

Surah: 5 Ayah: 27, Ayah: 28, Ayah: 29, Ayah: 30 & Ayah: 31

﴿ ۞ وَٱتْلُ عَلَيْهِمْ نَبَأَ ٱبْنَىْ ءَادَمَ بِٱلْحَقِّ إِذْ قَرَّبَا قُرْبَانًا فَتُقُبِّلَ مِنْ أَحَدِهِمَا وَلَمْ يُتَقَبَّلْ مِنَ ٱلْءَاخَرِ قَالَ لَأَقْتُلَنَّكَ قَالَ إِنَّمَا يَتَقَبَّلُ ٱللَّهُ مِنَ ٱلْمُتَّقِينَ ۞ ﴾

27. And (O Muhammad (peace be upon him)) recite to them (the Jews) the story of the two sons of Adam (Hâbil (Abel) and Qâbil (Cain)) in truth; when each offered a sacrifice (to Allâh), it was accepted from the one but not from the other. The latter said to the former: "I will surely kill you." The former said: "Verily, Allâh accepts only from those who are Al-Muttaqûn (the pious - see V.2:2)."

﴿ لَئِنۢ بَسَطتَ إِلَىَّ يَدَكَ لِتَقْتُلَنِى مَآ أَنَا۠ بِبَاسِطٍ يَدِىَ إِلَيْكَ لِأَقْتُلَكَ إِنِّىٓ أَخَافُ ٱللَّهَ رَبَّ ٱلْعَٰلَمِينَ ۞ ﴾

28. "If you do stretch your hand against me to kill me, I shall never stretch my hand against you to kill you : for I fear Allâh, the Lord of the 'Alamîn (mankind, jinn, and all that exists)."

$$\text{﴿ إِنِّي أُرِيدُ أَن تَبُوءَ بِإِثْمِي وَإِثْمِكَ فَتَكُونَ مِنْ أَصْحَابِ النَّارِ ۚ وَذَٰلِكَ جَزَاءُ الظَّالِمِينَ ﴾}$$

29. "Verily, I intend to let you draw my sin on yourself as well as yours, then you will be one of the dwellers of the Fire; and that is the recompense of the Zâlimûn (polytheists and wrong-doers)."

$$\text{﴿ فَطَوَّعَتْ لَهُ نَفْسُهُ قَتْلَ أَخِيهِ فَقَتَلَهُ فَأَصْبَحَ مِنَ الْخَاسِرِينَ ﴾}$$

30. So the Nafs (self) of the other (latter one) encouraged him and made fair-seeming to him the murder of his brother; he murdered him and became one of the losers.

$$\text{﴿ فَبَعَثَ اللَّهُ غُرَابًا يَبْحَثُ فِي الْأَرْضِ لِيُرِيَهُ كَيْفَ يُوَارِي سَوْءَةَ أَخِيهِ ۚ قَالَ يَا وَيْلَتَىٰ أَعَجَزْتُ أَنْ أَكُونَ مِثْلَ هَٰذَا الْغُرَابِ فَأُوَارِيَ سَوْءَةَ أَخِي ۖ فَأَصْبَحَ مِنَ النَّادِمِينَ ﴾}$$

31. Then Allâh sent a crow who scratched the ground to show him to hide the dead body of his brother. He (the murderer) said: "Woe to me! Am I not even able to be as this crow and to hide the dead body of my brother?" Then he became one of those who regretted.

Transliteration

27. Waotlu AAalayhim nabaa ibnay adama bialhaqqi ith qarraba qurbanan fatuqubbila min ahadihima walam yutaqabbal mina al-akhari qala laaqtulannaka qala innama yataqabbalu Allahu mina almuttaqeena 28. La-in basatta ilayya yadaka litaqtulanee ma ana bibasitin yadiya ilayka li-aqtulaka innee akhafu Allaha rabba alAAalameena 29. Innee oreedu an taboo-a bi-ithmee wa-ithmika fatakoona min as-habi alnnari wathalika jazao alththalimeena 30. FatawwaAAat lahu nafsuhu qatla akheehi faqatalahu faasbaha mina alkhasireena 31. FabaAAatha Allahu ghuraban yabhathu fee al-ardi liyuriyahu kayfa yuwaree saw-ata akheehi qala ya waylata aAAajaztu an akoona mithla hatha alghurabi faowariya saw-ata akhee faasbaha mina alnnadimeena

Tafsir Ibn Kathir

The Story of Habil (Abel) and Qabil (Cain)

Allah describes the evil end and consequence of transgression, envy and injustice in the story of the two sons of Adam, Habil and Qabil. One of them fought against the other and killed him out of envy and transgression, because of the bounty that Allah gave his brother and because the sacrifice that he sincerely offered to Allah was accepted. The murdered brother earned forgiveness for his sins and was admitted into Paradise, while the murderer failed and earned a losing deal in both the lives. Allah said,

Chapter 5: Al-Maidah (The Table, The Table Spread), Verses 001-081

(And recite to them the story of the two sons of Adam in truth;) meaning, tell these envious, unjust people, the brothers of swine and apes from the Jews and their likes among mankind, the story of the two sons of Adam, Habil and Qabil, as many scholars among the Salaf and later generations said. Allah's statement,

(in truth;) means, clearly and without ambiguity, alteration, confusion, change, addition or deletion. Allah said in other Ayat,

(Verily, this is the true narrative (about the story of `Isa),)

(We narrate unto you their story with truth,) and,

(Such is `Isa, son of Maryam. (It is) a statement of truth.) Several scholars among the Salaf and the later generations said that Allah allowed Adam to marry his daughters to his sons because of the necessity of such action. They also said that in every pregnancy, Adam was given a twin, a male and a female, and he used to give the female of one twin, to the male of the other twin, in marriage. Habil's sister was not beautiful while Qabil's sister was beautiful, resulting in Qabil wanting her for himself, instead of his brother. Adam refused unless they both offer a sacrifice, and he whose sacrifice was accepted, would marry Qabil's sister. Habil's sacrifice was accepted, while Qabil's sacrifice was rejected, and thus what Allah told us about them occurred. Ibn Abi Hatim recorded that Ibn `Abbas said -- that during the time of Adam -- "The woman was not allowed in marriage for her male twin, but Adam was commanded to marry her to any of her other brothers. In each pregnancy, Adam was given a twin, a male and a female. A beautiful daughter was once born for Adam and another one that was not beautiful. So the twin brother of the ugly daughter said, `Marry your sister to me and I will marry my sister to you.' He said, `No, for I have more right to my sister.' So they both offered a sacrifice. The sacrifice of the one who offered the sheep was accepted while the sacrifice of the other (the twin brother of the beautiful daughter), which consisted of some produce, was not accepted. So the latter killed his brother." This story has a better than good chain of narration. The statement,

("Verily, Allah accepts only from those who have Taqwa.) who fear Allah in their actions. Ibn Abi Hatim recorded that Abu Ad-Darda' said, "If I become certain that Allah has accepted even one prayer from me, it will be better for me than this life and all that in it. This is because Allah says,

(Verily, Allah accepts only from the those who have Taqwa.) The statement,

("If you do stretch your hand against me to kill me, I shall never stretch my hand against you to kill you, for I fear Allah; the Lord of all that exists.") Qabil's brother, the pious man whose sacrifice was accepted because of his piety, said to his brother, who threatened to kill him without justification,

(If you do stretch your hand against me to kill me, I shall never stretch my hand against you to kill you,) I will not commit the same evil act that you threaten to commit, so that I will not earn the same sin as you, (for I fear Allah; the Lord of the all that exists.) and, as a result, I will not commit the error that you threaten to commit. Rather, I will observe patience and endurance. `Abdullah bin `Amr said, "By Allah! Habil was the stronger of the two men. But, fear of Allah restricted his hand." The Prophet said in a Hadith recorded in the Two Sahihs,

》إِذَا تَوَاجَهَ الْمُسْلِمَانِ بِسَيْفَيْهِمَا فَالْقَاتِلُ وَالْمَقْتُولُ فِي النَّارِ《

(When two Muslims fight (meet) each other with their swords, both the murderer as well as the murdered will go to the Hellfire.) They said, "O Allah's Messenger! It is all right for the murderer, but what about the victim" Allah's Messenger replied,

》إِنَّهُ كَانَ حَرِيصًا عَلَى قَتْلِ صَاحِبِهِ《

(He surely had the intention to kill his comrade.) Imam Ahmad recorded that, at the beginning of the calamity that `Uthman suffered from, Sa`d bin Abi Waqqas said, "I bear witness that the Messenger of Allah said,

》إِنَّهَا سَتَكُونُ فِتْنَةٌ الْقَاعِدُ فِيهَا خَيْرٌ مِنَ الْقَائِمِ، وَالْقَائِمُ خَيْرٌ مِنَ الْمَاشِي، وَالْمَاشِي خَيْرٌ مِنَ السَّاعِي《

(There will be a Fitnah, and he who sits idle during it is better than he who stands up, and he who stands up in it is better than he who walks, and he who walks is better than he who is walking at a fast pace.) When he was asked, `What if someone enters my home and stretched his hand to kill me' He said,

》كُنْ كَابْنِ آدَمَ《

(Be just like (the pious) son of Adam.)" At-Tirmidhi also recorded it this way, and said, "This Hadith is Hasan, and similar is reported on this subject from Abu Hurayrah, Khabbab bin Al-Aratt, Abu Bakr, Ibn Mas`ud, Abu Waqid and Abu Musa." The Qur'an continues,

("Verily, I intend to let you draw my sin on yourself as well as yours, then you will be one of the dwellers of the Fire, and that is the recompense of the wrongdoers.") Ibn `Abbas, Mujahid, Ad-Dahhak, As-Suddi and Qatadah said that,

("Verily, I intend to let you draw my sin on yourself as well as yours...") means, the sin of murdering me, in addition to your previous sins. Ibn Jarir recorded this. Allah's statement,

(So the soul of the other encouraged him and made fair-seeming to him the murder of his brother; he murdered him and became one of the losers.) means, his conscience encouraged him to kill his brother by making it seem like a sensible thing to do, so he killed him, even after his brother admonished him. Ibn Jarir said, "When he wanted to kill his brother, he started to twist his neck. So Shaytan took an animal and placed its head on a rock, then he took another rock, and similar is reported on this subject from Abu Hurayrah, Khabbab bin Al-Aratt, Abu Bakr, Ibn Mas`ud, Abu Waqid and Abu Musa." The Qur'an continues,

("Verily, I intend to let you draw my sin on yourself as well as yours, then you will be one of the dwellers of the Fire, and that is the recompense of the wrongdoers.") Ibn `Abbas, Mujahid, Ad-Dahhak, As-Suddi and Qatadah said that,

("Verily, I intend to let you draw my sin on yourself as well as yours...") means, the sin of murdering me, in addition to your previous sins. Ibn Jarir recorded this. Allah's statement,

(So the soul of the other encouraged him and made fair-seeming to him the murder of his brother; he murdered him and became one of the losers.) means, his conscience encouraged him to kill his brother by making it seem like a sensible thing to do, so he killed him, even after his brother admonished him. Ibn Jarir said, "When he wanted to kill his brother, he started to twist his neck. So Shaytan took an animal and placed its head on a rock, then he took another rock, and smashed its head with it until he killed it while the son of Adam was looking. So he did the same thing to his brother." Ibn Abi Hatim also recorded this. `Abdullah bin Wahb said that `Abdur-Rahman bin Zayd bin Aslam said that his father said, "Qabil held Habil by the head to kill him, so Habil laid down for him and Qabil started twisting Habil's head, not knowing how to kill him. Shaytan came to Qabil and said, `Do you want to kill him' He said, `Yes.' Shaytan said, `Take that stone and throw it on his head.' So Qabil took the stone and threw it at his brother's head and smashed his head. Shaytan then went to Hawwa' in a hurry and said to her, `O Hawwa'! Qabil killed Habil.' She asked him, `Woe to you! What does `kill' mean' He said, `He will no longer eat, drink or move.' She said, `And that is death' He said, `Yes it is.' So she started to weep until Adam came to her while she was weeping and said, `What is the matter with you' She did not answer him. He asked her two more times, but she did not answer him. So he said, `You and your daughters will inherit the practice of weeping, while I and my sons are free of it.'" Ibn Abi Hatim recorded it. Allah's statement,

(And became one of the losers.) in this life and the Hereafter, and which loss is worse than this Imam Ahmad recorded that `Abdullah bin Mas`ud said that the Messenger of Allah said,

«لَا تُقْتَلُ نَفْسٌ ظُلْمًا إِلَّا كَانَ عَلَى ابْنِ آدَمَ الْأَوَّلِ كِفْلٌ مِنْ دَمِهَا،لِأَنَّهُ كَانَ أَوَّلَ مَنْ سَنَّ الْقَتْلِ»

(Any soul that is unjustly killed, then the first son of Adam will carry a burden of its shedding, for he was the first to practice the crime of murder.) The Group, with the exception of Abu Dawud, also recorded this Hadith. Ibn Jarir recorded that `Abdullah bin `Amr used to say, "The son of Adam, who killed his brother, will be the most miserable among men. There is no blood shed on earth since he killed his brother, until the Day of Resurrection, but he will carry a burden from it, for he was the first person to establish murder." Allah said,

(Then Allah sent a crow who scratched the ground to show him how to hide the dead body of his brother. He (the murderer) said, "Woe to me! Am I not even able to be as this crow and to hide the dead body of my brother" Then he became one of those who regretted.) As-Suddi said that the Companions said, "When his brother died, Qabil left him on the bare ground and did not know how to bury him. Allah sent two crows, which fought with each other until one of them killed the other. So it dug a hole and threw sand over the dead corpse (which it placed in the hole). When Qabil saw that, he said,

("Woe to me! Am I not even able to be as this crow and to hide the dead body of my brother") `Ali bin Abi Talhah reported that Ibn `Abbas said, "A crow came to the dead corpse of another crow and threw sand over it, until it hid it in the ground. He who killed his brother said,

(Woe to me! Am I not even able to be as this crow and to hide the dead body of my brother)" Al-Hasan Al-Basri commented on the statement,

(Then he became one of those who regretted.) "Allah made him feel sorrow after the loss that he earned."

The Swift Punishment for Transgression and Cutting the Relations of the Womb

A Hadith states that the Prophet said,

«مَا مِنْ ذَنْبٍ أَجْدَرُ أَنْ يُعَجِّلَ اللهُ عُقُوبَتَهُ فِي الدُّنْيَا مَعَ مَا يَدَّخِرُ لِصَاحِبِهِ فِي الْآخِرَةِ مِنَ الْبَغْيِ وَقَطِيعَةِ الرَّحِمِ»

(There is no sin that is more worthy of Allah hastening its punishment in this life, in addition to what He has in store for its offender in the Hereafter, more than transgression and cutting the relations of the womb.) The act of Qabil included both of these. We are Allah's and to Him is our return.

Surah: 5 Ayah: 32, Ayah: 33 & Ayah: 34

﴿ مِنْ أَجْلِ ذَٰلِكَ كَتَبْنَا عَلَىٰ بَنِىٓ إِسْرَٰٓءِيلَ أَنَّهُۥ مَن قَتَلَ نَفْسًۢا بِغَيْرِ نَفْسٍ أَوْ فَسَادٍ فِى ٱلْأَرْضِ فَكَأَنَّمَا قَتَلَ ٱلنَّاسَ جَمِيعًا وَمَنْ أَحْيَاهَا فَكَأَنَّمَآ أَحْيَا

﴿ ٱلنَّاسَ جَمِيعًا ۚ وَلَقَدْ جَآءَتْهُمْ رُسُلُنَا بِٱلْبَيِّنَـٰتِ ثُمَّ إِنَّ كَثِيرًا مِّنْهُم بَعْدَ ذَٰلِكَ فِى ٱلْأَرْضِ لَمُسْرِفُونَ ۝ ﴾

32. Because of that We ordained for the Children of Israel that if anyone killed a person not in retaliation of murder, or (and) to spread mischief in the land - it would be as if he killed all mankind, and if anyone saved a life, it would be as if he saved the life of all mankind. And indeed, there came to them Our Messengers with clear proofs, evidences, and signs, even then after that many of them continued to exceed the limits (e.g. by doing oppression unjustly and exceeding beyond the limits set by Allâh by committing the major sins) in the land!.

﴿ إِنَّمَا جَزَٰٓؤُا۟ ٱلَّذِينَ يُحَارِبُونَ ٱللَّهَ وَرَسُولَهُۥ وَيَسْعَوْنَ فِى ٱلْأَرْضِ فَسَادًا أَن يُقَتَّلُوٓا۟ أَوْ يُصَلَّبُوٓا۟ أَوْ تُقَطَّعَ أَيْدِيهِمْ وَأَرْجُلُهُم مِّنْ خِلَـٰفٍ أَوْ يُنفَوْا۟ مِنَ ٱلْأَرْضِ ۚ ذَٰلِكَ لَهُمْ خِزْىٌ فِى ٱلدُّنْيَا ۖ وَلَهُمْ فِى ٱلْأَخِرَةِ عَذَابٌ عَظِيمٌ ۝ ﴾

33. The recompense of those who wage war against Allâh and His Messenger and do mischief in the land is only that they shall be killed or crucified or their hands and their feet be cut off from opposite sides, or be exiled from the land. That is their disgrace in this world, and a great torment is theirs in the Hereafter.

﴿ إِلَّا ٱلَّذِينَ تَابُوا۟ مِن قَبْلِ أَن تَقْدِرُوا۟ عَلَيْهِمْ ۖ فَٱعْلَمُوٓا۟ أَنَّ ٱللَّهَ غَفُورٌ رَّحِيمٌ ۝ ﴾

34. Except for those who (having fled away and then) came back (as Muslims) with repentance before they fall into your power; in that case, know that Allâh is Oft-Forgiving, Most Merciful.

Transliteration

32. Min ajli thalika katabna AAala banee isra-eela annahu man qatala nafsan bighayri nafsin aw fasadin fee al-ardi fakaannama qatala alnnasa jameeAAan waman ahyaha fakaannama ahya alnnasa jameeAAan walaqad jaat-hum rusuluna bialbayyinati thumma inna katheeran minhum baAAda thalika fee al-ardi lamusrifoona 33. Innama jazao allatheena yuhariboona Allaha warasoolahu wayasAAawna fee al-ardi fasadan an yuqattaloo aw yusallaboo aw tuqattaAAa aydeehim waarjuluhum min khilafin aw yunfaw mina al-ardi thalika lahum khizyun fee alddunya walahum fee al-akhirati AAathabun AAatheemun 34. Illa allatheena taboo min qabli an taqdiroo AAalayhim faiAAlamoo anna Allaha ghafoorun raheemun

Tafsir Ibn Kathir

Human Beings Should Respect the Sanctity of Other Human Beings

Allah says, because the son of Adam killed his brother in transgression and aggression,

(We ordained for the Children of Israel...) meaning, We legislated for them and informed them,

(that if anyone killed a person not in retaliation of murder, or (and) to spread mischief in the land - it would be as if he killed all mankind, and if anyone saved a life, it would be as if he saved the life of all mankind.) The Ayah states, whoever kills a soul without justification -- such as in retaliation for murder or for causing mischief on earth -- will be as if he has killed all mankind, because there is no difference between one life and another.

(and if anyone saved a life...) by preventing its blood from being shed and believing in its sanctity, then all people will have been saved from him, so,

(it would be as if he saved the life of all mankind.) Al-A`mash and others said that Abu Salih said that Abu Hurayrah said, "I entered on `Uthman when he was under siege in his house and said, `I came to give you my support. Now, it is good to fight (defending you) O Leader of the Faithful!' He said, `O Abu Hurayrah! Does it please you that you kill all people, including me' I said, `No.' He said, `If you kill one man, it is as if you killed all people. Therefore, go back with my permission for you to leave. May you receive your reward and be saved from burden.' So I went back and did not fight.'" `Ali bin Abi Talhah reported that Ibn `Abbas said, "It is as Allah has stated,

(if anyone killed a person not in retaliation of murder, or (and) to spread mischief in the land - it would be as if he killed all mankind, and if anyone saved a life, it would be as if he saved the life of all mankind.) Saving life in this case occurs by not killing a soul that Allah has forbidden. So this is the meaning of saving the life of all mankind, for whoever forbids killing a soul without justification, the lives of all people will be saved from him." Similar was said by Mujahid;

(And if anyone saved a life...) means, he refrains from killing a soul. Al-`Awfi reported that Ibn `Abbas said that Allah's statement,

(it would be as if he killed all mankind. .) means, "Whoever kills one soul that Allah has forbidden killing, is just like he who kills all mankind." Sa`id bin Jubayr said, "He who allows himself to shed the blood of a Muslim, is like he who allows shedding the blood of all people. He who forbids shedding the blood of one Muslim, is like he who forbids shedding the blood of all people." In addition, Ibn Jurayj said that Al-A`raj said that Mujahid commented on the Ayah,

(it would be as if he killed all mankind,) "He who kills a believing soul intentionally, Allah makes the Fire of Hell his abode, He will become angry with him, and curse him, and has prepared a tremendous punishment for him, equal to if he had killed all people, his punishment will still be the same." Ibn Jurayj said that Mujahid said that the Ayah,

(and if anyone saved a life, it would be as if he saved the life of all mankind.) means, "He who does not kill anyone, then the lives of people are safe from him."

Warning Those who Commit Mischief

Allah said,

(And indeed, there came to them Our Messengers with Al-Bayyinat,) meaning, clear evidences, signs and proofs,

(even then after that many of them continued to exceed the limits in the land!) This Ayah chastises and criticizes those who commit the prohibitions, after knowing that they are prohibited from indulging in them. The Jews of Al-Madinah, such as Banu Qurayzah, An-Nadir and Qaynuqa`, used to fight along with either Khazraj or Aws, when war would erupt between them during the time of Jahiliyyah. When these wars would end, the Jews would ransom those who were captured and pay the blood money for those who were killed. Allah criticized them for this practice in Surat Al-Baqarah,

(And (remember) when We took your covenant (saying): Shed not your (people's) blood, nor turn out your own people from their dwellings. Then, (this) you ratified and (to this) you bear witness. After this, it is you who kill one another and drive out a party of your own from their homes, assist (their enemies) against them, in sin and transgression. And if they come to you as captives, you ransom them, although their expulsion was forbidden to you. Then do you believe in a part of the Scripture and reject the rest Then what is the recompense of those who do so among you, except disgrace in the life of this world, and on the Day of Resurrection they shall be consigned to the most grievous torment. And Allah is not unaware of what you do.) (2:84-85)

The Punishment of those Who Cause Mischief in the Land

Allah said next,

(The recompense of those who wage war against Allah and His Messenger and do mischief in the land is only that they shall be killed or crucified or their hands and their feet be cut off on the opposite sides, or be exiled from the land.) `Wage war' mentioned here means, oppose and contradict, and it includes disbelief, blocking roads and spreading fear in the fairways. Mischief in the land refers to various types of evil. Ibn Jarir recorded that `Ikrimah and Al-Hasan Al-Basri said that the Ayat,

(The recompense of those who wage war against Allah and His Messenger) until,

(Allah is Of-Forgiving, Most Merciful,) "Were revealed about the idolators. Therefore, the Ayah decrees that, whoever among them repents before you apprehend them, then you have no right to punish them. This Ayah does not save a Muslim from punishment if he kills, causes mischief in the land or wages war against Allah and His

Messenger and then joins rank with the disbelievers, before the Muslims are able to catch him. He will still be liable for punishment for the crimes he committed." Abu Dawud and An-Nasa'i recorded that `Ikrimah said that Ibn `Abbas said that the Ayah,

(The recompense of those who wage war against Allah and His Messenger and do mischief in the land...) "Was revealed concerning the idolators, those among them who repent before being apprehended, they will still be liable for punishment for the crimes they committed." The correct opinion is that this Ayah is general in meaning and includes the idolators and all others who commit the types of crimes the Ayah mentioned. Al-Bukhari and Muslim recorded that Abu Qilabah `Abdullah bin Zayd Al-Jarmi, said that Anas bin Malik said, "Eight people of the `Ukl tribe came to the Messenger of Allah and gave him their pledge to follow Islam. Al-Madinah's climate did not suit them and they became sick and complained to Allah's Messenger . So he said,

»أَلَا تَخْرُجُونَ مَعَ رَاعِينَا فِي إِبِلِهِ، فَتُصِيبُوا مِنْ أَبْوَالِهَا وَأَلْبَانِهَا«

(Go with our shephard to be treated by the milk and urine of his camels.) So they went as directed, and after they drank from the camels' milk and urine, they became healthy, and they killed the shepherd and drove away all the camels. The news reached the Prophet and he sent (men) in their pursuit and they were captured. He then ordered that their hands and feet be cut off (and it was done), and their eyes were branded with heated pieces of iron. Next, they were put in the sun until they died." This is the wording of Muslim. In another narration for this Hadith, it was mentioned that these people were from the tribes of `Ukl or `Uraynah. Another narration reported that these people were put in the Harrah area (of Al-Madinah), and when they asked for water, no water was given to them. Allah said,

(they shall be killed or crucified or their hands and their feet be cut off on the opposite sides, or be exiled from the land.) `Ali bin Abi Talhah said that Ibn `Abbas said about this Ayah, `He who takes up arms in Muslim land and spreads fear in the fairways and is captured, the Muslim Leader has the choice to either have him killed, crucified or cut off his hands and feet." Similar was said by Sa`id bin Al-Musayyib, Mujahid, `Ata', Al-Hasan Al-Basri, Ibrahim An-Nakha`i and Ad-Dahhak, as Abu Ja`far Ibn Jarir recorded. This view is supported by the fact that the word Aw (or), indicates a choice. As Allah said,

(The penalty is an offering, brought to the Ka`bah, of an eatable animal equivalent to the one he killed, as adjudged by two just men among you; or, for expiation, he should feed the poor, or its equivalent in fasting.)(5:95) Allah said,

(And whosoever of you is ill or has an ailment in his scalp (necessitating shaving), he must pay a ransom of either fasting or giving charity or offering a sacrifice.) and,

(...for its expiation feed ten of the poor, on a scale of the average of that with which you feed your own families, or clothe them, or free a slave.) All of these Ayat offer a choice, just as the Ayah above. As for Allah's statement, (or be exiled from the land.) some said that it means, he is actively pursued until he is captured, and thus receives his prescribed punishment, or otherwise he escapes from the land of Islam, as Ibn Jarir recorded from Ibn `Abbas, Anas bin Malik, Sa`id bin Jubayr, Ad-Dahhak, Ar-Rabi` bin Anas, Az-Zuhri, Al-Layth bin Sa`d and Malik bin Anas. Some said that the Ayah means these people are expelled to another land, or to another state by the Muslims authorities. Sa`id bin Jubayr, Abu Ash-Sha`tha', Al-Hasan, Az-Zuhri, Ad-Dahhak and Muqatil bin Hayyan said that he is expelled, but not outside of the land of Islam, while others said that he is to be imprisoned. Allah's statement,

(That is their disgrace in this world, and a great torment is theirs in the Hereafter.) means, the punishment We prescribed, killing these aggressors, crucifying them, cutting off their hands and feet on opposite sides, or expelling them from the land is a disgrace for them among mankind in this life, along with the tremendous torment Allah has prepared for them in the Hereafter. This view supports the opinion that these Ayat were revealed about the idolators. As for Muslims, in his Sahih, Muslim recorded that `Ubadah bin As-Samit said, "The Messenger of Allah took the same pledge from us that he also took from women: That we do not associate anything with Allah in worship, we do not steal, commit adultery, or kill our children, and that we do not spread falsehood about each other. He said that he who keeps this pledge, then his reward will be with Allah. He who falls into shortcomings and was punished, then this will be his expiation. And those whose errors were covered by Allah, then their matter is for Allah: If He wills, He will punish them and If He wills, He will pardon them." `Ali narrated that the Messenger of Allah said,

«مَنْ أَذْنَبَ ذَنْبًا فِي الدُّنْيَا فَعُوقِبَ بِهِ، فَاللهُ أَعْدَلُ مِنْ أَنْ يُثَنِّيَ عُقُوبَتَهُ عَلَى عَبْدِهِ، وَمَنْ أَذْنَبَ ذَنْبًا فِي الدُّنْيَا فَسَتَرَهُ اللهُ عَلَيْهِ وَعَفَا عَنْهُ، فَاللهُ أَكْرَمُ مِنْ أَنْ يَعُودَ عَلَيْهِ فِي شَيْءٍ قَدْ عَفَا عَنْه»

(He who sins in this life and was punished for it, then Allah is far more just than to combine two punishments on His servant. He who commits an error in this life and Allah hides this error and pardons him, then Allah is far more generous than to punish the servant for something that He has already pardoned.) iRecorded by Ahmad, Ibn Majah and At-Tirmidhi who said, "Hasan Gharib."Al-Hafiz Ad-Daraqutni was asked about this Hadith, and he said that it was related to the Prophet in some narrations, and it was related to the Companions in others, and that this narration from the Prophet is Sahih. Ibn Jarir commented on Allah's statement,

(That is their disgrace in this world,) "Meaning, shame, humiliation, punishment, contempt and torment in this life, before the Hereafter,

(and a great torment is theirs in the Hereafter.) if they do not repent from these errors until death overcomes them. In this case, they will be stricken by the punishment that We prescribed for them in this life and the torment that We prepared for them therein,

(a great torment) in the Fire of Jahannam."

The Punishment of those who Wage War Against Allah and His Messenger is Annulled if They Repent Before their Apprehension

Allah said,

(Except for those who (having fled away and then) came back (as Muslims) with repentance before they fall into your power; in that case, know that Allah is Oft-Forgiving, Most Merciful.) This Ayah is clear in its indication that it applies to the idolators. As for the Muslims who commit this crime and repent before they are apprehended, the punishment of killing, crucifixion and cutting the limbs will be waved. The practice of the Companions in this regard is that all of the punishments prescribed in this case will be waved, as is apparent from the wording of the Ayah. Ibn Abi Hatim recorded that Ash-Sha`bi said, "Harithah bin Badr At-Tamimi was living in Al-Basrah, and he committed the crime of mischief in the land. So he talked to some men from Quraysh, such as Al-Hasan bin `Ali, Ibn `Abbas and `Abdullah bin Ja`far, and they talked to `Ali about him so that he would grant him safety, but `Ali refused. So Harithah went to Sa`id bin Qays Al-Hamadani who kept him in his house and went to `Ali, saying, `O Leader of the Faithful! What about those who wage war against Allah and His Messenger and cause mischief in the land' So he recited the Ayah until he reached,

(Except for those who (having fled away and them) came back cas Muslims) with repentance before they fall into your power.) So `Ali wrote a document that granted safety, and Sa`id bin Qays said, `This is for Harithah bin Badr.'" Ibn Jarir recorded this Hadith. Ibn Jarir recorded that `Amir Ash-Sha`bi said, "A man from Murad came to Abu Musa, while he was the governor of Al-Kufah during the reign of `Uthman, and said to him after he offered the obligatory prayer, `O Abu Musa! I seek your help. I am so-and-so from Murad and I waged war against Allah and His Messenger and caused mischief in the land. I repented before you had any authority over me.' Abu Musa proclaimed, `This is so-and-so, who had waged war against Allah and His Messenger and caused mischief in the land, and he repented before we had authority over him. Therefore, anyone who meets him, should deal with him in a better way. If he is saying the truth, then this is the path of those who say the truth. If he is saying a lie, his sins will destroy him. So the man remained idle for as long as Allah willed, but he later rose against the leaders, and Allah punished him for his sins and he was killed." Ibn Jarir recorded that Musa bin Ishaq Al-Madani said that `Ali Al-Asadi waged war, blocked the roads, shed blood and plundered wealth. The leaders and the people alike, sought to capture him, but they could not do that until he came after he repented, after he heard a man reciting the Ayah,

(O My servants who have transgressed against themselves! Despair not of the mercy of Allah, verily, Allah forgives all sins. Truly, He is Oft-Forgiving, Most Merciful.) So he said to that man, "O servant of Allah! Recite it again." So he recited it again, and `Ali put down his sword and went to Al-Madinah in repentance, arriving during the night.

He washed up and went to the Masjid of the Messenger of Allah and prayed the dawn prayer. He sat next to Abu Hurayrah amidst his companions. In the morning, the people recognized him and went after him. He said, "You have no way against me. I came in repentance before you had any authority over me." Abu Hurayrah said, "He has said the truth," and he held his hand and went to Marwan bin Al-Hakam, who was the governor of Al-Madinah during the reign of Mu`awiyah. Abu Hurayrah said, "This is `Ali and he came in repentance and you do not have a way against him, nor can you have him killed." So `Ali was absolved of punishment and remained on his repentance and went to the sea to perform Jihad in Allah's cause. The Muslims met the Romans in battle, and the Muslims brought the ship `Ali was in to one of the Roman ships, and `Ali crossed to that ship and the Romans escaped from him to the other side of the ship, and the ship capsized and they all drowned."

Surah: 5 Ayah: 35, Ayah: 36 & Ayah: 37

﴿ يَٰٓأَيُّهَا ٱلَّذِينَ ءَامَنُواْ ٱتَّقُواْ ٱللَّهَ وَٱبْتَغُوٓاْ إِلَيْهِ ٱلْوَسِيلَةَ وَجَٰهِدُواْ فِى سَبِيلِهِۦ لَعَلَّكُمْ تُفْلِحُونَ ۝ ﴾

35. O you who believe! Do your duty to Allâh and fear Him. And seek the means of approach to Him, and strive hard in His Cause as much as you can. So that you may be successful.

﴿ إِنَّ ٱلَّذِينَ كَفَرُواْ لَوْ أَنَّ لَهُم مَّا فِى ٱلْأَرْضِ جَمِيعًا وَمِثْلَهُۥ مَعَهُۥ لِيَفْتَدُواْ بِهِۦ مِنْ عَذَابِ يَوْمِ ٱلْقِيَٰمَةِ مَا تُقُبِّلَ مِنْهُمْ وَلَهُمْ عَذَابٌ أَلِيمٌ ۝ ﴾

36. Verily, those who disbelieve, if they had all that is in the earth, and as much again therewith to ransom themselves thereby from the torment on the Day of Resurrection, it would never be accepted of them, and theirs would be a painful torment.

﴿ يُرِيدُونَ أَن يَخْرُجُواْ مِنَ ٱلنَّارِ وَمَا هُم بِخَٰرِجِينَ مِنْهَا وَلَهُمْ عَذَابٌ مُّقِيمٌ ۝ ﴾

37. They will long to get out of the Fire, but never will they get out therefrom; and theirs will be a lasting torment.

Transliteration

35. Ya ayyuha allatheena amanoo ittaqoo Allaha waibtaghoo ilayhi alwaseelata wajahidoo fee sabeelihi laAAallakum tuflihoona 36. Inna allatheena kafaroo law anna lahum ma fee al-ardi jameeAAan wamithlahu maAAahu liyaftadoo bihi min AAathabi yawmi alqiyamati ma tuqubbila minhum walahum AAathabun aleemun 37. Yureedoona an yakhrujoo mina alnnari wama hum bikharijeena minha walahum AAathabun muqeemun

Tafsir Ibn Kathir

Commanding Taqwa, Wasilah, and Jihad

Allah commands His faithful servants to fear Him in Taqwa, which if mentioned along with acts of obedience, it means to refrain from the prohibitions and the prohibited matters. Allah said next,

(seek the Wasilah to Him.) Sufyan Ath-Thawri said that Talhah said that `Ata' said that Ibn `Abbas said that Wasilah means `the means of approach'. Mujahid, Abu Wa'il, Al-Hasan, Qatadah, `Abdullah bin Kathir, As-Suddi, Ibn Zayd and others gave the same meaning for Wasilah. Qatadah said that the Ayah means, "Seek the means of approach to Him by obeying Him and performing the acts that please Him."

(Those whom they call upon seek a means of access to their Lord (Allah).) (17:57) Wasilah is a means of approach to achieve something, and it is also used to refer to the highest grade in Paradise, and it is the grade of the Messenger of Allah , his residence and the nearest grade in Paradise to Allah's Throne. Al-Bukhari recorded that Jabir bin `Abdullah said that the Messenger of Allah said,

«مَنْ قَالَ حِينَ يَسْمَعُ النِّدَاءَ: اللَّهُمَّ رَبَّ هذِهِ الدَّعْوَةِ التَّامَّةِ، وَالصَّلَاةِ الْقَائِمَةِ، آتِ مُحَمَّدًا الْوَسِيلَةَ وَالْفَضِيلَةَ، وَابْعَثْهُ مَقَامًا مَحْمُودًا الَّذِي وَعَدْتَهُ، إِلَّا حَلَّتْ لَهُ الشَّفَاعَةُ يَوْمَ الْقِيَامَةِ»

(Whoever, after hearing to the Adhan says, "O Allah! Lord of this perfect call and of the regular prayer which is going to be established! Grant Muhammad the Wasilah and superiority and send him (on the Day of Judgment) to the praiseworthy station which You have promised him," then intercession from me will be permitted for him on the Day of Resurrection.) Muslim recorded that `Abdullah bin `Amr bin Al-`As said that he heard the Prophet saying,

«إِذَا سَمِعْتُمُ الْمُؤَذِّنَ فَقُولُوا مِثْلَ مَا يَقُولُ، ثُمَّ صَلُّوا عَلَيَّ، فَإِنَّهُ مَنْ صَلَّى عَلَيَّ صَلَاةً صَلَّى اللهُ عَلَيْهِ عَشْرًا، ثُمَّ سَلُوا لِيَ الْوَسِيلَةَ، فَإِنَّهَا مَنْزِلَةٌ فِي الْجَنَّةِ لَا تَنْبَغِي إِلَّا لِعَبْدٍ مِنْ عِبَادِ اللهِ، وَأَرْجُو أَنْ أَكُونَ أَنَا هُوَ، فَمَنْ سَأَلَ لِيَ الْوَسِيلَةَ حَلَّتْ عَلَيْهِ الشَّفَاعَة»

(When you hear the Mu'adhdhin, repeat what he says, and then ask for Salah (blessing, mercy from Allah) for me. Verily, whoever asks for Salah for me, then Allah will grant ten Salah to him. Then, ask for the Wasilah for me, for it is a grade in

Paradise that only one servant of Allah deserves, and I hope that I am that servant. Verily, whoever asks (Allah) for Wasilah for me, he will earn the right of my intercession.) Allah said,

(and strive hard in His cause as much as you can. So that you may be successful.) After Allah commanded Muslims to avoid the prohibitions and to work towards obedience, He commanded them to fight against their enemies, the disbelievers and idolators who have deviated from the straight path and abandoned the correct religion. Allah encouraged the believers by reminding them of the unending success and great happiness that He prepared for them for the Day of Resurrection, which will never change or decrease for those who join Jihad in His cause. They will remain in the lofty rooms of Paradise that are safe and beautiful. Those who live in these dwellings will always be comfortable and will never be miserable, living, never dying, and their clothes will never grow thin, nor will their youth ever end.

No Amount of Ransom Shall Be Accepted from the Disbelievers on the Day of the Judgment and They Will Remain in the Fire

Allah then describes the painful torment and punishment that He has prepared for His disbelieving enemies for the Day of Resurrection. Allah said,

(Verily, those who disbelieve, if they had all that is in the earth, and as much again therewith to ransom themselves thereby from the torment on the Day of Resurrection, it would never be accepted of them. And theirs would be a painful torment.) So if a disbeliever brought the earth's fill of gold, and twice as much as that amount on the Day of Judgment to ransom himself from Allah's torment that has surrounded him, and he is certain that he will suffer from it, it will not be accepted of him. Rather, there is no escaping the torment, and he will not be able to evade or save himself from it. Hence Allah's statement,

(And theirs would be a painful torment.) meaning, hurtful,

(They will long to get out of the Fire, but never will they get out therefrom, and theirs will be a lasting torment.) In another Ayah, Allah said,

(Every time they seek to get away therefrom, in anguish, they will be driven back therein.) Therefore, they will still long to leave the torment because of the severity and the pain it causes. They will have no way of escaping it. The more the flames lift them to the upper part of Hell, the more the angels of punishment will strike them with iron bars and they will fall down to its depths,

(And theirs will be a lasting torment.) meaning, eternal and everlasting, and they will never be able to depart from it or avoid it. Anas bin Malik said that the Messenger of Allah said,

«يُؤْتَى بِالرَّجُلِ مِنْ أَهْلِ النَّارِ فَيُقَالُ لَهُ: يَا ابْنَ آدَمَ كَيْفَ وَجَدْتَ مَضْجَعَكَ؟ فَيَقُولُ: شَرَّ مَضْجَعٍ، فَيُقَالُ: هَلْ تَفْتَدِي بِقُرَابِ الْأَرْضِ ذَهَبًا؟ قَالَ: فَيَقُولُ:

نَعَمْ يَارَبِّ فَيَقُولُ اللهُ: كَذَبْتَ، قَدْ سَأَلْتُكَ أَقَلَّ مِنْ ذَلِكَ فَلَمْ تَفْعَلْ، فَيُؤْمَرُ بِهِ إِلَى النَّارِ»

(A man from the people of the Fire will be brought forth and will be asked, `O son of Adam! How did you find your dwelling' He will say, `The worst dwelling.' He will be told, `Would you ransom yourself with the earth's fill of gold' He will say, `Yes, O Lord!' Allah will say to him, `You have lied. I asked you for what is less than that and you did not do it,' and he will be ordered to the Fire.) Muslim and An-Nasa'i recorded it.

Surah: 5 Ayah: 38, Ayah: 39 & Ayah: 40

﴿ وَٱلسَّارِقُ وَٱلسَّارِقَةُ فَٱقْطَعُوٓاْ أَيْدِيَهُمَا جَزَآءًۢ بِمَا كَسَبَا نَكَٰلًۭا مِّنَ ٱللَّهِ ۗ وَٱللَّهُ عَزِيزٌ حَكِيمٌۭ ﴾

38. And (as for) the male thief and the female, cut off (from the wrist joint) their (right) hand as a recompense for that which they committed, a punishment by way of example from Allâh. And Allâh is All-Powerful, All-Wise.

﴿ فَمَن تَابَ مِنۢ بَعْدِ ظُلْمِهِۦ وَأَصْلَحَ فَإِنَّ ٱللَّهَ يَتُوبُ عَلَيْهِ ۗ إِنَّ ٱللَّهَ غَفُورٌۭ رَّحِيمٌ ﴾

39. But whosoever repents after his crime and does righteous good deeds (by obeying Allâh), then verily, Allâh will pardon him (accept his repentance). Verily, Allâh is Oft-Forgiving, Most Merciful.

﴿ أَلَمْ تَعْلَمْ أَنَّ ٱللَّهَ لَهُۥ مُلْكُ ٱلسَّمَٰوَٰتِ وَٱلْأَرْضِ يُعَذِّبُ مَن يَشَآءُ وَيَغْفِرُ لِمَن يَشَآءُ ۗ وَٱللَّهُ عَلَىٰ كُلِّ شَىْءٍۢ قَدِيرٌۭ ﴾

40. Know you not that to Allâh (Alone) belongs the dominion of the heavens and the earth! He punishes whom He wills and He forgives whom He wills. And Allâh is Able to do all things.

Transliteration

38. Waalssariqu waalssariqatu faiqtaAAoo aydiyahuma jazaan bima kasaba nakalan mina Allahi waAllahu AAazeezun hakeemun 39. Faman taba min baAAdi thulmihi waaslaha fa-inna Allaha yatoobu AAalayhi inna Allaha ghafoorun raheemun 40. Alam taAAlam anna Allaha lahu mulku alssamawati waal-ardi yuAAaththibu man yashao wayaghfiru liman yashao waAllahu AAala kulli shay-in qadeerun

Tafsir Ibn Kathir

The Necessity of Cutting off the Hand of the Thief

Allah commands and decrees that the hand of the thief, male or female be cut off. During the time of Jahiliyyah, this was also the punishment for the thief, and Islam upheld this punishment. In Islam, there are several conditions that must be met before this punishment is carried out, as we will come to know, Allah willing. There are other rulings that Islam upheld after modifying these rulings, such as that of blood money for example. When Does Cutting the Hand of the Thief Become Necessary In is recorded in the Two Sahihs that Abu Hurayrah said that the Messenger of Allah said,

«لَعَنَ اللهُ السَّارِقَ يَسْرِقُ الْبَيْضَةَ فَتُقْطَعُ يَدُهُ، وَيَسْرِقُ الْحَبْلَ فَتُقْطَعُ يَدُهُ»

(May Allah curse the thief who steals an egg and as a result his hand is cut off, and who steals rope and as a result his hand is cut off.) Al-Bukhari and Muslim recorded that `A'ishah said that the Messenger of Allah said,

«تُقْطَعُ يَدُ السَّارِقِ فِي رُبْعِ دِينَارٍ فَصَاعِدًا»

(The hand of the thief shall be cut off if he steals a quarter of a Dinar or more.) Muslim recorded that `A'ishah, may Allah be pleased with her, said that the Messenger of Allah said,

«لَا تُقْطَعُ يَدُ السَّارِقِ إِلَّا فِي رُبْعِ دِينَارٍ فَصَاعِدًا»

(The hand of the thief shall only be cut off if he steals a quarter of a Dinar or more.) This Hadith is the basis of the matter since it specifies (that the least amount of theft that deserves cutting the hand) is a quarter of a Dinar. So this Hadith fixes the value. And saying that it is three Dirhams is not a contradiction. This is because the Dinar in question was equal to twelve Dirhams, so three Dirhams equalled a fourth of a Dinar. So in this way it is possible to harmonize these two views. This opinion was reported from `Umar bin Al-Khattab, `Uthman bin `Affan,

When Does Cutting the Hand of the Thief Become Necessary

In is recorded in the Two Sahihs that Abu Hurayrah said that the Messenger of Allah said,

«لَعَنَ اللهُ السَّارِقَ يَسْرِقُ الْبَيْضَةَ فَتُقْطَعُ يَدُهُ، وَيَسْرِقُ الْحَبْلَ فَتُقْطَعُ يَدُهُ»

(May Allah curse the thief who steals an egg and as a result his hand is cut off, and who steals rope and as a result his hand is cut off.) Al-Bukhari and Muslim recorded that `A'ishah said that the Messenger of Allah said,

«تُقْطَعُ يَدُ السَّارِقِ فِي رُبْعِ دِينَارٍ فَصَاعِدًا»

(The hand of the thief shall be cut off if he steals a quarter of a Dinar or more.) Muslim recorded that `A'ishah, may Allah be pleased with her, said that the Messenger of Allah said,

«لَا تُقْطَعُ يَدُ السَّارِقِ إِلَّا فِي رُبْعِ دِينَارٍ فَصَاعِدًا»

(The hand of the thief shall only be cut off if he steals a quarter of a Dinar or more.) This Hadith is the basis of the matter since it specifies (that the least amount of theft that deserves cutting the hand) is a quarter of a Dinar. So this Hadith fixes the value. And saying that it is three Dirhams is not a contradiction. This is because the Dinar in question was equal to twelve Dirhams, so three Dirhams equalled a fourth of a Dinar. So in this way it is possible to harmonize these two views. This opinion was reported from `Umar bin Al-Khattab, `Uthman bin `Affan, `Ali bin Abi Talib - may Allah be pleased with them - and it is the view of `Umar bin `Abdul-`Aziz, Al-Layth bin Sa`d, Al-Awza`i, and Ash-Shafi`i and his companions. This is also the view of Imam Ahmad bin Hanbal and Ishaq bin Rahwayh in one of the narrations from him, as well as Abu Thawr, and Dawud bin `Ali Az-Zahari, may Allah have mercy upon them. As for Imam Abu Hanifah and his students Abu Yusuf, Muhammad and Zufar, along with Sufyan Ath-Thawri, they said that the least amount of theft that deserves cutting off the hand is ten Dirhams, whereas a Dinar was twelve Dirhams at that time. The first ruling is the correct one, that the least amount of theft is one forth of a Dinar or more. This meager amount was set as the limit for cutting the hand, so that the people would refrain from theft, and this is a wise decision to those who have sound comprehension. Hence Allah's statement,

(as a recompense for that which both committed, a punishment by way of example from Allah. And Allah is All-Powerful, All-Wise.) This is the prescribed punishment for the evil action they committed, by stealing the property of other people with their hands. Therefore, it is fitting that the tool they used to steal the people's wealth be cut off as punishment from Allah for their error.

(And Allah is All-Powerful,) in His torment,

(All-Wise.) in His commands, what he forbids, what He legislates and what He decrees.

Repentance of the Thief is Acceptable

Allah said next,

(But whosoever repents after his crime and does righteous good deeds, then verily, Allah will pardon him. Verily, Allah is Oft-Forgiving, Most Merciful.) Therefore, whoever repents and goes back to Allah after he commits theft, then Allah will forgive him. Imam Ahmad recorded that `Abdullah bin `Amr said that a woman committed theft during the time of the Messenger of Allah and those from whom she stole brought her and said, "O Allah's Messenger! This woman stole from us." Her people said, "We ransom her." The Messenger of Allah said,

《اقْطَعُوا يَدَهَا》

(Cut off her hand.) They said, "We ransom her with five hundred Dinars." The Prophet said,

《اقْطَعُوا يَدَهَا》

(Cut off her hand.) Her right hand was cut off and the woman asked, "O Messenger of Allah! Is there a chance for me to repent" He said,

《نَعَمْ أَنْتِ الْيَوْمَ مِنْ خَطِيئَتِكِ كَيَوْمَ وَلَدَتْكِ أُمُّكِ》

(Yes. This day, you are free from your sin just as the day your mother gave birth to you.) Allah sent down the verse in Surat Al-Ma'idah,

(But whosoever repents after his crime and does righteous good deeds (by obeying Allah), then verily, Allah will pardon him. Verily, Allah is Oft-Forgiving, Most Merciful.) This woman was from the tribe of Makhzum. Her story was narrated in the Two Sahihs from Az-Zuhri from `Urwah from `A'ishah, The incident caused concern for the Quraysh after she committed the theft during the time of the battle of the Conquest (of Makkah). They said, "Who can talk to Allah's Messenger about her matter" They then said, "Who dares speak to him about such matters other than Usamah bin Zayd, his loved one." When the woman was brought to the Messenger of Allah , Usamah bin Zayd talked to him about her and the face of the Messenger changed color (because of anger) and he said,

《أَتَشْفَعُ فِي حَدٍ مِنْ حُدُودِ اللهِ عَزَّ وَجَلَّ؟》

(Do you intercede in a punishment prescribed by Allah) Usamah said to him, "Ask Allah to forgive me, O Allah's Messenger!" During that night, the Messenger of Allah stood up and gave a speech and praised Allah as He deserves to be praised. He then said,

《أَمَّا بَعْدُ فَإِنَّمَا أَهْلَكَ الَّذِينَ مِنْ قَبْلِكُمْ أَنَّهُمْ كَانُوا إِذَا سَرَقَ فِيهِمُ الشَّرِيفُ تَرَكُوهُ، وَإِذَا سَرَقَ فِيهِمُ الضَّعِيفُ أَقَامُوا عَلَيْهِ الْحَدَّ، وَإِنِّي وَالَّذِي نَفْسِي بِيَدِهِ لَوْ أَنَّ فَاطِمَةَ بِنْتَ مُحَمَّدٍ سَرَقَتْ لَقَطَعْتُ يَدَهَا》

(Those who were before you were destroyed because when an honorable person among them would steal, they would leave him. But, when a weak man among them stole, they implemented the prescribed punishment against him. By Him in Whose Hand is my soul! If Fatimah the daughter of Muhammad stole, I will have her hand cut off.) The Prophet commanded that the hand of the woman who stole be cut off, and it was cut off. `A'ishah said, `Her repentance was sincere afterwards, and she got married and she used to come to me so that I convey her needs to the Messenger of Allah." This is the wording that Muslim collected, and in another narration by Muslim, `A'ishah said, "She was a woman from Makhzum who used to borrow things and deny that she took them. So the Prophet ordered that her hand be cut off." Allah then said,

(Know you not that to Allah (Alone) belongs the dominion of the heavens and the earth!) He owns everything and decides what He wills for it and no one can resist His judgment,

(He forgives whom He wills and punishes whom He wills. And Allah is able to do all things.)

Surah: 5 Ayah: 41, Ayah: 42, Ayah: 43 & Ayah: 44

﴿ ۞ يَٰٓأَيُّهَا ٱلرَّسُولُ لَا يَحْزُنكَ ٱلَّذِينَ يُسَٰرِعُونَ فِى ٱلْكُفْرِ مِنَ ٱلَّذِينَ قَالُوٓاْ ءَامَنَّا بِأَفْوَٰهِهِمْ وَلَمْ تُؤْمِن قُلُوبُهُمْ ۛ وَمِنَ ٱلَّذِينَ هَادُواْ ۛ سَمَّٰعُونَ لِلْكَذِبِ سَمَّٰعُونَ لِقَوْمٍ ءَاخَرِينَ لَمْ يَأْتُوكَ ۖ يُحَرِّفُونَ ٱلْكَلِمَ مِنۢ بَعْدِ مَوَاضِعِهِۦ ۖ يَقُولُونَ إِنْ أُوتِيتُمْ هَٰذَا فَخُذُوهُ وَإِن لَّمْ تُؤْتَوْهُ فَٱحْذَرُواْ ۚ وَمَن يُرِدِ ٱللَّهُ فِتْنَتَهُۥ فَلَن تَمْلِكَ لَهُۥ مِنَ ٱللَّهِ شَيْـًٔا ۚ أُوْلَٰٓئِكَ ٱلَّذِينَ لَمْ يُرِدِ ٱللَّهُ أَن يُطَهِّرَ قُلُوبَهُمْ ۚ لَهُمْ فِى ٱلدُّنْيَا خِزْىٌ ۖ وَلَهُمْ فِى ٱلْءَاخِرَةِ عَذَابٌ عَظِيمٌ ﴿٤١﴾

41. O Messenger (Muhammad (peace be upon him))! Let not those who hurry to fall into disbelief grieve you, of such who say: "We believe" with their mouths but their hearts have no faith. And of the Jews are men who listen much and eagerly to lies - listen to others who have not come to you. They change the words from their places; they say, "If you are given this, take it, but if you are not given this, then beware!" And whomsoever Allâh wants to put in Al-Fitnah (error, because of his rejecting of Faith), you can do nothing for him against Allâh. Those are the ones whose hearts Allâh does not want to purify (from disbelief and hypocrisy); for them there is a disgrace in this world, and in the Hereafter a great torment.

$$\begin{array}{c}
\text{﴿ سَمَّاعُونَ لِلْكَذِبِ أَكَّالُونَ لِلسُّحْتِ ۚ فَإِن جَاءُوكَ فَٱحْكُم بَيْنَهُمْ أَوْ أَعْرِضْ} \\
\text{عَنْهُمْ ۖ وَإِن تُعْرِضْ عَنْهُمْ فَلَن يَضُرُّوكَ شَيْئًا ۖ وَإِنْ حَكَمْتَ فَٱحْكُم بَيْنَهُم بِٱلْقِسْطِ ۚ} \\
\text{إِنَّ ٱللَّهَ يُحِبُّ ٱلْمُقْسِطِينَ ۝ ﴾}
\end{array}$$

42. (They like to) listen to falsehood, to devour anything forbidden. So if they come to you (O Muhammad (peace be upon him)) either judge between them, or turn away from them. If you turn away from them, they cannot hurt you in the least. And if you judge, judge with justice between them. Verily, Allâh loves those who act justly.

$$\text{﴿ وَكَيْفَ يُحَكِّمُونَكَ وَعِندَهُمُ ٱلتَّوْرَىٰةُ فِيهَا حُكْمُ ٱللَّهِ ثُمَّ يَتَوَلَّوْنَ مِنۢ بَعْدِ ذَٰلِكَ ۚ وَمَا أُو۟لَـٰٓئِكَ بِٱلْمُؤْمِنِينَ ۝ ﴾}$$

43. But how do they come to you for decision while they have the Taurât (Torah), in which is the (plain) Decision of Allâh; yet even after that, they turn away. For they are not (really) believers.

$$\text{﴿ إِنَّآ أَنزَلْنَا ٱلتَّوْرَىٰةَ فِيهَا هُدًى وَنُورٌ ۚ يَحْكُمُ بِهَا ٱلنَّبِيُّونَ ٱلَّذِينَ أَسْلَمُوا۟ لِلَّذِينَ هَادُوا۟ وَٱلرَّبَّـٰنِيُّونَ وَٱلْأَحْبَارُ بِمَا ٱسْتُحْفِظُوا۟ مِن كِتَـٰبِ ٱللَّهِ وَكَانُوا۟ عَلَيْهِ شُهَدَآءَ ۚ فَلَا تَخْشَوُا۟ ٱلنَّاسَ وَٱخْشَوْنِ وَلَا تَشْتَرُوا۟ بِـَٔايَـٰتِى ثَمَنًا قَلِيلًا ۚ وَمَن لَّمْ يَحْكُم بِمَآ أَنزَلَ ٱللَّهُ فَأُو۟لَـٰٓئِكَ هُمُ ٱلْكَـٰفِرُونَ ۝ ﴾}$$

44. Verily, We did send down the Taurât (Torah) (to Mûsâ (Moses)) therein was guidance and light, by which the Prophets, who submitted themselves to Allâh's Will, judged for the Jews. And the rabbis and the priests (too judged for the Jews by the Taurât (Torah) after those Prophets), for to them was entrusted the protection of Allâh's Book, and they were witnesses thereto. Therefore fear not men but fear Me (O Jews) and sell not My Verses for a miserable price. And whosoever does not judge by what Allâh has revealed, such are the Kâfirûn (i.e. disbelievers - of a lesser degree as they do not act on Allâh's Laws).

Transliteration

41. Ya ayyuha alrrasoolu la yahzunka allatheena yusariAAoona fee alkufri mina allatheena qaloo amanna bi-afwahihim walam tu/min quloobuhum wamina allatheena hadoo sammaAAoona lilkathibi sammaAAoona liqawmin akhareena lam ya/tooka yuharrifoona alkalima min baAAdi mawadiAAihi yaqooloona in ooteetum hatha fakhuthoohu wa-in lam tu/tawhu faihtharoo waman yuridi Allahu fitnatahu falan tamlika lahu mina Allahi shay-an ola-ika allatheena lam yuridi Allahu an yutahhira quloobahum lahum fee alddunya khizyun walahum fee al-akhirati AAathabun AAatheemun 42. SammaAAoona lilkathibi akkaloona lilssuhti fa-in jaooka faohkum

baynahum aw aAArid AAanhum wa-in tuAArid AAanhum falan yadurrooka shay-an wa-in hakamta faohkum baynahum bialqisti inna Allaha yuhibbu almuqsiteena 43. Wakayfa yuhakkimoonaka waAAindahumu alttawratu feeha hukmu Allahi thumma yatawallawna min baAAdi thalika wama ola-ika bialmu/mineena 44. Inna anzalna alttawrata feeha hudan wanoorun yahkumu biha alnnabiyyoona allatheena aslamoo lillatheena hadoo waalrrabbaniyyoona waal-ahbaru bima istuhfithoo min kitabi Allahi wakanoo AAalayhi shuhadaa fala takhshawoo alnnasa waikhshawni wala tashtaroo bi-ayatee thamanan qaleelan waman lam yahkum bima anzala Allahu faola-ika humu alkafiroona

Tafsir Ibn Kathir

Do Not Feel Sad Because of the Behavior of the Jews and Hypocrites

These honorable Ayat were revealed about those who rush into disbelief, deviating from the obedience of Allah, His Messenger, prefering their opinions and lusts to what Allah has legislated,

(of such who say, "We believe" with their mouths but their hearts have no faith.) These people pretend to be faithful with their words, but their hearts are empty from faith, and they are the hypocrites.

(And of the Jews...) the enemies of Islam and its people, they and the hypocrites all,

(listen much and eagerly to lies...) and they accept and react to it positively,

(listening to others who have not come to you,) meaning, they listen to some people who do not attend your meetings, O Muhammad. Or, the Ayah might mean, they listen to what you say and convey it to your enemies who do not attend your audience.

The Jews Alter and Change the Law, Such As Stoning the Adulterer

(They change the words from their places:) by altering their meanings and knowingly distorting them after they comprehended them,

(they say, "If you are given this, take it, but if you are not given this, then beware!") It was reported that this part of the Ayah was revealed about some Jews who committed murder and who said to each other, "Let us ask Muhammad to judge between us, and if he decides that we pay the Diyah, accept his judgement. If he decides on capital punishment, do not accept his judgement." The correct opinion is that this Ayah was revealed about the two Jews who committed adultery. The Jews changed the law they had in their Book from Allah on the matter of punishment for adultery, from stoning to death, to a hundred flogs and making the offenders ride a donkey facing the back of the donkey. When this incident of adultery occurred after the Hijrah, they said to each other, "Let us go to Muhammad and seek his judgement. If he gives a ruling of flogging, then implement his decision and make it a proof for you with Allah. This way, one of Allah's Prophets will have upheld this ruling amongst you. But if he decides that the punishment should be stoning to death, then do not accept his decision." There are several Hadiths mentioning this story. Malik reported

Chapter 5: Al-Maidah (The Table, The Table Spread), Verses 001-081   125

that Nafi` said that `Abdullah bin `Umar said, "The Jews came to Allah's Messenger and mentioned that a man and a woman from them committed adultery. Allah's Messenger said to them,

«مَا تَجِدُونَ فِي التَّوْرَاةِ فِي شَأْنِ الرَّجْمِ؟»

(What do find of the ruling about stoning in the Tawrah) They said, `We only find that they should be exposed and flogged.' `Abdullah bin Salam said, `You lie. The Tawrah mentions stoning, so bring the Tawrah.' They brought the Tawrah and opened it but one of them hid the verse about stoning with his hand and recited what is before and after that verse. `Abdullah bin Salam said to him, `Remove your hand,' and he removed it, thus uncovering the verse about stoning. So they said, He (`Abdullah bin Salam) has said the truth, O Muhammad! It is the verse about stoning.' The Messenger of Allah decided that the adulterers be stoned to death and his command was carried out. I saw that man shading the woman from the stones with his body." Al-Bukhari and Muslim also collected this Hadith and this is the wording collected by Al-Bukhari. In another narration by Al-Bukhari, the Prophet said to the Jews,

«مَا تَصْنَعُونَ بِهِمَا؟»

(What would you do in this case) They said, "We would humiliate and expose them." The Prophet recited,

(Bring here the Tawrah and recite it, if you are truthful.) So they brought a man who was blind in one eye and who was respected among them and said to him, "Read (from the Tawrah)." So he read until he reached a certain verse and then covered it with his hand. He was told, "Remove your hand," and it was the verse about stoning. So that man said, "O Muhammad! This is the verse about stoning, and we had hid its knowledge among us." So the Messenger ordered that the two adulterers be stoned, and they were stoned. Muslim recorded that a Jewish man and a Jewish woman were brought before Allah's Messenger because they committed adultery. The Messenger of Allah went to the Jews and asked them,

«مَا تَجِدُونَ فِي التَّوْرَاةِ عَلَى مَنْ زَنَى؟»

(What is the ruling that you find in the Tawrah for adultery) hThey said, "We expose them, carry them (on donkeys) backwards and parade them in public." The Prophet recited;

(Bring here the Tawrah and recite it, if you are truthful.) So they brought the Tawrah and read from it until the reader reached the verse about stoning. Then he placed his hand on that verse and read what was before and after it. `Abdullah bin Salam, who was with the Messenger of Allah , said, "Order him to remove his hand," and he removed his hand and under it was the verse about stoning. So the Messenger of Allah commanded that the adulterers be stoned, and they were stoned. `Abdullah bin

`Umar said, "I was among those who stoned them and I saw the man shading the woman from the stones with his body." Abu Dawud recorded that Ibn `Umar said, "Some Jews came to the Messenger of Allah and invited him to go to the Quff area. So he went to the house of Al-Midras and they said, `O Abu Al-Qasim! A man from us committed adultery with a woman, so decide on their matter.' They arranged a pillow for the Messenger of Allah and he sat on it and said,

»ائْتُونِي بِالتَّوْرَاةِ«

(Bring the Tawrah to me.) He was brought the Tawrah and he removed the pillow from under him and placed the Tawrah on it, saying,

»آمَنْتُ بِكِ وَبِمَنْ أَنْزَلَكِ«

(I trust you and He Who revealed it to you.) He then said,

»ائْتُونِي بِأَعْلَمِكُمْ«

(Bring me your most knowledgeable person.) So he was brought a young man..." and then he mentioned the rest of the story that Malik narrated from Nafi`. These Hadiths state that the Messenger of Allah issued a decision that conforms with the ruling in the Tawrah, not to honor the Jews in what they believe in, for the Jews were commanded to follow the Law of Muhammad only. Rather, the Prophet did this because Allah commanded him to do so. He asked them about the ruling of stoning in the Tawrah to make them admit to what the Tawrah contains and what they collaborated to hide, deny and exclude from implementing for all that time. They had to admit to what they did, although they did it while having knowledge of the correct ruling. What made them go to the Prophet for judgement in this matter was their lusts and desires, hoping that the Prophet would agree with their opinion, not that they believed in the correctness of his judgment. This is why they said,

(If you are given this,) referring to flogging, then take it,

(but if you are not given this, then beware!) and do not accept or implement it. Allah said next,

(And whomsoever Allah wants to put in Fitnah, you can do nothing for him against Allah. Those are the ones whose hearts Allah does not want to purify; for them there is a disgrace in this world, and in the Hereafter a great torment. They (like to) listen to falsehood, to devour Suht) `Suht' refers to bribes, as Ibn Mas`ud and others stated. The Ayah states that if one is like this, how can Allah cleanse his heart and accept his supplication Allah said to His Prophet ,

(So if they come to you...) so that you judge between them,

(either judge between them, or turn away from them. If you turn away from them, they cannot hurt you in the least.) meaning, there is no harm if you do not judge between them. This is because when they came to you to judge between them, they did not seek to follow the truth, but only what conformed to their lusts. We should mention here that Ibn `Abbas, Mujahid, `Ikrimah, Al-Hasan, Qatadah, As-Suddi, Zayd bin Aslam, `Ata' Al-Khurasani, and several others said that this part of the Ayah was abrogated by Allah's statement,

(And so judge among them by what Allah has revealed.)

(And if you judge, judge with justice between them.) and with fairness, even if the Jews were unjust and outcasts from the path of fairness,

(Verily, Allah loves those who act justly.)

Chastising the Jews for Their Evil Lusts and Desires, While Praising the Tawrah

Allah then chastises the Jews for their false ideas and deviant desires to abandon what they believe is true in their Book, and which they claim is their eternal Law that they are always commanded to adhere to. Yet, they do not adhere to the Tawrah, but they prefer other laws over it, although they believe that these other laws are not correct and do not apply to them. Allah said,

(But how do they come to you for decision while they have the Tawrah, in which is the decision of Allah; yet even after that they turn away. For they are not believers.) Allah next praises the Tawrah that He sent down to His servant and Messenger Musa, son of `Imran,

(Verily, We did send down the Tawrah (to Musa), therein was guidance and light, by which the Prophets who submitted themselves to Allah's will, judged the Jews.) and these Prophets did not deviate from the law of the Tawrah, change or alter it,

(And (also) the Rabbaniyyun and the Ahbar...) wherein Rabbaniyyun refers to the worshippers who are learned and religious, and Ahbar refers to the scholars,

(for to them was entrusted the protection of Allah's Book,) meaning, they were entrusted with the Book of Allah, and they were commanded to adhere to it and not hide any part of,

(and they were witnesses thereto. Therefore fear not men but fear Me and sell not My verses for a miserable price. And whosoever does not judge by what Allah has revealed, such are the disbelievers.) There are two ways to explain this Ayah and we will mention the later.

Another Reason Behind Revealing these Honorable Ayat

Imam Ahmad recorded that Ibn `Abbas said, "Allah sent down the Ayat,

(And whosoever does not judge by what Allah has revealed, such are the disbelievers,)

(Such are the unjust,) and,

(Such are the rebellious.) about two groups among the Jews. During the time of Jahiliyyah, one of them had defeated the other. As a result, they made a treaty that they would pay blood money totaling fifty Wasaq (of gold) (each Wasaq approx. 3 kg) for every dead person from the defeated group killed by the victors, and a hundred Wasaq for every dead person the defeated group killed from the victors. This treaty remained in effect until the Prophet came to Al-Madinah and both of these groups became subservient under the Prophet . Yet, when the mighty group once suffered a casualty at the hands of the weaker group, the mighty group sent a delegation demanding the hundred Wasaq. The weaker group said, `How can two groups who have the same religion, one ancestral lineage and a common land, have a Diyah that for some of them is half of that of the others We only agreed to this because you oppressed us and because we feared you. Now that Muhammad has come, we will not give you what you asked.' So war was almost rekindled between them, but they agreed to seek Muhammad's judgement in their dispute. The mighty group among them said (among themselves), `By Allah! Muhammad will never give you double the Diyah that you pay to them compared to what they pay to you. They have said the truth anyway, for they only gave us this amount because we oppressed and overpowered them. Therefore, send someone to Muhammad who will sense what his judgement will be. If he agrees to give you what you demand, accept his judgment, and if he does not give you what you seek, do not refer to him for judgement.' So they sent some hypocrites to the Messenger of Allah to try and find out the Messenger's judgement. When they came to the Messenger , Allah informed him of their matter and of their plot. Allah sent down,

(O Messenger! Let not those who hurry to fall into disbelief grieve you,) until,

(Such are the rebellious.) By Allah! It is because of their problem that Allah sent down these verses and it is they whom Allah meant." Abu Dawud collected a similar narration for this Hadith. Abu Ja`far Ibn Jarir recorded that Ibn `Abbas said that the Ayah in Surat Al-Ma'idah,

(either judge between them, or turn away from them...) until,

(Those who act justly.) was revealed concerning the problem of blood money between Bani An-Nadir and Bani Qurayzah. The dead of Bani An-Nadir were being honored more and they received the full amount of Diyah, while Qurayzah received half the Diyah for their dead. So they referred to the Messenger of Allah for judgement and Allah sent down these verses about them. The Messenger of Allah compelled them to adhere to the true judgement in this matter and made the Diyah the same for both groups and Allah knows best about that matter." Ahmad, Abu Dawud and An-Nasa'i also recorded this Hadith from Abu Ishaq. Al-`Awfi and `Ali bin Abi Talhah reported that Ibn `Abbas said that these Ayat were revealed about the two Jews who committed adultery, and we mentioned the Hadiths about this story before.

It appears that both of these were the reasons behind revealing these Ayat, and Allah knows best. This is why Allah said afterwards,

(And We ordained therein for them: Life for life, eye for eye) until the end of the Ayah, which strengthens the opinion that the story of the Diyah was behind revealing the Ayat as we explained above. Allah knows best. Allah said,

(And whosoever does not judge by what Allah has revealed, such are the disbelievers.) Al-Bara' bin `Azib, Hudhayfah bin Al-Yaman, Ibn `Abbas, Abu Mijlaz, Abu Raja' Al-`Utaridi, `Ikrimah, `Ubaydullah bin `Abdullah, Al-Hasan Al-Basri and others said that this Ayah was revealed about the People of the Book. Al-Hasan Al-Basri added that this Ayah also applies to us. `Abdur-Razzaq said that Ath-Thawri said that Mansur said that Ibrahim said that these Ayat, "Were revealed about the Children of Israel, and Allah accepted them for this Ummah." Ibn Jarir recorded this statement. `Ali bin Abi Talhah also stated that Ibn `Abbas commented on Allah's statement,

(And whosoever does not judge by what Allah has revealed, such are the disbelievers,) "Whoever rejects what Allah has revealed, will have committed Kufr, and whoever accepts what Allah has revealed, but did not rule by it, is a Zalim (unjust) and a Fasiq (rebellious) and a sinner." Ibn Jarir recorded this statement. `Abdur-Razzaq said, "Ma`mar narrated to us that Tawus said that Ibn `Abbas was asked about Allah's statement,

(And whosoever does not judge...) He said, `It is an act of Kufr.' Ibn Tawus added, `It is not like those who disbelieve in Allah, His angels, His Books and His Messengers.' Ath-Thawri narrated that Ibn Jurayj said that `Ata' said, `There is Kufr and Kufr less than Kufr, Zulm and Zulm less than Zulm, Fisq and Fisq less than Fisq.'" Waki` said that Sa`id Al-Makki said that Tawus said that,

(And whosoever does not judge by what Allah has revealed, such are the disbelievers,) "This is not the Kufr that annuls one's religion."

Surah: 5 Ayah: 45

﴿ وَكَتَبْنَا عَلَيْهِمْ فِيهَا أَنَّ ٱلنَّفْسَ بِٱلنَّفْسِ وَٱلْعَيْنَ بِٱلْعَيْنِ وَٱلْأَنفَ بِٱلْأَنفِ وَٱلْأُذُنَ بِٱلْأُذُنِ وَٱلسِّنَّ بِٱلسِّنِّ وَٱلْجُرُوحَ قِصَاصٌ فَمَن تَصَدَّقَ بِهِۦ فَهُوَ كَفَّارَةٌ لَّهُۥ وَمَن لَّمْ يَحْكُم بِمَآ أَنزَلَ ٱللَّهُ فَأُو۟لَٰٓئِكَ هُمُ ٱلظَّٰلِمُونَ

45. And We ordained therein for them: "Life for life, eye for eye, nose for nose, ear for ear, tooth for tooth, and wounds equal for equal." But if anyone remits the retaliation by way of charity, it shall be for him an expiation. And whosoever does not judge by that which Allâh has revealed, such are the Zâlimûn (polytheists and wrong-doers - of a lesser degree).

Transliteration

45. Wakatabna AAalayhim feeha anna alnnafsa bialnnafsi waalAAayna bialAAayni waal-anfa bial-anfi waalothuna bialothuni waalssinna bialssinni waaljurooha qisasun faman tasaddaqa bihi fahuwa kaffaratun lahu waman lam yahkum bima anzala Allahu faola-ika humu alththalimoona

Tafsir Ibn Kathir

This Ayah also chastises and criticizes the Jews because in the Tawrah, they have the law of a life for a life. Yet, they defied this ruling by transgression and rebellion. They used to apply this ruling when a person from Bani An-Nadir was killed by a Qurayzah person, but this was not the case when the opposite occurred. Rather, they would revert to Diyah in this case. They also defied the ruling in the Tawrah to stone the adulterer and instead came up with their own form of punishment, flogging, humiliation and parading them in public. This is why Allah said in the previous Ayah, t

(And whosoever does not judge by what Allah has revealed, such are the disbelievers.) because they rejected Allah's command with full intention and with transgression and rebellion. In this Ayah, Allah said,

(such are the unjust.) because they did not exact the oppressed his due rights from the oppressor in a matter which Allah ordered that all be treated equally and fairly. Instead, they defied that command, committed injustice and transgressed against each other.

A Man is Killed for a Woman Whom He Kills

Imam Abu Nasr bin As-Sabbagh stated in his book, Ash-Shamil, that the scholars agree that this Ayah (5:45) should be implemented, and the Imams agree that the man is killed for a woman whom he kills, according to the general indications of this Ayah. A Hadith that An-Nasa'i recorded states that the Messenger of Allah had this statement written in the book that he gave `Amr bin Hazm,

»أَنَّ الرَّجُلَ يُقْتَلُ بِالْمَرْأَة«

(The man is killed for the woman (whom he kills).) In another Hadith, the Messenger said,

»الْمُسْلِمُونَ تَتَكَافَأُ دِمَاؤُهُم«

(Muslims are equal regarding the sanctity of their blood.) This is also the opinion of the majority of the scholars. What further supports what Ibn As-Sabbagh said is the Hadith that Imam Ahmad recorded that Anas bin Malik said, "Ar-Rabi` (his aunt) broke the tooth of a girl, and the relatives of Ar-Rabi` requested the girl's relatives to forgive (the offender), but they refused. So, they went to the Prophet who ordered them to bring about retaliation. Anas bin An-Nadr, her brother, asked, `O Allah's Messenger! Will the tooth of Ar-Rabi` be broken' The Messenger of Allah said, `O

Anas! The Book of Allah prescribes retaliation.' Anas said, `No, by Him Who has sent you with the Truth, her tooth will not be broken.' Later the relatives of the girl agreed to forgive Ar-Rabi` and forfeit their right to retaliation. The Messenger of Allah said,

«إن من عباد الله من لو أقسم على الله لأبره»

(There are some of Allah's servants who, if they take an oath by Allah, Allah fullfils them.)" It was recorded in the Two Sahihs.

Retaliation for Wounds

Allah said,

(and wounds equal for equal.) `Ali bin Abi Talhah reported that Ibn `Abbas said, "Life for life, an eye for an eye, a nose, if cut off, for a nose, a tooth broken for a tooth and wounds equal for wound." The free Muslims, men and women, are equal in this matter. And their slaves, male and female, are equal in this matter. And this ruling is the same regarding intentional murder and lesser offenses, as Ibn Jarir and Ibn Abi Hatim recorded.

An Important Ruling

The retaliation for wounds should not be implemented until the wounds of the victim heal. If retaliation occurs before the wound heals, and then the wound becomes aggravated, the victim will have no additional rights in this case. The proof for this ruling is what Imam Ahmad narrated from `Amr bin Shu`ayb, from his father, from his grandfather that a man once stabbed another man in his leg using a horn. The victim came to the Prophet asking for retaliation, and the Prophet said,

«حَتَّى تَبْرَأَ»

(Not until you heal.) The man again came to the Prophet and asked for equality in retaliation and the Prophet allowed him that. Later on, that man said, "O Messenger of Allah! I limp now." The Messenger said,

«قَدْ نَهَيْتُكَ فَعَصَيْتَنِي، فَأَبْعَدَكَ اللهُ وَبَطَلَ عَرَجُكَ»

(I had asked you to wait, but you disobeyed me. Therefore, Allah cast you away and your limp has no compensation.) Afterwards, the Messenger of Allah forbade that the wound be retaliated for until the wound of the victim heals. If the victim is allowed to retaliate for his wound caused by the aggressor and the aggressor dies as a result, there is no compensation in this case, according to the majority of the Companions and their followers.

The Pardon is Expiation for Such Offenses

Allah said,

(But if anyone remits the retaliation by way of charity, it shall be for him an expiation.) `Ali bin Abi Talhah reported that Ibn `Abbas commented that

(But if anyone remits the retaliation by way of charity) means; "If one pardons by way of charity, it will result in expiation for the aggressor and reward for the victim." Sufyan Ath-Thawri said that `Ata' bin As-Sa'ib said that Sa`id bin Jubayr said that Ibn `Abbas said, `He who pardons the retaliation by way of charity, it will be an expiation for the aggressor and a reward for the victim with Allah." Ibn Abi Hatim recorded this statement. Jabir bin `Abdullah said that Allah's statement,

(But if anyone remits the retaliation by way of charity, it shall be for him an expiation,) "For the victim." This is also the opinion of Al-Hasan Al-Basri, Ibrahim An-Nakha`i and Abu Ishaq Al-Hamdani. Imam Ahmad recorded that `Ubadah bin As-Samit said, "I heard the Messenger of Allah saying,

«مَا مِنْ رَجُلٍ يُجْرَحُ مِنْ جَسَدِهِ جَرَاحَةً فَيَتَصَدَّقُ بِهَا، إِلَّا كَفَّرَ اللهُ عَنْهُ مِثْلَ مَا تَصَدَّقَ بِهِ»

(Any man who suffers a wound on his body and forfeits his right of retaliation as way of charity, then Allah will pardon him that which is similar to what he forfeited.) An-Nasa'i and Ibn Jarir recorded this Hadith. Allah's statement,

(And whosoever does not judge by that which Allah has revealed, such are the unjust.) Earlier we mentioned the statements of `Ata' and Tawus that there is Kufr and lesser Kufr, injustice and lesser injustice and Fisq and lesser Fisq.

Surah: 5 Ayah: 46 & Ayah: 47

﴿ وَقَفَّيْنَا عَلَىٰ ءَاثَٰرِهِم بِعِيسَى ٱبْنِ مَرْيَمَ مُصَدِّقًا لِّمَا بَيْنَ يَدَيْهِ مِنَ ٱلتَّوْرَىٰةِ وَءَاتَيْنَٰهُ ٱلْإِنجِيلَ فِيهِ هُدًى وَنُورٌ وَمُصَدِّقًا لِّمَا بَيْنَ يَدَيْهِ مِنَ ٱلتَّوْرَىٰةِ وَهُدًى وَمَوْعِظَةً لِّلْمُتَّقِينَ ﴾

46. And in their footsteps, We sent 'Isâ (Jesus), son of Maryam (Mary), confirming the Taurât (Torah) that had come before him, and We gave him the Injeel (Gospel), in which was guidance and light and confirmation of the Taurât (Torah) that had come before it, a guidance and an admonition for Al-Muttaqûn (the pious - see V.2:2).

Chapter 5: Al-Maidah (The Table, The Table Spread), Verses 001-081

﴿ وَلْيَحْكُمْ أَهْلُ ٱلْإِنجِيلِ بِمَآ أَنزَلَ ٱللَّهُ فِيهِ ۚ وَمَن لَّمْ يَحْكُم بِمَآ أَنزَلَ ٱللَّهُ فَأُوْلَٰٓئِكَ هُمُ ٱلْفَٰسِقُونَ ﴾

47. Let the people of the Injeel (Gospel) judge by what Allâh has revealed therein. And whosoever does not judge by what Allâh has revealed (then) such (people) are the Fâsiqûn (the rebellious i.e. disobedient (of a lesser degree)) to Allâh.

Transliteration

46. Waqaffayna AAala atharihim biAAeesa ibni maryama musaddiqan lima bayna yadayhi mina alttawrati waataynahu al-injeela feehi hudan wanoorun wamusaddiqan lima bayna yadayhi mina alttawrati wahudan wamawAAithatan lilmuttaqeena 47. Walyahkum ahlu al-injeeli bima anzala Allahu feehi waman lam yahkum bima anzala Allahu faola-ika humu alfasiqoona

Tafsir Ibn Kathir

Allah Mentions `Isa and Praises the Injil

Allah said,

(and We sent...) meaning, We sent

(in their footsteps) meaning the Prophets of the Children of Israel,

(`Isa, son of Maryam, confirming the Tawrah that had come before him,) meaning, he believed in it and ruled by it.

(and We gave him the Injil, in which was guidance and light) a guidance that directs to the truth and a light that removes the doubts and solves disputes,

(and confirmation of the Tawrah that had come before it,) meaning, he adhered to the Tawrah, except for the few instances that clarified the truth where the Children of Israel differed. Allah states in another Ayah that `Isa said to the Children of Israel,

(. ..and to make lawful to you part of what was forbidden to you.) So the scholars say that the Injil abrogated some of the rulings of the Tawrah. Allah's statement,

(a guidance and an admonition for those who have Taqwa.) means, We made the Injil guidance and an admonition that prohibits committing sins and errors, for those who have Taqwa of Allah and fear His warning and torment. Allah said next,

(Let the people of the Injil judge by what Allah has revealed therein.) meaning, so that He judges the people of the Injil by it in their time. Or, the Ayah means, so that they believe in all that is in it and adhere to all its commands, including the good news about the coming of Muhammad and the command to believe in and follow him when he is sent. Allah said in other Ayat,

(Say "O People of the Scripture! You have nothing (guidance) until you act according to the Tawrah, the Injil, and what has been sent down to you from your Lord.") and,

(Those who follow the Messenger, the Prophet who can neither read nor write whom they find written with them in the Tawrah...) until,

(...successful.) Here, Allah said,

(And whosoever does not judge by what Allah has revealed, such are the rebellious.) meaning, the rebellious and disobedient of Allah who prefer falsehood and abandon truth. We mentioned before that this Ayah was revealed about the Christians, and this is evident from the context of the Ayah.

Surah: 5 Ayah: 48, Ayah: 49 & Ayah: 50

﴿ وَأَنزَلْنَا إِلَيْكَ ٱلْكِتَـٰبَ بِٱلْحَقِّ مُصَدِّقًا لِّمَا بَيْنَ يَدَيْهِ مِنَ ٱلْكِتَـٰبِ وَمُهَيْمِنًا عَلَيْهِ ۖ فَٱحْكُم بَيْنَهُم بِمَآ أَنزَلَ ٱللَّهُ ۖ وَلَا تَتَّبِعْ أَهْوَآءَهُمْ عَمَّا جَآءَكَ مِنَ ٱلْحَقِّ ۚ لِكُلٍّ جَعَلْنَا مِنكُمْ شِرْعَةً وَمِنْهَاجًا ۚ وَلَوْ شَآءَ ٱللَّهُ لَجَعَلَكُمْ أُمَّةً وَٰحِدَةً وَلَـٰكِن لِّيَبْلُوَكُمْ فِى مَآ ءَاتَىٰكُمْ ۖ فَٱسْتَبِقُوا۟ ٱلْخَيْرَٰتِ ۚ إِلَى ٱللَّهِ مَرْجِعُكُمْ جَمِيعًا فَيُنَبِّئُكُم بِمَا كُنتُمْ فِيهِ تَخْتَلِفُونَ ۞ ﴾

48. And We have sent down to you (O Muhammad (peace be upon him)) the Book (this Qur'ân) in truth, confirming the Scripture that came before it and Muhaymin (trustworthy in highness and a witness) over it (old Scriptures). So judge among them by what Allâh has revealed, and follow not their vain desires, diverging away from the truth that has come to you. To each among you, We have prescribed a law and a clear way. If Allâh had willed, He would have made you one nation, but that (He) may test you in what He has given you; so compete in good deeds. The return of you (all) is to Allâh; then He will inform you about that in which you used to differ.

﴿ وَأَنِ ٱحْكُم بَيْنَهُم بِمَآ أَنزَلَ ٱللَّهُ وَلَا تَتَّبِعْ أَهْوَآءَهُمْ وَٱحْذَرْهُمْ أَن يَفْتِنُوكَ عَنۢ بَعْضِ مَآ أَنزَلَ ٱللَّهُ إِلَيْكَ ۖ فَإِن تَوَلَّوْا۟ فَٱعْلَمْ أَنَّمَا يُرِيدُ ٱللَّهُ أَن يُصِيبَهُم بِبَعْضِ ذُنُوبِهِمْ ۗ وَإِنَّ كَثِيرًا مِّنَ ٱلنَّاسِ لَفَـٰسِقُونَ ۞ ﴾

49. And so judge (you O Muhammad (peace be upon him)) among them by what Allâh has revealed and follow not their vain desires, but beware of them lest they turn you (O Muhammad (peace be upon him)) far away from some of that which Allâh has sent down to you. And if they turn away, then know that Allâh's Will is to punish them for some sins of theirs. And truly, most of men are Fâsiqûn (rebellious and disobedient to Allâh).

﴿ أَفَحُكْمَ ٱلْجَـٰهِلِيَّةِ يَبْغُونَ ۚ وَمَنْ أَحْسَنُ مِنَ ٱللَّهِ حُكْمًا لِّقَوْمٍ يُوقِنُونَ ۞ ﴾

50. Do they then seek the judgement of (the Days of) Ignorance? And who is better in judgement than Allâh for a people who have firm Faith.

Transliteration

48. Waanzalna ilayka alkitaba bialhaqqi musaddiqan lima bayna yadayhi mina alkitabi wamuhayminan AAalayhi faohkum baynahum bima anzala Allahu wala tattabiAA ahwaahum AAamma jaaka mina alhaqqi likullin jaAAalna minkum shirAAatan waminhajan walaw shaa Allahu lajaAAalakum ommatan wahidatan walakin liyabluwakum feema atakum faistabiqoo alkhayrati ila Allahi marjiAAukum jameeAAan fayunabbi-okum bima kuntum feehi takhtalifoona 49. Waani ohkum baynahum bima anzala Allahu wala tattabiAA ahwaahum waihtharhum an yaftinooka AAan baAAdi ma anzala Allahu ilayka fa-in tawallaw faiAAlam annama yureedu Allahu an yuseebahum bibaAAdi thunoobihim wa-inna katheeran mina alnnasi lafasiqoona 50. Afahukma aljahiliyyati yabghoona waman ahsanu mina Allahu hukman liqawmin yooqinoona

Tafsir Ibn Kathir

Praising the Qur'an; the Command to Refer to the Qur'an for Judgment

Allah mentioned the Tawrah that He sent down to His Prophet Musa, the one whom He spoke directly to, praising it, commanding that it should be implemented, before it was abrogated. Allah then mentioned the Injil, praised it and commanded its people to adhere to it and follow it, as we stated. He next mentioned the Glorious Qur'an that He sent down to His honorable servant and Messenger. Allah said,

(And We have sent down to you the Book in truth...) meaning, with the truth that, no doubt, is coming from Allah,

(confirming the Scripture that came before it) meaning, the Divinely Revealed Books that praised the Qur'an and mentioned that it would be sent down from Allah to His servant and Messenger Muhammad . The Qur'an was revealed as was foretold in the previous Scriptures. This fact increased faith in the previous Scriptures for the sincere who have knowledge of these Scriptures, those who adhered to Allah's commands and Laws and believed in His Messengers. Allah said,

(Say: "Believe in it or do not believe (in it). Verily, those who were given knowledge before it, when it is recited to them, fall down on their faces in humble prostration." And they say: "Glory be to our Lord! Truly, the promise of our Lord must be fulfilled.") meaning that they say, the promise of our Lord, concerning the coming of Muhammad by the words of His previous Messengers, will certainly be fulfilled. Allah's statement,

(and Muhayminan over it) means entrusted over it, according to Sufyan Ath-Thawri who narrated it from Abu Ishaq from At-Tamimi from Ibn `Abbas. `Ali bin Abi Talhah reported that Ibn `Abbas said, "Muhaymin is, `the Trustworthy'. Allah says that the Qur'an is trustworthy over every Divine Book that preceded it." This was reported from `Ikrimah, Sa`id bin Jubayr, Mujahid, Muhammad bin Ka`b, `Atiyyah, Al-Hasan, Qatadah, `Ata' Al-Khurasani, As-Suddi and Ibn Zayd. Ibn Jarir said, "The Qur'an is trustworthy over the Books that preceded it. Therefore, whatever in these previous Books conforms to the Qur'an is true, and whatever disagrees with the Qur'an is false." Al-Walibi said that Ibn `Abbas said that Muhayminan means, `Witness'. Mujahid, Qatadah and As-Suddi said the same. Al-`Awfi said that Ibn `Abbas said that Muhayminan means, `dominant over the previous Scriptures'. These meanings are similar, as the word Muhaymin includes them all. Consequently, the Qur'an is trustworthy, a witness, and dominant over every Scripture that preceded it. This Glorious Book, which Allah revealed as the Last and Final Book, is the most encompassing, glorious and perfect Book of all times. The Qur'an includes all the good aspects of previous Scriptures and even more, which no previous Scripture ever contained. This is why Allah made it trustworthy, a witness and dominant over all Scriptures. Allah promised that He will protect the Qur'an and swore by His Most Honorable Self,

(Verily, We, it is We Who have sent down the Dhikr and surely, We will guard it (from corruption).) Allah said,

(So judge between them by what Allah has revealed.) The Ayah commands: O Muhammad! Rule between the people, Arabs and non-Arabs, lettered and unlettered, by what Allah has revealed to you in this Glorious Book and what it approves of for you from the Law of the previous Prophets, as Ibn Jarir said. Ibn Abi Hatim reported that Ibn `Abbas said, "The Prophet had the choice to judge between them or to turn away from them and refer them to their own Law. Then this Ayah was revealed,

(So judge between them by what Allah has revealed, and follow not their vain desires. ..) and he was commanded to judge between them by our Book.". Allah's statement

(and follow not their vain desires...) This means the ideas they promote, because of which they turned away from what Allah revealed to His Messengers. This is why Allah said,

(And follow not their vain desires, diverging away from the truth that has come to you.) The Ayah commands: Do not diverge from the truth that Allah has ordained for you, to the vain desires of these miserable, ignorant people. Allah's statement,

(To each among you, We have prescribed a law and a clear way.)

(To each among you, We have prescribed a law) Shir`at meaning, a clear path, as Ibn Abi Hatim recorded from Ibn `Abbas.

(If Allah willed, He would have made you one nation.) This is a general proclamation to all nations informing them of Allah's mighty ability. If Allah wills, He would make all mankind follow one religion and one Law, that would never be abrogated. Allah decided that every Prophet would have his own distinct law that is later abrogated partially or totally with the law of a latter Prophet. Later on, all previous laws were abrogated by the Law that Allah sent with Muhammad , His servant and Messenger, whom Allah sent to the people of earth as the Final Prophet. Allah said,

(If Allah willed, He would have made you one nation, but that (He) may test you in what He has given you.) This Ayah means, Allah has instituted different laws to test His servants' obedience to what He legislates for them, thus, He rewards or punishes them according to their actions and what they intend. `Abdullah bin Kathir said that the Ayah,

(In what He has given you.) means, of the Book. Next, Allah encouraged rushing to perform good deeds,

(so strive as in a race in good deeds.) which are obedience to Allah, following His Law that abrogated the laws that came before it, and believing in His Book, the Qur'an, which is the Final Book that He revealed. Allah said next,

(The return of you (all) is to Allah;) Therefore, O people, your return and final destination is to Allah on the Day of Resurrection,

(then He will inform you about that in which you used to differ.) Allah will inform you about the truth in which you used to differ and will reward the sincere, as compensation for their sincerity, and will punish the disbelieving, rebellious people who rejected the truth and deviated from it to other paths, without proof or evidence to justify their actions. Rather, they have rejected the clear evidences, unequivocal proofs and established signs. Ad-Dahhak said that,

(So strive as in a race in good deeds.) is directed at the Ummah of Muhammad , but the first view is more apparent. Allah's statement,

(And so judge between them by what Allah has revealed and follow not their vain desires,) emphasizes this command and forbids ignoring it. Allah said next,

(but beware of them lest they turn you far away from some of that which Allah has sent down to you.) meaning; beware of the Jews, your enemies, lest they distort the truth for you in what they convey to you. Therefore, do not be deceived by them, for they are liars, treacherous and disbelievers.

(And if they turn away,) from the judgement that you pass in their disputes, and they defy Allah's Law,

(then know that Allah's will is to punish them for some sins of theirs.) meaning, know that this will occur according to the decree of Allah, and because out of His wisdom they have deviated from the truth, and because of their previous sins.

(And truly, most men are rebellious.) Therefore, the majority of humans are disobedient to their Lord, defiant of the truth and deviate away from it. Allah said in other Ayat,

(And most people will not believe even if you desire it eagerly,) and,

(And if you obey most of those on the earth they will mislead you far away from Allah's path.) Muhammad bin Ishaq reported that Ibn `Abbas said, "Ka`b bin Asad, Ibn Saluba, `Abdullah bin Surya and Shas bin Qays said to each other, `Let us go to Muhammad to try and misguide him from his religion.' So they went to the Prophet and said, `O Muhammad! You know that we are the scholars, noblemen and chiefs of the Jews. If we follow you, the Jews will follow suit and will not contradict us. But, there is enmity between us and some of our people, so we will refer to you for judgement in this matter, and you should rule in our favor against them and we will believe in you.' The Messenger of Allah refused the offer and Allah sent down these Ayat about them,

(And so judge between them by what Allah has revealed and follow not their vain desires, but beware of them lest they turn you far away from some of that which Allah has sent down to you.) until,

(for a people who have firm faith.)" Ibn Jarir and Ibn Abi Hatim recorded this Hadith. Allah continues,

(Do they then seek the judgement of (the days of) ignorance And who is better in judgement than Allah for a people who have firm faith) Allah criticizes those who ignore Allah's commandments, which include every type of righteous good thing and prohibit every type of evil, but they refer instead to opinions, desires and customs that people themselves invented, all of which have no basis in Allah's religion. During the time of Jahiliyyah, the people used to abide by the misguidance and ignorance that they invented by sheer opinion and lusts. The Tatar (Mongols) abided by the law that they inherited from their king Genghis Khan who wrote Al-Yasiq, for them. This book contains some rulings that were derived from various religions, such as Judaism, Christianity and Islam. Many of these rulings were derived from his own opinion and desires. Later on, these rulings became the followed law among his children, preferring them to the Law of the Book of Allah and the Sunnah of His Messenger . Therefore, whoever does this, he is a disbeliever who deserves to be fought against, until he reverts to Allah's and His Messenger's decisions, so that no law, minor or major, is referred to except by His Law. Allah said,

(Do they then seek the judgement of (the days of) ignorance) meaning, they desire and want this and ignore Allah's judgement,

(And who is better in judgement than Allah for a people who have firm faith) Who is more just in decision than Allah for those who comprehend Allah's Law, believe in Him, who are certain that Allah is the best among those who give decisions and that He is more merciful with His creation than the mother with her own child Allah has perfect knowledge of everything, is able to do all things, and He is just in all matters. Al-Hafiz Abu Al-Qasim At-Tabarani recorded that Ibn `Abbas said that the Messenger of Allah said,

«أَبْغَضُ النَّاسِ إِلَى اللهِ عَزَّ وَجَلَّ، مَنْ يَبْتَغِي فِي الْإِسْلَامِ سُنَّةَ الْجَاهِلِيَّةِ، وَطَالِبُ دَمِ امْرِىءٍ بِغَيْرِ حَقَ لِيُرِيقَ دَمَه»

(The most hated person to Allah is the Muslim who seeks the ways of the days of ignorance and he who seeks to shed the blood of a person without justification.) Al-Bukhari recorded Abu Al-Yaman narrating a similar Hadith, with some addition.

Surah: 5 Ayah: 51, Ayah: 52 & Ayah: 53

﴿ يَـٰٓأَيُّهَا ٱلَّذِينَ ءَامَنُوا۟ لَا تَتَّخِذُوا۟ ٱلْيَهُودَ وَٱلنَّصَـٰرَىٰٓ أَوْلِيَآءَ ۘ بَعْضُهُمْ أَوْلِيَآءُ بَعْضٍ ۚ وَمَن يَتَوَلَّهُم مِّنكُمْ فَإِنَّهُۥ مِنْهُمْ ۗ إِنَّ ٱللَّهَ لَا يَهْدِى ٱلْقَوْمَ ٱلظَّـٰلِمِينَ ﴿٥١﴾ ﴾

51. O you who believe! Take not the Jews and the Christians as Auliyâ' (friends, protectors, helpers), they are but Auliyâ' of one another. And if any amongst you takes them (as Auliyâ'), then surely he is one of them. Verily, Allâh guides not those people who are the Zâlimûn (polytheists and wrong-doers and unjust).

﴿ فَتَرَى ٱلَّذِينَ فِى قُلُوبِهِم مَّرَضٌ يُسَـٰرِعُونَ فِيهِمْ يَقُولُونَ نَخْشَىٰٓ أَن تُصِيبَنَا دَآئِرَةٌ ۚ فَعَسَى ٱللَّهُ أَن يَأْتِىَ بِٱلْفَتْحِ أَوْ أَمْرٍ مِّنْ عِندِهِۦ فَيُصْبِحُوا۟ عَلَىٰ مَآ أَسَرُّوا۟ فِىٓ أَنفُسِهِمْ نَـٰدِمِينَ ﴿٥٢﴾ ﴾

52. And you see those in whose hearts there is a disease (of hypocrisy), they hurry to their friendship, saying: "We fear lest some misfortune of a disaster may befall us." Perhaps Allâh may bring a victory or a decision according to His Will. Then they will become regretful for what they have been keeping as a secret in themselves.

﴿ وَيَقُولُ ٱلَّذِينَ ءَامَنُوٓا۟ أَهَـٰٓؤُلَآءِ ٱلَّذِينَ أَقْسَمُوا۟ بِٱللَّهِ جَهْدَ أَيْمَـٰنِهِمْ ۙ إِنَّهُمْ لَمَعَكُمْ ۚ حَبِطَتْ أَعْمَـٰلُهُمْ فَأَصْبَحُوا۟ خَـٰسِرِينَ ﴿٥٣﴾ ﴾

53. And those who believe will say: "Are these the men (hypocrites) who swore their strongest oaths by Allâh that they were with you (Muslims)?" All that they did has been in vain (because of their hypocrisy), and they have become the losers.

Transliteration

51. Ya ayyuha allatheena amanoo la tattakhithoo alyahooda waalnnasara awliyaa baAAduhum awliyao baAAdin waman yatawallahum minkum fa-innahu minhum inna Allaha la yahdee alqawma alththalimeena   52. Fatara allatheena fee quloobihim maradun yusariAAoona feehim yaqooloona nakhsha an tuseebana da-iratun faAAasa Allahu an ya/tiya bialfathi aw amrin min AAindihi fayusbihoo AAala ma asarroo fee anfusihim nadimeena 53. Wayaqoolu allatheena amanoo ahaola-i allatheena aqsamoo biAllahi jahda aymanihim innahum lamaAAakum habitat aAAmaluhum faasbahoo khasireena

Tafsir Ibn Kathir

The Prohibition of Taking the Jews, Christians and Enemies of Islam as Friends

Allah forbids His believing servants from having Jews and Christians as friends, because they are the enemies of Islam and its people, may Allah curse them. Allah then states that they are friends of each other and He gives a warning threat to those who do this,

(And if any among you befriends them, then surely he is one of them.) Ibn Abi Hatim recorded that `Umar ordered Abu Musa Al-Ash`ari to send him on one sheet of balance the count of what he took in and what he spent. Abu Musa then had a Christian scribe, and he was able to comply with `Umar's demand. `Umar liked what he saw and exclaimed, "This scribe is proficient. Would you read in the Masjid a letter that came to us from Ash-Sham" Abu Musa said, `He cannot." `Umar said, "Is he not pure" Abu Musa said, "No, but he is Christian." Abu Musa said, "So `Umar admonished me and poked my thigh (with his finger), saying, `Drive him out (from Al-Madinah).' He then recited,

(O you who believe! Take not the Jews and the Christians as friends...)" Then he reported that `Abdullah bin `Utbah said, "Let one of you beware that he might be a Jew or a Christian, while unaware." The narrator of this statement said, "We thought that he was referring to the Ayah,

(O you who believe! Take not the Jews and the Christians as friends,)" Allah said,

(And you see those in whose hearts there is a disease...) A disease of doubt, hesitation and hypocrisy.

(they hurry to their friendship,) meaning, they rush to offer them their friendship and allegiances in secret and in public,

(saying: "We fear lest some misfortune of a disaster may befall us.") They thus offer this excuse for their friendship and allegiances to the disbelievers, saying that they fear that the disbelievers might defeat the Muslims, so they want to be in favor with the Jews and Christians, to use this favor for their benefit in that eventuality! Allah replied,

(Perhaps Allah may bring a victory...) referring to the conquering of Makkah, according to As-Suddi.

(or a decision according to His will) requiring the Jews and Christians to pay the Jizyah, as As-Suddi stated,

(Then they will become) meaning, the hypocrites who gave their friendship to the Jews and Christians, will become,

(for what they have been keeping as a secret in themselves) of allegiances, (regretful,) for their friendship with the Jews and Christians which did not benefit them or protect them from any harm. Rather, it was nothing but harm, as Allah exposed their true reality to His faithful servants in this life, although they tried to conceal it. When the signs that exposed their hypocrisy were compiled against them, their matter became clear to Allah's faithful servants. So the believers were amazed at these hypocrites who pretended to be believers, swearing to their faithfulness, yet their claims were all lies and deceit. This is why Allah said, s

(And those who believe will say, "Are these the men who swore their strongest oaths by Allah that they were with you" All that they did has been in vain, and they have become the losers.)

Surah: 5 Ayah: 54, Ayah: 55 & Ayah: 56

﴿ يَٰٓأَيُّهَا ٱلَّذِينَ ءَامَنُواْ مَن يَرْتَدَّ مِنكُمْ عَن دِينِهِۦ فَسَوْفَ يَأْتِي ٱللَّهُ بِقَوْمٍ يُحِبُّهُمْ وَيُحِبُّونَهُۥٓ أَذِلَّةٍ عَلَى ٱلْمُؤْمِنِينَ أَعِزَّةٍ عَلَى ٱلْكَٰفِرِينَ يُجَٰهِدُونَ فِى سَبِيلِ ٱللَّهِ وَلَا يَخَافُونَ لَوْمَةَ لَآئِمٍ ذَٰلِكَ فَضْلُ ٱللَّهِ يُؤْتِيهِ مَن يَشَآءُ وَٱللَّهُ وَٰسِعٌ عَلِيمٌ ﴿٥٤﴾ ﴾

54. O you who believe! Whoever from among you turns back from his religion (Islâm), Allâh will bring a people whom He will love and they will love Him; humble towards the believers, stern towards the disbelievers, fighting in the Way of Allâh, and never fear of the blame of the blamers. That is the Grace of Allâh which He bestows on whom He wills. And Allâh is All-Sufficient for His creatures' needs, All-Knower.

﴿ إِنَّمَا وَلِيُّكُمُ ٱللَّهُ وَرَسُولُهُۥ وَٱلَّذِينَ ءَامَنُواْ ٱلَّذِينَ يُقِيمُونَ ٱلصَّلَوٰةَ وَيُؤْتُونَ ٱلزَّكَوٰةَ وَهُمْ رَٰكِعُونَ ﴿٥٥﴾ ﴾

55. Verily, your Walî (Protector or Helper) is none other than Allâh, His Messenger, and the believers, - those who perform As-Salât (Iqâmat-as-Salât), and give Zakât, and they are Râki'ûn (those who bow down or submit themselves with obedience to Allâh in prayer).

﴿ وَمَن يَتَوَلَّ ٱللَّهَ وَرَسُولَهُۥ وَٱلَّذِينَ ءَامَنُواْ فَإِنَّ حِزْبَ ٱللَّهِ هُمُ ٱلْغَٰلِبُونَ ﴿٥٦﴾ ﴾

56. And whosoever takes Allâh, His Messenger, and those who have believed, as Protectors, then the party of Allâh will be the victorious.

Transliteration

54. Ya ayyuha allatheena amanoo man yartadda minkum AAan deenihi fasawfa ya/tee Allahu biqawmin yuhibbuhum wayuhibboonahu athillatin AAala almu/mineena aAAizzatin AAala alkafireena yujahidoona fee sabeeli Allahi wala yakhafoona lawmata la-imin thalika fadlu Allahi yu/teehi man yashao waAllahu wasiAAun AAaleemun 55. Innama waliyyukumu Allahu warasooluhu waallatheena amanoo allatheena

yuqeemoona alssalata wayu/toona alzzakata wahum rakiAAoona 56. Waman yatawalla Allaha warasoolahu waallatheena amanoo fa-inna hizba Allahi humu alghaliboona

Tafsir Ibn Kathir

Threatening to Replace the Believers With Another People if They Revert from Islam

Allah emphasizes His mighty ability and states that whoever reverts from supporting His religion and establishing His Law, then Allah will replace them with whomever is better, mightier and more righteous in Allah's religion and Law. Allah said in other Ayat,

(And if you turn away, He will exchange you for some other people and they will not be your likes.) and,

(Do you not see that Allah has created the heavens and the earth with truth If He will, He can remove you and bring (in your place) a new creation! And for Allah that is not hard or difficult.)(14:19-20). Verily this is not difficult or hard on Allah. Allah said here,

(O you who believe! Whoever from among you turns back from his religion...) and turns back from the truth to falsehood, from now until the commencement of the Last Hour. Allah said next,

(humble towards the believers, stern towards the disbelievers.) These are the qualities of perfect believers, as they are humble with their believing brothers and allies, stern with their enemies and adversaries. In another Ayah, Allah said,

(Muhammad is the Messenger of Allah. And those who are with him are severe against disbelievers, and merciful among themselves.) The Prophet is described as the smiling fighter, smiling to his allies and fighting his enemies. Allah's statement,

(Fighting in the way of Allah, and never fearing the blame of the blamers.) Nothing prevents them from obeying Allah, establishing His Law, fighting His enemies, enjoining righteousness and forbidding evil. Certainly, nothing prevents them from taking this path, neither someone who seeks to hinder them, nor one who blames or chastises them. Imam Ahmad recorded that Abu Dharr said, "My Khalil (intimate friend, the Messenger) has commanded me to do seven deeds. He commanded me to love the poor and to be close to them. He commanded me to look at those who are less than me and not those who are above me. He commanded me to keep the relations of the womb, even if they cut it. He commanded me not to ask anyone for anything, to say the truth even if it was bitter, and to not fear the blame of anyone for the sake of Allah. He commanded me to often repeat, `La hawla wa la quwwata illa billah (There is no strength or power except from Allah)', for these words are from a treasure under the Throne (of Allah)." It is confirmed in the Sahih;

«مَا يَنْبَغِي لِلْمُؤْمِنِ أَنْ يُذِلَّ نَفْسَه»

Chapter 5: Al-Maidah (The Table, The Table Spread), Verses 001-081

(The believer is not required to humiliate himself.) He was asked; "How does one humiliate himself, O Messenger of Allah" So he replied;

«يَتَحَمَّلُ مِنَ الْبَلَاءِ مَا لَا يُطِيق»

(He takes on tests that he cannot bear.)

(That is the grace of Allah which He bestows on whom He wills.) meaning, those who have these qualities, acquired it by Allah's bounty and favor and because He granted them these qualities.

(And Allah is All-Sufficient for His creatures' needs, All-Knower,) His favor is ever extending, and He has perfect knowledge of those who deserve or do not deserve His favor and bounty. Allah's statement,

(Verily, your Protector is Allah, His Messenger, and the believers...) means, the Jews are not your friends. Rather, your allegiance is to Allah, His Messenger and the faithful believers.

(those who perform the Salah, and give the Zakah...) referring to the believers who have these qualities and establish the prayer, which is one of the most important pillars of Islam, for it includes worshipping Allah alone without partners. They pay Zakah, which is the right of the creation and a type of help extended to the needy and the poor. As for Allah's statement,

(and they bow down,) some people thought that they give the Zakah while bowing down. If this were the case, then paying the Zakah while bowing would be the best form of giving Zakah. No scholar from whom religious rulings are taken says this, as much as we know. Therefore,

(and they bow down,) means, they attend the prayer in congregation in Allah's Masjids and spend by way of charity on the various needs of Muslims. Allah said;

(And whosoever takes Allah, His Messenger, and those who have believed, as protectors, then the party of Allah will be the victorious.) similarly Allah said;

(Allah has decreed: "Verily, it is I and My Messengers who shall be the victorious." Verily, Allah is All-Powerful, Almighty. You will not find any people who believe in Allah and the Last Day, making friendship with those who oppose Allah and His Messenger, even though they were their fathers or their sons or their brothers or their kindred (people). For such He has written faith in their hearts, and strengthened them with a Ruh (proof) from Himself. And He will admit them to Gardens (Paradise) under which rivers flow to dwell therein (forever). Allah is pleased with them, and they with Him. They are the party of Allah. Verily, it is the party of Allah that will be the successful.) Therefore, those who accept the allegiance of Allah - His Messenger and the faithful believers - will gain success in this life and the Hereafter. Hence Allah's statement here,

(And whosoever takes Allah, His Messenger, and those who have believed, as protectors, then the party of Allah will be the victorious.)

Surah: 5 Ayah: 57 & Ayah: 58

﴿ يَـٰٓأَيُّهَا ٱلَّذِينَ ءَامَنُوا۟ لَا تَتَّخِذُوا۟ ٱلَّذِينَ ٱتَّخَذُوا۟ دِينَكُمْ هُزُوًا وَلَعِبًا مِّنَ ٱلَّذِينَ أُوتُوا۟ ٱلْكِتَـٰبَ مِن قَبْلِكُمْ وَٱلْكُفَّارَ أَوْلِيَآءَ وَٱتَّقُوا۟ ٱللَّهَ إِن كُنتُم مُّؤْمِنِينَ ﴾ ۝

57. O you who believe! Take not as Auliyâ' (protectors and helpers) those who take your religion as a mockery and fun from among those who received the Scripture (Jews and Christians) before you, and nor from among the disbelievers; and fear Allâh if you indeed are true believers.

﴿ وَإِذَا نَادَيْتُمْ إِلَى ٱلصَّلَوٰةِ ٱتَّخَذُوهَا هُزُوًا وَلَعِبًا ذَٰلِكَ بِأَنَّهُمْ قَوْمٌ لَّا يَعْقِلُونَ ﴾ ۝

58. And when you proclaim the call for As-Salât (call for the prayer (Adhân)) they take it (but) as a mockery and fun; that is because they are a people who understand not.

Transliteration

57. Ya ayyuha allatheena amanoo la tattakhithoo allatheena ittakhathoo deenakum huzuwan walaAAiban mina allatheena ootoo alkitaba min qablikum waalkuffara awliyaa waittaqoo Allaha in kuntum mu/mineena 58. Wa-itha nadaytum ila alssalati ittakhathooha huzuwan walaAAiban thalika bi-annahum qawmun la yaAAqiloona

Tafsir Ibn Kathir

The Prohibition of Being Loyal Friends with Disbelievers

This Ayah discourages and forbids taking the enemies of Islam and its people, such as the People of the Book and the polytheists, as friends. These disbelievers mock the most important acts that any person could ever perform, the honorable, pure acts of Islam which include all types of good for this life and the Hereafter. They mock such acts and make them the subject of jest and play, because this is what these acts represent in their misguided minds and cold hearts. Allah said;

(from those who received the Scriptures before you and (nor) the disbelievers...) This is to clarify the particular category (of disbelievers). As Allah said,

(So shun the evil of the idols...) (22:30) So some recited it "Kuffari", making it an object of the preposition, and others recited it "Kuffara", making it a predicate noun;

(Take not as friends those who take your religion for a mockery and fun from those who received the Scriptures before you...) with the meaning of "nor",

Chapter 5: Al-Maidah (The Table, The Table Spread), Verses 001-081   *145*

(nor the disbelievers as friends) That is, do not take these people nor those people as friends. The meaning here of "Kuffar" (disbelievers) is idolators. Similarly, Ibn Jarir recorded that in the recitation of Ibn Mas`ud (in place of "Kuffar" he recited it: "and those who commit Shirk. Allah's statement,

(And have Taqwa of Allah if you indeed are true believers.) means, fear Allah and do not take the enemies of you and your religion as friends, if you believe in Allah's Law and religion that these people mocked and jested about. Allah said in another Ayah,

(Let not the believers take the disbelievers as friends instead of the believers, and whoever does that, will never be helped by Allah in any way, except if you indeed fear a danger from them. And Allah warns you against Himself, and to Allah is the final return.)

The Disbelievers Mock the Prayer and the Adhan

Allah said,

(And when you proclaim the call for the Salah, they take it (but) as a mockery and fun;) When you proclaim the Adhan for the prayer, which is the best action there is, for those who have sound minds and good comprehension,

(they take it...) also,

(as a mockery and fun; that is because they are a people who understand not.) the acts of worship and Allah's Law. These are the characteristics of the followers of Shaytan who,

»إِذَا سَمِعَ الْأَذَانَ أَدْبَرَ وَلَهُ حُصَاصٌ، أَيْ ضُرَاطٌ، حَتَّى لَا يَسْمَعَ التَّأْذِينَ فَإِذَا قُضِيَ التَّأْذِينُ، أَقْبَلَ فَإِذَا ثُوِّبَ لِلصَّلَاةِ أَدْبَرَ، فَإِذَا قُضِيَ التَّثْوِيبُ أَقْبَلَ حَتَّى يَخْطُرَ بَيْنَ الْمَرْءِ وَقَلْبِهِ، فَيَقُولُ: اذْكُرْ كَذَا اذْكُرْ كَذَا، لِمَا لَمْ يَكُنْ يَذْكُرْ حَتَّى يَظَلَّ الرَّجُلُ لَا يَدْرِي كَمْ صَلَّى، فَإِذَا وَجَدَ أَحَدُكُمْ ذَلِكَ، فَلْيَسْجُدْ سَجْدَتَيْنِ قَبْلَ السَّلَامِ«

(When the call for prayer is made, Shaytan takes to his heels passing wind so that he may not hear the Adhan. When the call is finished he comes back, and when the Iqamah is pronounced, Shaytan again takes to his heels. When the Iqamah is finished he comes back again and tries to interfere with the person and his thoughts and to say, `Remember this and that,' which he has not thought of before the prayer, until the praying person forgets how much he has prayed. If anyone of you does not remember, then he should perform two prostrations before pronouncing the Salam.) This Hadith is agreed upon. Az-Zuhri said, "Allah mentioned the Adhan in His Book,

(And when you proclaim the call for the Salah, they take it (but) as a mockery and fun; that is because they are a people who understand not.)" Ibn Abi Hatim recorded this statement.

Surah: 5 Ayah: 59, Ayah: 60, Ayah: 61, Ayah: 62 & Ayah: 63

﴿ قُلْ يَٰٓأَهْلَ ٱلْكِتَٰبِ هَلْ تَنقِمُونَ مِنَّآ إِلَّآ أَنْ ءَامَنَّا بِٱللَّهِ وَمَآ أُنزِلَ إِلَيْنَا وَمَآ أُنزِلَ مِن قَبْلُ وَأَنَّ أَكْثَرَكُمْ فَٰسِقُونَ ۝ ﴾

59. Say: "O people of the Scripture (Jews and Christians)! Do you criticize us for no other reason than that we believe in Allâh, and in (the revelation) which has been sent down to us and in that which has been sent down before (us), and that most of you are Fâsiqûn (rebellious and disobedient (to Allâh))"

﴿ قُلْ هَلْ أُنَبِّئُكُم بِشَرٍّ مِّن ذَٰلِكَ مَثُوبَةً عِندَ ٱللَّهِ مَن لَّعَنَهُ ٱللَّهُ وَغَضِبَ عَلَيْهِ وَجَعَلَ مِنْهُمُ ٱلْقِرَدَةَ وَٱلْخَنَازِيرَ وَعَبَدَ ٱلطَّٰغُوتَ أُوْلَٰٓئِكَ شَرٌّ مَّكَانًا وَأَضَلُّ عَن سَوَآءِ ٱلسَّبِيلِ ۝ ﴾

60. Say (O Muhammad (peace be upon him) to the people of the Scripture): "Shall I inform you of something worse than that, regarding the recompense from Allâh: those (Jews) who incurred the Curse of Allâh and His Wrath, and those of whom (some) He transformed into monkeys and swines, and those who worshipped Tâghût (false deities); such are worse in rank (on the Day of Resurrection in the Hell-fire), and far more astray from the Right Path (in the life of this world)."

﴿ وَإِذَا جَآءُوكُمْ قَالُوٓا۟ ءَامَنَّا وَقَد دَّخَلُوا۟ بِٱلْكُفْرِ وَهُمْ قَدْ خَرَجُوا۟ بِهِۦ وَٱللَّهُ أَعْلَمُ بِمَا كَانُوا۟ يَكْتُمُونَ ۝ ﴾

61. When they come to you, they say: "We believe." But in fact they enter with (an intention of) disbelief and they go out with the same. And Allâh knows all what they were hiding.

﴿ وَتَرَىٰ كَثِيرًا مِّنْهُمْ يُسَٰرِعُونَ فِى ٱلْإِثْمِ وَٱلْعُدْوَٰنِ وَأَكْلِهِمُ ٱلسُّحْتَ لَبِئْسَ مَا كَانُوا۟ يَعْمَلُونَ ۝ ﴾

62. And you see many of them (Jews) hurrying for sin and transgression, and eating illegal things

﴿ لَوْلَا يَنْهَاهُمُ ٱلرَّبَّـٰنِيُّونَ وَٱلْأَحْبَارُ عَن قَوْلِهِمُ ٱلْإِثْمَ وَأَكْلِهِمُ ٱلسُّحْتَ لَبِئْسَ مَا كَانُوا۟ يَصْنَعُونَ ۝ ﴾

63. Why do not the rabbis and the religious learned men forbid them from uttering sinful words and from eating illegal things. Evil indeed is that which they have been performing.

Transliteration

59. Qul ya ahla alkitabi hal tanqimoona minna illa an amanna biAllahi wama onzila ilayna wama onzila min qablu waanna aktharakum fasiqoona   60. Qul hal onabbi-okum bisharrin min thalika mathoobatan AAinda Allahi man laAAanahu Allahu waghadiba AAalayhi wajaAAala minhumu alqiradata waalkhanazeera waAAabada alttaghooti ola-ika sharrun makanan waadallu AAan sawa-i alssabeeli 61. Wa-itha jaookum qaloo amanna waqad dakhaloo bialkufri wahum qad kharajoo bihi waAllahu aAAlamu bima kanoo yaktumoona   62. Watara katheeran minhum yusariAAoona fee al-ithmi waalAAudwani waaklihimu alssuhta labi/sa ma kanoo yaAAmaloona   63. Lawla yanhahumu alrrabbaniyyoona waal-ahbaru AAan qawlihimu al-ithma waaklihimu alssuhta labi/sa ma kanoo yasnaAAoona

Tafsir Ibn Kathir

The People of the Book are Enraged at the Believers Because of their Faith in Allah

Allah commands: Say, O Muhammad, to those who mock and jest about your religion from among the People of the Scriptures,

(Do you criticize us for no other reason than that we believe in Allah, and in what has been sent down to us and in that which has been sent down before (us)) Do you have any criticism or cause of blame for us, other than this This, by no means, is cause of blame or criticism. Allah said in other Ayat,

(And they had no fault except that they believed in Allah, the Almighty, Worthy of all praise!) and,

(and they could not find any cause to do so except that Allah and His Messenger had enriched them of His bounty.)(9:74) In an agreed upon Hadith, the Prophet said,

«مَا يَنْقِمُ ابْنُ جَمِيلٍ إِلَّا أَنْ كَانَ فَقِيرًا فَأَغْنَاهُ الله»

(What caused Ibn Jamil to Yanqim (refuse to give Zakah), although he was poor and Allah made him rich) Allah's statement,

(and that most of you are rebellious. ..) is connected to

(that we believe in Allah, and in that which has been sent down to us and in that which has been sent down before (us).) Therefore, the meaning of this part of the

Ayah is: we also believe that most of you are rebellious and deviated from the straight path.

The People of the Scriptures Deserve the Worst Torment on the Day of Resurrection

Allah said next,

(Say: "Shall I inform you of something worse than that, regarding the recompense from Allah") The Ayah commands the Prophet to say: Shall I inform you about a worse people with Allah on the Day of Resurrection than what you think of us They are you, with these characteristics,

(those who incurred the curse of Allah) were expelled from His mercy,

(and who incurred His wrath) and anger, after which He will never be pleased with them,

(those of whom He transformed into monkeys and swine,) as we mentioned in Surat Al-Baqarah (2) and as we will mention in Surat Al-A`raf (7). Sufyan Ath-Thawri narrated that Ibn Mas`ud said, "Allah's Messenger was asked if the current monkeys and swine were those whom Allah transformed. He said,

«إنَّ اللهَ لَمْ يُهْلِكْ قَوْمًا، أَوْ لَمْ يَمْسَخْ قَوْمًا فَيَجْعَلَ لَهُمْ نَسْلًا وَلَا عَقِبًا، وَإِنَّ الْقِرَدَةَ وَالْخَنَازِيرَ كَانَتْ قَبْلَ ذلِكَ»

(Allah never destroyed a people by transforming them and making offspring or descendants for them. The monkeys and swine existed before that.)" This was also recorded by Muslim. Allah said,

(Those who worshipped Taghut...) and served them, becoming their servants. The meaning of this Ayah is: you, O People of the Scriptures, who mock our religion, which consists of Allah's Tawhid, and singling Him out in worship without others, how can you mock us while these are your characteristics This is why Allah said,

(such are worse in rank...) than what you -- People of the Scriptures -- think of us Muslims,

(and far more astray from the straight path.) `More' in the Ayah does not mean that the other party is `less' astray, but it means that the People of the Scriptures are far astray. In another Ayah, Allah said,

(The dwellers of Paradise will, on that Day, have the best abode, and have the fairest of places for repose.)

The Hypocrites Pretend to be Believers but Hide their Kufr

Allah said,

Chapter 5: Al-Maidah (The Table, The Table Spread), Verses 001-081   149

(When they come to you, they say, "We believe." But in fact they enter with (an intention of) disbelief and they go out with the same.) This is the description of the hypocrites, for they pretend to be believers while their hearts hide Kufr. So Allah said;

(But in fact they enter) on you, O Muhammad,

(with disbelief) in their hearts and they depart with Kufr, and this is why they do not benefit from the knowledge they hear from you, nor does the advice and reminder move them. So,

(and they go out with the same) meaning, they alone,

(and Allah knows all that they were hiding.) Allah knows their secrets and what their hearts conceal, even if they pretend otherwise with His creatures, thus pretending to be what they are not. Allah, Who has perfect knowledge of the seen and unseen, has more knowledge about the hypocrites than any of His creatures do and He will recompense them accordingly. Allah's statement,

(And you see many of them (Jews) hurrying for sin and transgression, and eating illegal things.) They hurry to devour prohibited and illegal things, all the while transgressing against people, unjustly consuming their property through bribes and Riba,

(Evil indeed is that which they have been doing.) Indeed, horrible is that which they used to do and the transgression that they committed.

Criticizing Rabbis and Learned Religious Men for Giving up on Forbidding Evil

Allah said,

(Why do not the Rabbaniyyun and the Ahbar forbid them from uttering sinful words and from eating illegal things. Evil indeed is that which they have been performing.) meaning why don't the Rabbaniyyun and the Ahbar forbid them from this evil The Rabbaniyyun are the scholars who are in positions of authority, while the Ahbar are the regular scholars.

(Evil indeed is that which they have been performing.) referring to the Rabbaniyyun, as `Ali bin Abi Talhah reported from Ibn `Abbas, because they abandoned forbidding evil. Ibn Jarir recorded that Ibn `Abbas said, "There is no Ayah in the Qur'an that has more severe admonition than this Ayah, (Why do not the Rabbaniyyun and the Ahbar forbid them from uttering sinful words and from eating illegal things. Evil indeed is that which they have been performing.)" Ibn Abi Hatim recorded that Yahya bin Ya`mar said, " `Ali bin Abi Talib once gave a speech, which he started by praising Allah and thanking Him. He then said, `O people! Those who were before you were destroyed because they committed sins and the Rabbaniyyun and Ahbar did not forbid them from evil. When they persisted in sin, they were overcome by punishment. Therefore, enjoin righteousness and forbid evil before what they suffered also strikes you. Know that enjoining righteousness and forbidding evil does not reduce the provision or shorten the term of life." Imam Ahmad recorded that Jarir said that the Messenger of Allah said,

«مَا مِنْ قَوْمٍ يَكُونُ بَيْنَ أَظْهُرِهِمْ مَنْ يَعْمَلُ بِالْمَعَاصِي هُمْ أَعَزُّ مِنْهُ وَأَمْنَعُ، وَلَمْ يُغَيِّرُوا إِلَّا أَصَابَهُمُ اللهُ مِنْهُ بِعَذَاب»

(There is no people among whom there are those who commit sins, while the rest are more powerful and mightier than the sinners, yet they do not stop them, but Allah will send a punishment upon them.) Ahmad was alone with this wording. Abu Dawud recorded it, but in his narration Jarir said, "I heard the Messenger of Allah saying,

«مَا مِنْ رَجُلٍ يَكُونُ فِي قَوْمٍ يُعْمَلُ فِيهِمْ بِالْمَعَاصِي، يَقْدِرُونَ أَنْ يُغَيِّرُوا عَلَيْهِ، فَلَا يُغَيِّرُوا إِلَّا أَصَابَهُمُ اللهُ بِعِقَابٍ قَبْلَ أَنْ يَمُوتُوا»

(There is no one who resides among people commiting evil among them, and they do not stop him though they are able to do so, but Allah will punish them (all) before they die.)" Ibn Majah also recorded this Hadith.

Surah: 5 Ayah: 64, Ayah: 65 & Ayah: 66

﴿ وَقَالَتِ ٱلْيَهُودُ يَدُ ٱللَّهِ مَغْلُولَةٌ غُلَّتْ أَيْدِيهِمْ وَلُعِنُوا بِمَا قَالُوا بَلْ يَدَاهُ مَبْسُوطَتَانِ يُنفِقُ كَيْفَ يَشَاءُ وَلَيَزِيدَنَّ كَثِيرًا مِّنْهُم مَّا أُنزِلَ إِلَيْكَ مِن رَّبِّكَ طُغْيَانًا وَكُفْرًا وَأَلْقَيْنَا بَيْنَهُمُ ٱلْعَدَاوَةَ وَٱلْبَغْضَاءَ إِلَىٰ يَوْمِ ٱلْقِيَامَةِ كُلَّمَا أَوْقَدُوا نَارًا لِّلْحَرْبِ أَطْفَأَهَا ٱللَّهُ وَيَسْعَوْنَ فِي ٱلْأَرْضِ فَسَادًا وَٱللَّهُ لَا يُحِبُّ ٱلْمُفْسِدِينَ ﴿٦٤﴾

64. The Jews say: "Allâh's Hand is tied up (i.e. He does not give and spend of His Bounty)." Be their hands tied up and be they accursed for what they uttered. Nay, both His Hands are widely outstretched. He spends (of His Bounty) as He wills. Verily, the Revelation that has come to you from your Lord (Allâh) increases in most of them (their) obstinate rebellion and disbelief. We have put enmity and hatred amongst them till the Day of Resurrection. Every time they kindled the fire of war, Allâh extinguished it; and they (ever) strive to make mischief on the earth. And Allâh does not like the Mufsidûn (mischief-makers).

﴿ وَلَوْ أَنَّ أَهْلَ ٱلْكِتَٰبِ ءَامَنُوا وَٱتَّقَوْا لَكَفَّرْنَا عَنْهُمْ سَيِّئَاتِهِمْ وَلَأَدْخَلْنَٰهُمْ جَنَّٰتِ ٱلنَّعِيمِ ﴿٦٥﴾

65. And if only the people of the Scripture (Jews and Christians) had believed (in Muhammad (peace be upon him)) and warded off evil (sin, ascribing partners to Allâh) and had become Al-Muttaqûn (the pious - see V.2:2) We would indeed have expiated from them their sins and admitted them to Gardens of pleasure (in Paradise).

﴿ وَلَوْ أَنَّهُمْ أَقَامُواْ ٱلتَّوْرَىٰةَ وَٱلْإِنجِيلَ وَمَآ أُنزِلَ إِلَيْهِم مِّن رَّبِّهِمْ لَأَكَلُواْ مِن فَوْقِهِمْ وَمِن تَحْتِ أَرْجُلِهِم مِّنْهُمْ أُمَّةٌ مُّقْتَصِدَةٌ وَكَثِيرٌ مِّنْهُمْ سَآءَ مَا يَعْمَلُونَ ۝ ﴾

66. And if only they had acted according to the Taurât (Torah), the Injeel (Gospel), and what has (now) been sent down to them from their Lord (the Qur'ân), they would surely have gotten provision from above them and from underneath their feet. There are from among them people who are on the right course (i.e. they act on the revelation and believe in Prophet Muhammad (peace be upon him) like 'Abdullâh bin Salâm (may Allah be pleased with him)) but many of them do evil deeds.

Transliteration

64. Waqalati alyahoodu yadu Allahi maghloolatun ghullat aydeehim waluAAinoo bima qaloo bal yadahu mabsootatani yunfiqu kayfa yashao walayazeedanna katheeran minhum ma onzila ilayka min rabbika tughyanan wakufran waalqayna baynahumu alAAadawata waalbaghdaa ila yawmi alqiyamati kullama awqadoo naran lilharbi atfaaha Allahu wayasAAawna fee al-ardi fasadan waAllahu la yuhibbu almufsideena
65. Walaw anna ahla alkitabi amanoo waittaqaw lakaffarna AAanhum sayyi-atihim walaadkhalnahum jannati alnnaAAeemi   66. Walaw annahum aqamoo alttawrata waal-injeela wama onzila ilayhim min rabbihim laakaloo min fawqihim wamin tahti arjulihim minhum ommatun muqtasidatun wakatheerun minhum saa ma yaAAmaloona

Tafsir Ibn Kathir

The Jews Say That Allah's Hand is Tied up!

Allah states that the Jews, may Allah's continuous curses descend on them until the Day of Resurrection, describe Him as a miser. Allah is far holier than what they attribute to Him. The Jews also claim that Allah is poor, while they are rich. `Ali bin Abi Talhah reported that Ibn `Abbas commented on Allah's statement,

(The Jews say, "Allah's Hand is tied up.") "They do not mean that Allah's Hand is literally tied up. Rather, they mean that He is a miser and does not spend from what He has. Allah is far holier than what they attribute to Him." Similar was reported from Mujahid, `Ikrimah, Qatadah, As-Suddi and Ad-Dahhak. Allah said in another Ayah,

(And let not your hand be tied (like a miser) to your neck, nor stretch it forth to its utmost reach (like a spendthrift), so that you become blameworthy and in severe poverty.) In this Ayah, Allah prohibits stinginess and extravagance, which includes unnecessary and improper expenditures. Allah describes stinginess by saying,

(And let not your hand be tied (like a miser) to your neck.) Therefore, this is the meaning that the Jews meant, may Allah's curses be on them. `Ikrimah said that this Ayah was revealed about Finhas, one of the Jews, may Allah curse him. We mentioned before that Finhas said,

("Truly, Allah is poor and we are rich!") and that Abu Bakr smacked him. Allah has refuted what the Jews attribute to Him and cursed them in retaliation for their lies and fabrications about Him. Allah said,

(Be their hands tied up and be they accursed for what they uttered.) What Allah said occurred, for the Jews are indeed miserly, envious, cowards and tremendously humiliated. Allah said in other Ayat,

(Or have they a share in the dominion Then in that case they would not give mankind even a Naqir. Or do they envy men for what Allah has given them of His bounty Then, We had already given the family of Ibrahim the Book and the Hikmah, and conferred upon them a great kingdom.) and, n

(Indignity is put over them.)

Allah's Hands are Widely Outstretched

Allah said next,

(Nay, both His Hands are widely outstretched. He spends (of His bounty) as He wills.) Allah's favors are ample, His bounty unlimited, as He owns the treasures of everything. Any good that reaches His servants is from Him alone, without partners. He has created everything that we need by night or by day, while traveling or at home and in all situations and conditions. Allah said,

(And He gave you of all that you asked for, and if you count the blessings of Allah, never will you be able to count them. Verily, man is indeed an extreme wrongdoer, an extreme ingrate.) There are many other Ayat on this subject. Imam Ahmad bin Hanbal said that `Abdur-Razzaq narrated to him that Ma`mar said that Hammam bin Munabbih said, "This is what Abu Hurayrah narrated to us that the Messenger of Allah said,

«إِنَّ يَمِينَ اللهِ مَلْأَى، لَا يَغِيضُهَا نَفَقَةٌ، سَحَّاءُ اللَّيْلَ وَالنَّهَارَ، أَرَأَيْتُمْ مَا أَنْفَقَ مُنْذُ خَلَقَ السَّمَوَاتِ وَالْأَرْضَ، فَإِنَّهُ لَمْ يَغِضْ مَا فِي يَمِينِهِ قال : وَعَرْشُهُ عَلَى الْمَاءِ، وَفِي يَدِهِ الْأُخْرى الْقَبْضُ يَرْفَعُ وَيَخْفِض»

(Allah's Right Hand is perfectly full, and no amount of spending can decrease what He has, even though He spends by night and by day. Do you see how much Allah has spent since He created the heavens and earth Yet surely it has not decreased what He has in His Right Hand. His Throne is over the water and in His Other Hand is the hold by which He raises and lowers.) He also said,

«أَنْفِقْ، أُنْفِقْ عَلَيْك»

(Allah said, `Spend and I will spend on you.')" This Hadith was recorded in the Two Sahihs.

The Revelation to the Muslims only Adds to the Transgression and Disbelief of the Jews

Allah said,

(Verily, the revelation that has come to you from your Lord makes many of them increase in rebellion and disbelief.) meaning, the bounty that comes to you, O Muhammad, is a calamity for your enemies, the Jews and their kind. The more the revelation increases the believers in faith, good works, and beneficial knowledge, the more the disbelievers increase in envy for you and your Ummah, the more they increase in Tughyan -- which is to exceed the ordained limits for things -- and in disbelief -- meaning denial of you. Allah said in other Ayat,

(Say: "It is for those who believe, a guide and a healing. And as for those who disbelieve, there is heaviness (deafness) in their ears, and it is blindness for them. They are those who are called from a place far away.") and,

(And We send down of the Qur'an that which is a healing and a mercy to those who believe, and it increases wrongdoers in nothing but loss.) Allah said next,

(We have put enmity and hatred among them till the Day of Resurrection.) Therefore, their hearts are never united. Rather, their various groups and sects will always have enmity and hatred for each other, because they do not agree on the truth, and because they opposed you and denied you. Allah's statement,

(Every time they kindled the fire of war, Allah extinguished it;) means, every time they try to plot against you and kindled the fire of war, Allah extinguishes it and makes their plots turn against them. Therefore, their evil plots will return to harm them.

(and they (ever) strive to make mischief on earth. And Allah does not like the mischief-makers.) It is their habit to always strive to cause mischief on the earth, and Allah does not like those with such behavior.

Had the People of the Book Adhered to their Book, they Would Have Acquired the Good of this Life and the Hereafter

Allah said next,

(And if only the People of the Scripture had believed and had Taqwa...) Consequently, had the People of the Book believed in Allah and His Messenger and avoided the sins and prohibitions that they committed;

(We would indeed have expiated for them their sins and admitted them to Gardens of pleasure (in Paradise).) meaning We would have removed the dangers from them and granted them their objectives.

(And if only they had acted according to the Tawrah, the Injil, and what has (now) been sent down to them from their Lord,) meaning, the Qur'an, as Ibn `Abbas and others said.

(they would surely have gotten provision from above them and from underneath their feet.) Had they adhered to the Books that they have with them which they inherited from the Prophets, without altering or changing these Books, these would have directed them to follow the truth and implement the revelation that Allah sent Muhammad with. These Books testify to the Prophet's truth and command that he must be followed. Allah's statement,

(they would surely have gotten provision from above them and from underneath their feet.) refers to the tremendous provision that would have descended to them from the sky and grown for them on the earth. Allah said in another Ayah,

(And if the people of the towns had believed and had Taqwa, certainly, We should have opened for them blessings from the heaven and the earth.) Allah's statement,

(And among them is a Muqtasid Ummah, but for most of them; evil is their work.) is similar to Allah's statement,

(And of the people of Musa there is a community who lead (the men) with truth and establish justice therewith.)(7:159) and His statement about the followers of `Isa, peace be upon him,

(So We gave those among them who believed, their (due) reward.) Therefore, Allah gave them the highest grade of Iqtisad, which is the middle course, given to this Ummah. Above them there is the grade of Sabiqun, as Allah described in His statement;

(Then We gave the Book as inheritance to such of Our servants whom We chose. Then of them are some who wrong themselves, and of them are some who follow a middle course, and of them are some who, by Allah's permission, are Sabiq (foremost) in good deeds. That itself is indeed a great grace. `Adn (Eden) Paradise (everlasting Gardens) will they enter, therein will they be adorned with bracelets of gold and pearls, and their garments there will be of silk.)(35:32-33)

Surah: 5 Ayah: 67

﴿يَٰٓأَيُّهَا ٱلرَّسُولُ بَلِّغْ مَآ أُنزِلَ إِلَيْكَ مِن رَّبِّكَ ۖ وَإِن لَّمْ تَفْعَلْ فَمَا بَلَّغْتَ رِسَالَتَهُۥ ۚ وَٱللَّهُ يَعْصِمُكَ مِنَ ٱلنَّاسِ ۗ إِنَّ ٱللَّهَ لَا يَهْدِى ٱلْقَوْمَ ٱلْكَٰفِرِينَ ۝﴾

67. O Messenger (Muhammad (peace be upon him))! Proclaim (the Message) which has been sent down to you from your Lord. And if you do not, then you have not conveyed His Message. Allâh will protect you from mankind. Verily, Allâh guides not the people who disbelieve.

Transliteration

67. Ya ayyuha alrrasoolu balligh ma onzila ilayka min rabbika wa-in lam tafAAal fama ballaghta risalatahu waAllahu yaAAsimuka mina alnnasi inna Allaha la yahdee alqawma alkafireena

Tafsir Ibn Kathir

Commanding the Prophet to Convey the Message; Promising Him Immunity and Protection

Allah addresses His servant and Messenger Muhammad by the title `Messenger' and commands him to convey all that He has sent him, a command that the Prophet has fulfilled in the best manner. Al-Bukhari recorded that `A'ishah said, "Whoever says to you that Muhammad hid any part of what Allah revealed to him, then he is uttering a lie. Allah said,

(O Messenger! Convey what has been sent down to you from your Lord.)" Al-Bukhari collected the short form of this story here, but mentioned the full narration in another part of his book. Muslim in the Book of Iman, At-Tirmidhi, and An-Nasa'i in the Book of Tafsir of their Sunans also collected this Hadith. In is recorded in the Two Sahihs that `A'ishah said, "If Muhammad hid anything from the Qur'an, he would have hidden this Ayah,

(But you did hide in yourself that which Allah will make manifest, you did fear the people while Allah had a better right that you should fear Him.)" Al-Bukhari recorded that Az-Zuhri said, "From Allah comes the Message, for the Messenger is its deliverance and for us is submission to it." The Ummah of Muhammad has testified that he has delivered the Message and fulfilled the trust, when he asked them during the biggest gathering in his speech during the Farewell Hajj. At that time, there were over forty thousand of his Companions. Muslim recorded that Jabir bin `Abdullah said that the Messenger of Allah said in his speech on that day,

«أَيُّهَا النَّاسُ إِنَّكُمْ مَسْؤُولُونَ عَنِّي، فَمَا أَنْتُمْ قَائِلُونَ؟»

(O people! You shall be asked about me, so what are you going to reply) They said, "We bear witness that you have conveyed (the Message), fulfilled (the trust) and offered sincere advice." The Prophet kept raising his finger towards the sky and then pointing at them, saying,

«اللَّهُمَّ هَلْ بَلَّغْتُ؟ اللَّهُمَّ هَلْ بَلَّغْتُ؟»

(O Allah! Did I convey O Allah! Did I convey) Allah's statement,

(And if you do not, then you have not conveyed His Message.) meaning: If you do not convey to the people what I sent to you, then you have not conveyed My Message. Meaning, the Prophet knows the consequences of this failure. `Ali bin Abi Talhah reported that Ibn `Abbas commented on the Ayah,

(And if you do not, then you have not conveyed His Message.) "It means, if you hide only one Ayah that was revealed to you from your Lord, then you have not conveyed His Message." Allah's statement,

(Allah will protect you from mankind.) means, you convey My Message and I will protect, aid and support you over your enemies and will grant you victory over them. Therefore, do not have any fear or sadness, for none of them will be able to touch you with harm. Before this Ayah was revealed, the Prophet was being guarded, as Imam Ahmad recorded that `A'ishah said that the Prophet was vigilant one night when she was next to him; she asked him, "What is the matter, O Allah's Messenger" He said,

«لَيْتَ رَجُلًا صَالِحًا مِنْ أَصْحَابِي يَحْرُسُنِي اللَّيْلَةَ»

(Would that a pious man from my companions guard me tonight!) She said, "Suddenly we heard the clatter of arms. The Prophet said,

«مَنْ هَذَا؟»

(Who is that".) He (the new comer) replied, "I am Sa`d bin Malik (Sa`d bin Abi Waqqas)." The Prophet asked,

«مَا جَاءَ بِكَ؟»

(What brought you here) He said, "I have come to guard you, O Allah's Messenger." `A'ishah said, "So, the Prophet slept (that night) and I heard the noise of sleep coming from him.)" This Hadith is recorded in Two Sahihs. Another narration for this Hadith reads, "The Messenger of Allah was vigilant one night, after he came to Al-Madinah...", meaning, after the Hijrah and after the Prophet consummated his marriage to `A'ishah in the second year of Hijrah. Ibn Abi Hatim recorded that `A'ishah said, "The Prophet was being guarded until this Ayah,

(Allah will protect you from mankind) was revealed." She added; "The Prophet raised his head from the room and said;

> «يَا أَيُّهَا النَّاسُ انْصَرِفُوا فَقَدْ عَصَمَنِي اللهُ عَزَّ وَجَلَ»

(O people! Go away, for Allah will protect me.)"' At-Tirmidhi recorded it and said,"This Hadith is Gharib." It was also recorded by Ibn Jarir, and Al-Hakim in his Mustadrak, where he said, "Its chain is Sahih, but they did not record it." Allah's statement,

(Verily, Allah guides not those who disbelieve.) means, O Muhammad, you convey, and Allah guides whom He wills, and misguides whom He wills. In other Ayat, Allah said,

(Not upon you is their guidance, but Allah guides whom He wills,) and,

(Your duty is only to convey and on Us is the reckoning.)

Surah: 5 Ayah: 68 & Ayah: 69

﴿ قُلْ يَٰٓأَهْلَ ٱلْكِتَٰبِ لَسْتُمْ عَلَىٰ شَىْءٍ حَتَّىٰ تُقِيمُوا۟ ٱلتَّوْرَىٰةَ وَٱلْإِنجِيلَ وَمَآ أُنزِلَ إِلَيْكُم مِّن رَّبِّكُمْ ۚ وَلَيَزِيدَنَّ كَثِيرًا مِّنْهُم مَّآ أُنزِلَ إِلَيْكَ مِن رَّبِّكَ طُغْيَٰنًا وَكُفْرًا ۖ فَلَا تَأْسَ عَلَى ٱلْقَوْمِ ٱلْكَٰفِرِينَ ﴾

68. Say (O Muhammad (peace be upon him)) "O people of the Scripture (Jews and Christians)! You have nothing (as regards guidance) till you act according to the Taurât (Torah), the Injeel (Gospel), and what has (now) been sent down to you from your Lord (the Qur'ân)." Verily, that which has been sent down to you (Muhammad (peace be upon him)) from your Lord increases in most of them (their) obstinate rebellion and disbelief. So be not sorrowful over the people who disbelieve.

﴿ إِنَّ ٱلَّذِينَ ءَامَنُوا۟ وَٱلَّذِينَ هَادُوا۟ وَٱلصَّٰبِـُٔونَ وَٱلنَّصَٰرَىٰ مَنْ ءَامَنَ بِٱللَّهِ وَٱلْيَوْمِ ٱلْءَاخِرِ وَعَمِلَ صَٰلِحًا فَلَا خَوْفٌ عَلَيْهِمْ وَلَا هُمْ يَحْزَنُونَ ﴾

69. Surely, those who believe (in the Oneness of Allâh, in His Messenger Muhammad (peace be upon him) and all that was revealed to him from Allâh), and those who are the Jews and the Sabians and the Christians, - whosoever believed in Allâh and the Last Day, and worked righteousness, on them shall be no fear, nor shall they grieve.

Transliteration

68. Qul ya ahla alkitabi lastum AAala shay-in hatta tuqeemoo alttawrata waal-injeela wama onzila ilaykum min rabbikum walayazeedanna katheeran minhum ma onzila ilayka min rabbika tughyanan wakufran fala ta/sa AAala alqawmi alkafireena 69. Inna

allatheena amanoo waallatheena hadoo waalssabi-oona waalnnasara man amana biAllahi waalyawmi al-akhiri waAAamila salihan fala khawfun AAalayhim wala hum yahzanoona

Tafsir Ibn Kathir

There is no Salvation Except through Faith in the Qur'an

Allah says: O Muhammad, say,

(O People of the Scripture! You have nothing...) meaning no real religion until you adhere to and implement the Tawrah and the Injil. That is, until you believe in all the Books that you have that Allah revealed to the Prophets. These Books command following Muhammad and believing in his prophecy, all the while adhering to his Law. Before, we explained Allah's statement,

(Verily, the revelation that has come to you from your Lord makes many of them increase in rebellion and disbelief.)

(So do not grieve for the people who disbelieve), Do not be sad or taken aback by their disbelief. Allah said next,

(Surely, those who believe) referring to Muslims,

(those who are the Jews) who were entrusted with the Tawrah,

(and the Sabians. ..) a sect from the Christians and Magians who did not follow any particular religion, as Mujahid stated. As for the Christians, they are known and were entrusted with the Injil. The meaning here is that if each of these groups believed in Allah and the Hereafter, which is the Day of Judgement and Reckoning, and performed good actions, which to be so, must conform to Muhammad's Law, after Muhammad was sent to all mankind and the Jinns. If any of these groups held these beliefs, then they shall have no fear of what will come or sadness regarding what they lost, nor will grief ever affect them. We discussed a similar Ayah before in Surat Al-Baqarah (2:62).

Surah: 5 Ayah: 70 & Ayah: 71

﴿ لَقَدْ أَخَذْنَا مِيثَاقَ بَنِى إِسْرَءِيلَ وَأَرْسَلْنَآ إِلَيْهِم رُسُلاً كُلَّمَا جَآءَهُمْ رَسُولٌ بِمَا لَا تَهْوَىٰ أَنفُسُهُمْ فَرِيقًا كَذَّبُواْ وَفَرِيقًا يَقْتُلُونَ ۝ ﴾

70. Verily, We took the covenant of the Children of Israel and sent Messengers to them. Whenever there came to them a Messenger with what they themselves desired not, - a group of them they called liars, and others among them they killed.

﴿ وَحَسِبُوٓاْ أَلَّا تَكُونَ فِتْنَةٌ فَعَمُواْ وَصَمُّواْ ثُمَّ تَابَ ٱللَّهُ عَلَيْهِمْ ثُمَّ عَمُواْ وَصَمُّواْ كَثِيرٌ مِّنْهُمْ وَٱللَّهُ بَصِيرٌۢ بِمَا يَعْمَلُونَ ۝ ﴾

71. They thought there will be no Fitnah (trial or punishment), so they became blind and deaf; after that Allâh turned to them (with Forgiveness); yet again many of them became blind and deaf. And Allâh is the All-Seer of what they do.

Transliteration

70. Laqad akhathna meethaqa banee isra-eela waarsalna ilayhim rusulan kullama jaahum rasoolun bima la tahwa anfusuhum fareeqan kaththaboo wafareeqan yaqtuloona 71. Wahasiboo alla takoona fitnatun faAAamoo wasammoo thumma taba Allahu AAalayhim thumma AAamoo wasammoo katheerun minhum waAllahu baseerun bima yaAAmaloona

Tafsir Ibn Kathir

Allah reminds that He took the covenant and pledges from the Children of Israel to hear and obey Him and His Messenger. They broke these pledges and covenants and followed their lusts and desires instead of the law, and whichever part of the law they agreed with, they took it. Otherwise, they abandoned it, if it did not conform to their desires. This is why Allah said,

(Whenever there came to them a Messenger with what they themselves desired not - a group of them they called liars, and others among them they killed. They thought there will be no Fitnah (trial or punishment) so they became blind and deaf.) thinking that they would suffer no repercussions for of the evil that they committed. Consequently, they were blinded from the truth and became deaf, incapable of hearing the truth. For these reasons they were unable to be guided by it. Allah forgave that, then,

(yet they became blind and deaf) again, (many of them, and Allah is the All-Seer of what they do.) He has perfect knowledge of what they do and whomever among them deserves the guidance and whomever deserves misguidance.

Surah: 5 Ayah: 72, Ayah: 73, Ayah: 74 & Ayah: 75

﴿ لَقَدْ كَفَرَ ٱلَّذِينَ قَالُوٓاْ إِنَّ ٱللَّهَ هُوَ ٱلْمَسِيحُ ٱبْنُ مَرْيَمَ وَقَالَ ٱلْمَسِيحُ يَٰبَنِىٓ إِسْرَٰٓءِيلَ ٱعْبُدُواْ ٱللَّهَ رَبِّى وَرَبَّكُمْ إِنَّهُ مَن يُشْرِكْ بِٱللَّهِ فَقَدْ حَرَّمَ ٱللَّهُ عَلَيْهِ ٱلْجَنَّةَ وَمَأْوَىٰهُ ٱلنَّارُ وَمَا لِلظَّٰلِمِينَ مِنْ أَنصَارٍ ۝ ﴾

72. Surely, they have disbelieved who say: "Allâh is the Messiah ('Isâ (Jesus)) son of Maryam (Mary)." But the Messiah ('Isâ (Jesus)) said: "O Children of Israel! Worship Allâh, my Lord and your Lord." Verily, whosoever sets up partners (in worship) with Allâh, then Allâh has forbidden Paradise to him, and the Fire will be

his abode. And for the Zâlimûn (polytheists and wrong-doers) there are no helpers.

$$\textit{﴿ لَقَدْ كَفَرَ ٱلَّذِينَ قَالُوٓا۟ إِنَّ ٱللَّهَ ثَالِثُ ثَلَٰثَةٍ ۘ وَمَا مِنْ إِلَٰهٍ إِلَّآ إِلَٰهٌ وَٰحِدٌ ۚ وَإِن لَّمْ يَنتَهُوا۟ عَمَّا يَقُولُونَ لَيَمَسَّنَّ ٱلَّذِينَ كَفَرُوا۟ مِنْهُمْ عَذَابٌ أَلِيمٌ ﴾}$$

73. Surely, disbelievers are those who said: "Allâh is the third of the three (in a Trinity)." But there is no Iilâh (god) (none who has the right to be worshipped) but One Ilâh (God -Allâh). And if they cease not from what they say, verily, a painful torment will befall on the disbelievers among them.

$$\textit{﴿ أَفَلَا يَتُوبُونَ إِلَى ٱللَّهِ وَيَسْتَغْفِرُونَهُۥ ۚ وَٱللَّهُ غَفُورٌ رَّحِيمٌ ﴾}$$

74. Will they not turn with repentance to Allâh and ask His Forgiveness? For Allâh is Oft-Forgiving, Most Merciful.

$$\textit{﴿ مَّا ٱلْمَسِيحُ ٱبْنُ مَرْيَمَ إِلَّا رَسُولٌ قَدْ خَلَتْ مِن قَبْلِهِ ٱلرُّسُلُ وَأُمُّهُۥ صِدِّيقَةٌ ۖ كَانَا يَأْكُلَانِ ٱلطَّعَامَ ۗ ٱنظُرْ كَيْفَ نُبَيِّنُ لَهُمُ ٱلْءَايَٰتِ ثُمَّ ٱنظُرْ أَنَّىٰ يُؤْفَكُونَ ﴾}$$

75. The Messiah ('Isâ (Jesus)) son of Maryam (Mary), was no more than a Messenger; many were the Messengers that passed away before him. His mother (Maryam (Mary)) was a Siddiqah (i.e. she believed in the words of Allâh and His Books (see Verse 66:12)) They both used to eat food (as any other human being, while Allâh does not eat). Look how We make the Ayât (proofs, evidences, verses, lessons, signs, revelations, etc.) clear to them, yet look how they are deluded away (from the truth).

Transliteration

72. Laqad kafara allatheena qaloo inna Allaha huwa almaseehu ibnu maryama waqala almaseehu ya banee isra-eela oAAbudoo Allaha rabbee warabbakum innahu man yushrik biAllahi faqad harrama Allahu AAalayhi aljannata wama/wahu alnnaru wama lilththalimeena min ansarin

73. Laqad kafara allatheena qaloo inna Allaha thalithu thalathatin wama min ilahin illa ilahun wahidun wa-in lam yantahoo AAamma yaqooloona layamassanna allatheena kafaroo minhum AAathabun aleemun   74. Afala yatooboona ila Allahi wayastaghfiroonahu waAllahu ghafoorun raheemun   75. Ma almaseehu ibnu maryama illa rasoolun qad khalat min qablihi alrrusulu waommuhu siddeeqatun kana ya/kulani alttaAAama onthur kayfa nubayyinu lahumu al-ayati thumma onthur anna yu/fakoona

Tafsir Ibn Kathir

The Disbelief of the Christians; `Isa Only called to Tawhid

Allah states that the Christians such sects as Monarchite, Jacobite and Nestorite are disbelievers, those among them who say that `Isa is Allah. Allah is far holier than what they attribute to Him. They made this claim in spite of the fact that `Isa made it known that he was the servant of Allah and His Messenger. The first words that `Isa uttered when he was still a baby in the cradle were, "I am `Abdullah (the servant of Allah)." He did not say, "I am Allah," or, "I am the son of Allah." Rather, he said,

(Verily, I am a servant of Allah, He has given me the Scripture and made me a Prophet.) until he said,

("And verily Allah is my Lord and your Lord. So worship Him (Alone). That is the straight path.") He also proclaimed to them when he was a man, after he was sent as a Prophet, commanding them to worship his Lord and their Lord, alone without partners,

(But the Messiah said, "O Children of Israel! worship Allah, my Lord and your Lord." Verily, whosoever sets up partners with Allah...) in worship;

(...then Allah has forbidden Paradise for him, and the Fire will be his abode.) as He will send him to the Fire and forbid Paradise for him. Allah also said;

(Verily, Allah forgives not that partners should be set up with Him (in worship), but He forgives except that (anything else) to whom He wills.) and,

(And the dwellers of the Fire will call to the dwellers of Paradise; "Pour on us some water or anything that Allah has provide you with." They will say: "Allah has forbidden both to the disbelievers.") It is recorded in the Sahih that the Prophet had someone proclaim to the people,

«إِنَّ الْجَنَّةَ لَا يَدْخُلُهَا إِلَّا نَفْسٌ مُسْلِمَةٌ»

(Only a Muslim soul shall enter Paradise.) In another narration,

«مُؤْمِنَةٌ»

(Only a believing soul...) This is why Allah said that `Isa said to the Children of Israel,

(Verily, whosoever sets up partners with Allah, then Allah has forbidden Paradise for him, and the Fire will be his abode. And there are no helpers for the wrongdoers.) There is no help from Allah, nor anyone who will support or protect them from the state they will be in. Allah's statement,

(Surely, they have disbelieved who say: "Allah is the third of three.") Mujahid and several others said that this Ayah was revealed about the Christians in particular. As-

Suddi and others said that this Ayah was revealed about taking `Isa and his mother as gods besides Allah, thus making Allah the third in a trinity. As-Suddi said, "This is similar to Allah's statement towards the end of the Surah,

(And (remember) when Allah will say: "O `Isa, son of Maryam! Did you say unto men: `Worship me and my mother as two gods besides Allah' He will say, "Glory be to You!")(5:116). Allah replied,

(But there is no god but One God.) meaning there are not many worthy of worship but there is only One God without partners, and He is the Lord of all creation and all that exists. Allah said next, while threatening and admonishing them,

(And if they cease not from what they say,) their lies and false claims,

(verily, a painful torment will befall the disbelievers among them.) in the Hereafter, shackled and tormented. Allah said next,

(Will they not repent to Allah and ask His Forgiveness For Allah is Oft-Forgiving, Most Merciful.) This demonstrates Allah's generosity, kindness and mercy for His creatures, even though they committed this grave sin and invented such a lie and false allegation. Despite all of this, Allah calls them to repent so that He will forgive them, for Allah forgives those who sincerely repent to Him.

`Isa is Allah's Servant and His Mother is a Truthful Believer

Allah said,

(The Messiah, son of Maryam, was no more than a Messenger; many were the Messengers that passed away before him.) `Isa is just like the previous Prophets, and he is one of the servants of Allah and one of His honorable Messengers. Allah said in another Ayah,

(He (`Isa) was not more than a servant. We granted Our favor to him, and We made him an example for the Children of Israel.) Allah said next,

(His mother was a Siddiqah) for she believed in Allah with complete trust in Him. This is the highest rank she was given, which proves that she was not a Prophet. Allah said next,

(They both used to eat food) needing nourishment and to relieve the call of nature. Therefore, they are just servants like other servants, not gods as ignorant Christian sects claim, may Allah's continued curses cover them until the Day of Resurrection. Allah said next,

(Look how We make the Ayat clear to them.) making them unequivocal and plain,

(yet look how they are deluded away (from the truth).) look at the opinions, misguided ideas, and claims they cling to, even after Our clarification and plain, unequivocal explanation.

Surah: 5 Ayah: 76 & Ayah: 77

﴿ قُلْ أَتَعْبُدُونَ مِن دُونِ ٱللَّهِ مَا لَا يَمْلِكُ لَكُمْ ضَرًّا وَلَا نَفْعًا ۚ وَٱللَّهُ هُوَ ٱلسَّمِيعُ ٱلْعَلِيمُ ۝ ﴾

76. Say (O Muhammad (peace be upon him) to mankind): "How do you worship besides Allâh something which has no power either to harm or to benefit you? But it is Allâh Who is the All-Hearer, All-Knower."

﴿ قُلْ يَٰٓأَهْلَ ٱلْكِتَٰبِ لَا تَغْلُوا۟ فِى دِينِكُمْ غَيْرَ ٱلْحَقِّ وَلَا تَتَّبِعُوٓا۟ أَهْوَآءَ قَوْمٍ قَدْ ضَلُّوا۟ مِن قَبْلُ وَأَضَلُّوا۟ كَثِيرًا وَضَلُّوا۟ عَن سَوَآءِ ٱلسَّبِيلِ ۝ ﴾

77. Say (O Muhammad (peace be upon him)) "O people of the Scripture (Jews and Christians)! Exceed not the limits in your religion (by believing in something) other than the truth, and do not follow the vain desires of people who went astray in times gone by, and who misled many, and strayed (themselves) from the Right Path."

Transliteration

76. Qul ataAAbudoona min dooni Allahi ma la yamliku lakum darran wala nafAAan waAllahu huwa alssameeAAu alAAaleemu   77. Qul ya ahla alkitabi la taghloo fee deenikum ghayra alhaqqi wala tattabiAAoo ahwaa qawmin qad dalloo min qablu waadalloo katheeran wadalloo AAan sawa-i alssabeeli

Tafsir Ibn Kathir

The Prohibition of Shirk (Polytheism) and Exaggeration in the Religion

Allah admonishes those who take up rivals with Him and worship the idols, monuments and false deities. Allah states that such false deities do not deserve any degree of Divinity. Allah said,

(Say) O Muhammad, to those from among the Children of Adam, such as the Christians, who worship other than Allah,

(How do you worship besides Allah something which has no power either to harm or to benefit you) meaning, which cannot prevent harm for you nor bring about your benefit,

(But it is Allah Who is the All-Hearer, All-Knower.) He hears what His servants say and has knowledge of all things. Therefore, how did you worship inanimate objects that do not hear, see or know anything - having no power to bring harm or benefit to themselves let alone others - instead of worshipping Allah Allah then said,

(Say: "O People of the Scipture! Exceed not the limits in your religion beyond the truth,) Meaning: Do not exceed the limits concerning the truth and exaggeration in praising whom you were commanded to honor. You exaggerated in his case and elevated him from the rank of Prophet to the rank of a god. You did this with `Isa, who was a Prophet, yet you claimed that he is god besides Allah. This error occurred because you followed your teachers, the advocates of misguidance who came before your time and who,

(...and who misled many, and strayed (themselves) from the right path,) deviated from the straight path, to the path of misguidance and deviation.

Surah: 5 Ayah: 78, Ayah: 79, Ayah: 80 & Ayah: 81

﴿ لُعِنَ ٱلَّذِينَ كَفَرُواْ مِنْ بَنِىٓ إِسْرَٰٓءِيلَ عَلَىٰ لِسَانِ دَاوُۥدَ وَعِيسَى ٱبْنِ مَرْيَمَ ذَٰلِكَ بِمَا عَصَواْ وَّكَانُواْ يَعْتَدُونَ ۝ ﴾

78. Those among the Children of Israel who disbelieved were cursed by the tongue of Dâwûd (David) and 'Isâ (Jesus), son of Maryam (Mary). That was because they disobeyed (Allâh and the Messengers) and were ever transgressing beyond bounds.

﴿ كَانُواْ لَا يَتَنَاهَوْنَ عَن مُّنكَرٍ فَعَلُوهُ لَبِئْسَ مَا كَانُواْ يَفْعَلُونَ ۝ ﴾

79. They used not to forbid one another from Al-Munkar (wrong, evil-doing, sins, polytheism, disbelief) which they committed. Vile indeed was what they used to do.

﴿ تَرَىٰ كَثِيرًا مِّنْهُمْ يَتَوَلَّوْنَ ٱلَّذِينَ كَفَرُواْ لَبِئْسَ مَا قَدَّمَتْ لَهُمْ أَنفُسُهُمْ أَن سَخِطَ ٱللَّهُ عَلَيْهِمْ وَفِى ٱلْعَذَابِ هُمْ خَٰلِدُونَ ۝ ﴾

80. You see many of them taking the disbelievers as their Auliyâ' (protectors and helpers). Evil indeed is that which their own selves have sent forward before them; for that (reason) Allâh's Wrath fell upon them, and in torment they will abide.

﴿ وَلَوْ كَانُواْ يُؤْمِنُونَ بِٱللَّهِ وَٱلنَّبِىِّ وَمَآ أُنزِلَ إِلَيْهِ مَا ٱتَّخَذُوهُمْ أَوْلِيَآءَ وَلَٰكِنَّ كَثِيرًا مِّنْهُمْ فَٰسِقُونَ ۝ ﴾

81. And had they believed in Allâh, and in the Prophet (Muhammad (peace be upon him)) and in what has been revealed to him, never would they have taken them (the disbelievers) as Auliyâ' (protectors and helpers); but many of them are the Fâsiqûn (rebellious, disobedient to Allâh).

Transliteration

78. LuAAina allatheena kafaroo min banee isra-eela AAala lisani dawooda waAAeesa ibni maryama thalika bima AAasaw wakanoo yaAAtadoona 79. Kanoo la yatanahawna AAan munkarin faAAaloohu labi/sa ma kanoo yafAAaloona   80. Tara katheeran minhum yatawallawna allatheena kafaroo labi/sa ma qaddamat lahum anfusuhum an sakhita Allahu AAalayhim wafee alAAathabi hum khalidoona 81. Walaw kanoo yu/minoona biAllahi waalnnabiyyi wama onzila ilayhi ma ittakhathoohum awliyaa walakinna katheeran minhum fasiqoona

Tafsir Ibn Kathir

Allah Cursed the Disbelievers Among the Children of Israel

Allah states that He has cursed the disbelievers among the Children of Israel long ago, and revealed this fact to His Prophets Dawud and `Isa, son of Maryam. He cursed them because they disobeyed Allah and transgressed against His creatures. Al-`Awfi reported that Ibn `Abbas said, "They were cursed in the Tawrah, the Injil, the Zabur (Psalms) and the Furqan (Qur'an)." Allah then states that during their time, their habit was that,

(They used not to forbid one another from the evil they committed.) They did not forbid each other from committing sins and the prohibitions. Allah chastised them for this behavior, so that their behavior would not be imitated. Allah said,

(Vile indeed was what they used to do.)

Hadiths that Order Enjoining Righteousness and Forbidding Evil

There are many Hadiths that order enjoining righteousness and forbidding evil. Imam Ahmad recorded that Hudhayfah bin Al-Yaman said that the Prophet said,

«وَالَّذِي نَفْسِي بِيَدِهِ، لَتَأْمُرُنَّ بِالْمَعْرُوفِ، وَلَتَنْهَوُنَّ عَنِ الْمُنْكَرِ، أَوْ لَيُوشِكَنَّ اللهُ أَنْ يَبْعَثَ عَلَيْكُمْ عِقَابًا مِنْ عِنْدِهِ، ثُمَّ لَتَدْعُنَّهُ فَلَا يَسْتَجِيبَ لَكُمْ»

(By He in Whose Hand is my soul! You will enjoin righteousness and forbid evil, or Allah will send a punishment on you from Him. Then, you will supplicate to Him, but He will not accept your supplication.) At-Tirmidhi also recorded it and said, "This Hadith is Hasan." Muslim recorded that Abu Sa`id Al-Khudri said that the Messenger of Allah said,

«مَنْ رَأَى مِنْكُمْ مُنْكَرًا فَلْيُغَيِّرْهُ بِيَدِهِ، فَإِنْ لَمْ يَسْتَطِعْ فَبِلِسَانِهِ، فَإِنْ لَمْ يَسْتَطِعْ فَبِقَلْبِهِ، وَذَلِكَ أَضْعَفُ الْإِيمَانِ»

(He among you who witnesses an evil, let him change it with his hand, if he cannot do that, then by his tongue, if he cannot do even that, then with his heart, and this is the weakest faith.) Abu Dawud said that Al-`Urs, meaning Ibn `Amirah, said that the Prophet said,

«إِذَا عُمِلَتِ الْخَطِيئَةُ فِي الْأَرْضِ كَانَ مَنْ شَهِدَهَا فَكَرِهَهَا، وَقَالَ مَرَّةً فَأَنْكَرَهَا كَانَ كَمَنْ غَابَ عَنْهَا، وَمَنْ غَابَ عَنْهَا فَرَضِيَهَا كَانَ كَمَنْ شَهِدَهَا»

(When sin is committed on the earth, then whoever witnesses it and hates - (once he said): forbids it, will be like those who did not witness it. Whoever was absent from it, but agreed with it, will be like those who witness it.) Only Abu Dawud recorded this Hadith. Abu Dawud recorded that one of the Companions said that the Prophet said,

«لَنْ يَهْلِكَ النَّاسُ حَتَّى يَعْذِرُوا أَوْ يُعْذِرُوا مِنْ أَنْفُسِهِم»

(The people will not perish until they do not leave -or- have any excuse for themselves.) Ibn Majah recorded that Abu Sa`id Al-Khudri said that the Messenger of Allah gave a speech once and said,

«أَلَا لَا يَمْنَعَنَّ رَجُلًا هَيْبَةُ النَّاسِ أَنْ يَقُولَ الْحَقَّ إِذَا عَلِمَه»

(Behold! Fear from people should not prevent one from saying the truth if he knows it.) Abu Sa`id then cried and said, "By Allah! We have seen some errors, but we feared (the people)." Another Hadith that Abu Sa`id narrated states that the Messenger of Allah said,

«أَفْضَلُ الْجِهَادِ كَلِمَةُ حَقٍّ عِنْدَ سُلْطَانٍ جَائِر»

(The best Jihad is a word of truth proclaimed before an unjust ruler.) Recorded by Abu Dawud, At-Tirmidhi, and Ibn Majah. At-Tirmidhi said, "Hasan Gharib from this route of narration." Imam Ahmad recorded that Hudhayfah said that the Prophet said,

«لَا يَنْبَغِي لِمُسْلِمٍ أَنْ يُذِلَّ نَفْسَه»

(It is not required of the Muslim that he humiliate himself.) They said, `How does one humiliate himself'' he said;

«يَتَعَرَّضُ مِنَ الْبَلَاءِ لِمَا لَا يُطِيق»

(He takes on trials that he is not capable of enduring.) This was recorded by At-Tirmidhi and Ibn Majah, and At-Tirmidhi said, "This Hadith is Hasan Sahih Gharib."

Censuring the Hypocrites

Allah said,

(You see many of them taking the disbelievers as their friends.) Mujahid said that this Ayah refers to the hypocrites. Allah's statement,

(Evil indeed is that which they have sent forward before themselves;) by giving their loyalty and support to the disbelievers, instead of the believers. This evil act caused them to have hypocrisy in their hearts and brought them the anger of Allah, that will remain with them until the Day of Return. Allah said;

(for that (reason) Allah is wrath with them) because of what they did. Allah next said that,

(in torment they will abide) on the Day of Resurrection. Allah's statement,

(And had they believed in Allah, and in the Prophet and in what has been revealed to him, never would they have taken them as friends.) meaning, had they sincerely believed in Allah, His Messenger and the Qur'an, they would not have committed the evil act of supporting the disbelievers in secret and being enemies with those who believe in Allah, the Prophet and what was revealed to him,

(but many of them are rebellious). disobedient to Allah and His Messenger and defiant of the Ayat of His revelation that He sent down.

www.ingramcontent.com/pod-product-compliance
Lightning Source LLC
Chambersburg PA
CBHW081110080526
44587CB00021B/3522